Communicating Ideas with Film, Video, and Multimedia

Communicating Ideas with Film, Video, and Multimedia

A Practical Guide to
Information Motion-Media

S. Martin Shelton

Southern Illinois University Press • Carbondale

Library of Congress Cataloging-in-Publication Data
Shelton, S. Martin, date.
Communicating ideas with film, video, and multimedia : a
practical guide to information motion-media / S. Martin
Shelton.
       p. cm.
Includes bibliographical references and index.
1. Documentary films—Production and direction.
2. Documentary television programs—Production and
direction. 3. Multimedia systems. I. Title.
PN1995.9.D6S493 2004
070.1'8—dc22
ISBN 0-8093-2601-9 (hardcover : alk. paper)
ISBN 0-8093-2603-5 (pbk. : alk. paper)   2004007226

I dedicate this book to my wife, Mary Allene Shelton, and my daughter, Rachel Valerie Shelton. Both have given me unstinting support in my career as a filmmaker and in the preparation of this book. I could not have done either successfully without their encouragement, help, and understanding.

Contents

Illustrations

Figures

Following page 233

Preface

I've been active in the information motion-media (kinetic sight-and-sound media) for almost all my adult life, and I love it. I'm truly fortunate to have found my life's calling in a profession that has posed interesting challenges every day. I always learned new things. Met interesting folks. Traveled the world several times over and had a great time doing it. Fortunately, the Hollywood movie bug never bit me. I was always focused on the information motion-media rather than the narrative film, the "movies." My fiscal rewards were adequate, but the real reward was the love and satisfaction I got from working in this wonderful profession. Perhaps more important, my reward was the pride and fulfillment I experienced seeing my shows on the screen. Watching audiences react positively. Garnering praise from clients. And even dealing with my share of "learning experiences." On the whole, it doesn't get any better than this.

During my long career, I was fortunate to have attended fine schools and to have had demanding teachers, great mentors, exceptional professional associates, empathetic managers, tolerant clients (mostly), an understanding family, and the God-given wherewithal to learn, to work with industry and verve, and to be what I am.

Eventually, time caught me. A few years ago, I retired from active script design, production, and management. On reflection, I'd do it all over again—perhaps a few things differently but essentially all the same. Nowadays, I'm consulting, hosting seminars, and working with the Nevada State Museum building a database of all the historic sites, ghost towns, and mining camps in the state.

Actually, this book on filmic communication has been a work-in-progress for some twenty-five-odd years. It's a synthesis of material I've written as formal papers for professional journals, magazine articles, editorials, newsletter columns, jottings, and scribbles on notecards. This book isn't organized like a textbook or a "how-to" book. It's a series of essays on motion-media that I've edited and arranged into a coherent pattern in five modules or sections. Each section deals with one major topic. The book can be used as a handy reference for quick perusal to get the kernel of an idea on a particular topic, or it can be used as a "sit-down" study in which all the ideas are set in perspective for in-depth thought. In appendix 7, I've summarized the major points in this book. And, to lighten the scene, in appendix 9, I list memorable quotes about our profession that I've heard and read.

Frequently, I cite old-time classic films rather than contemporary ones. The pioneers and giants of our profession produced these films with communication skill, artistic finesse, and adroit filmic design. I'll concede that the films are sometimes old, timeworn, and out of style; nonetheless, they set the standards for our profession.

The primary reason I'm writing this book is to speak my mind in a forthright manner on the status of our profession and to encourage newcomers and old-timers alike to consider and adapt the ideas I'm proffering in order to enhance their professional growth and our profession. Another reason is to fulfill my obligation to my profession.

I step on a lot of toes in this book and debunk a host of "sacred doctrines." There is much "how-to" in it, but more than anything else, this book is an editorial. By nature, I'm a contrarian, so please bear with me. Your patience and understanding will be rewarded.

Acknowledgments

Over the many years of my career, I've had caring mentors who have given me expert guidance and counsel and who have shared their expertise willingly and patiently. My peers and fellow professionals have challenged me to do better. Teachers whetted my appetite for this wonderful sight-and-sound profession of ours, stimulating me to constantly extend my professional development. Fellow members in professional societies, such as the Society for Technical Communication, the Information Film Producers of America, and the International Television Association, have inspired me to emulate their creative, technical, and managerial achievements.

Without the help of all these people, many now deceased, I would have long ago withered in this profession. It is they who make this book possible. Heartfelt thanks to one and all. In particular, I want to remember the following longtime friends and mentors:

My supervisors in the Pacific Fleet Combat Camera Group in the early 1950s, Lt. (jg) Charles "Chuck" Kircher, USN (ret.) and Chief Photographer's Mates Frank "Kaz" Kazakatis, USN (ret.), and the late Patrick "Pat" Cady, who demanded my very best and sparked my passion for this profession.

Melvin "Mel" Sloan, professor in the University of Southern California Cinema Department, who taught me the basic wherewithal of our profession and instilled in me the maxim that communication is paramount in information film.

The late Elizabeth "Betty" Scheibel Dunn, longtime friend and reporter for *Life* magazine, whose critiques and encouragement were the sparks that inspired me to see the beauty of our language.

The late Erskin "Gil" Gilbert, information-film scriptwriter, who with patience and skill guided my filmic-design skills.

Alberta "Berti" Cox, former president of the Society for Technical Information, who demanded that my writing be sharp, sharper, and sharpest.

Marilyn Morgan, who was instrumental in integrating my articles, papers, and jottings into a coherent whole that became this book.

Emilie Boguchwal and Janice Kasperson, members of the Society for Technical Communication, Sierra Panamint chapter, who over the years edited my ramblings into publishable manuscripts.

Louise Burnham for her script *The Scarf: The Perennial Fashion Statement*.

Ken Albright, intrepid ghost-town hunter and longtime associate, for his insightful critique.

Olivia Francis, for the storyboard for *The Scarf*.

Ron Marryott Jr., former associate and longtime friend, for his sage counsel.

Brian McCaleb, Consulting Professionals United, for his detailed review of this book and his singular assistance in making it ready for publication.

Richard "Dick" McCurdy of McCurdy Editorial for his review and comments on chapter 21, "The Sound Track."

Mark Pahuta, former associate and longtime friend, for his comprehensive review of and cogent comments on the first draft of this book.

James Simmons, former acquisitions editor at Southern Illinois University Press, for his sage counsel, patience, and encouragement.

Margaret Dalrymple, editor par excellence, who honed the manuscript into a smooth-reading text.

Carol A. Burns, who with consummate skill and patience guided this manuscript (and me) through the editing processes at Southern Illinois University Press.

Mary Lou Kowaleski, editor par excellence, who with her eagle eye and insightful queries was instrumental in making this book coherent, readable, and all 'round excellent.

Barb Martin, production manager at Southern Illinois University Press, who with her adept skill and artistic finesse transformed my manuscript into an easily readable and harmonious book.

Barbara E. Cohen, who with superior talent and in-depth perception developed the detailed index to this book.

Thanks are also owed to the following for their gracious permission to use materials reproduced in this book:

Sunbreak Inc., for permission to reprint its promotional script "Vision Lab"; the Margaret Herrick Library of the Academy of Motion Picture Arts and Sciences; Mrs. William Wyler; the National Film Board of Canada; the National Archives and Records Administration; and the Bildarchiv of the Deutsche Presse-Agentur.

Part One

Introduction

1

Prologue

I'm sorely disappointed at the state of our profession, the information motion-media profession. *We're not doing so well.* Far too many of our films, videos, and multimedia shows are amateurish in concept, technically inept, and fail in their primary objective of communicating ideas to our audience. Unfortunately, many of today's films, videos, and multimedia shows sparkle with "creative" whiz-bang-and-pop multichannel surround-sound, but they don't communicate much except, perhaps, "Gee, isn't technology wonderful?" Rapidly advancing technology has made it so easy to produce a film, video, or multimedia show that we no longer have to think very hard about it. We've lost track of what we're up to: We're not supposed to be producing films, videos, and multimedia shows; we're supposed to be communicating ideas to our target audiences, implanting our messages firmly in their minds so that when the lights come on, they will speak, think, or act the way we want them to.

We're in the communication business. All else is irrelevant. We use film, video, and multimedia simply as the carriers of our encoded messages. It's the message and our audience that count. That's what this book is about: how to optimize communication using motion-media (integrated sight-and-sound kinetic media). This book is not about technology. There's not one thought about f-stops, key lights, chrominance, bit rate, gamma curves, white balance, decibels, auteur concepts, or the Strasberg acting method. If you're looking for the latest technical "how-to," this tome is not it. There are plenty of excellent books on these specialized subjects in print. Rather, this book takes an in-depth look at just what our profession is about—communication. It's my perspective—part theory, part philosophy, analysis, history, personal opinion, and application. I approach the topic from a reality-based understanding and philosophy of the media. In this book, I'm including the entire genre of *information* motion-media, whose purpose is to inform rather than to entertain. Occasionally, I'll discuss experimental, enrichment, or personal-statement shows. Excluded are narrative motion-media (theatrical and television storytelling). I'm using *show* to refer to the generic, all-encompassing information motion-media product.

Fully realizing that I'm challenging some of today's most sacred tenets and widespread practices, I stand pat. My opinions are based on a long-term successful career in all aspects of information motion-media production and on viewing dozens of motion-media shows a year. For the past thirty years, I've been a preliminary and blue-ribbon judge in several national motion-media competitions. For twelve consecutive years, I managed a major international competition for one of the nation's largest professional communication societies, and I make it a point to view shows of various genres from other competitions and from government and industry. Unfortunately, I've seen distressingly few shows that match the communications beauty of *To Be Alive* by Francis Thompson, *Why Man Creates* by Saul Bass, *Man with a Thousand Hands* by Cap Palmer, *Universe* by Lester Novoros, and dozens of others that engender effective communication in a creative way.

Why is this so? Why are we inundated with "good enough" mediocrity and wholesale incompetence? Where are today's Thompsons, Basses, Palmers, and Novoroses? One possible answer is that many of today's media designers and producers have forgotten or don't understand that they're in the communications profession rather than the entertainment industry.

I'm not suggesting that our shows must be dull, lack innovation, or not excel technically. I'm suggesting that we need to analyze critically every technical and artistic element planned for our shows: to evaluate the communication value of each individual element and its contribution to overall effect in generating empathy. Those technical and artistic elements that contribute significantly to enhancing communication, and that promise high return on the investment in resources, should be employed to make maximum use of the power of our medium in all its variants.

All factors being equal, we optimize the power of our communication medium when the messages are contained in a relevant filmic design fashioned by carefully crafted montage editing. We use words sparingly. We use narration or dialogue only to tell the audience what it needs to know but cannot perceive from the visuals. Today's audiences need to be trained, informed, and motivated— perhaps more so in our high-tech, communication-age society. It's our job, and our client's job, to do it and to do it professionally. We need to unleash the power of our communication medium from script to screen monitor with creative effectiveness, competence, and understanding. We must use our sight-and-sound kinetic media to communicate relevant messages that stick in the minds of the target audience and cause them to achieve the goals that are set for our shows: goals that are *fitting, realistic,* and *worthwhile.* In other words, in order to communicate effectively, we must engender empathy in our audience. The audience needs to identify with a personal experience, either vicariously or intellectually, with the people, emotions, places, and situations that we're depicting in our show's *mise en scène.* The more empathetic our message is, the more effective our communication. We must understand to the depth of our being that we are in the communication profession, not the film, video, or multimedia profession. We must *care.*

2

The Message and Motion-Media

Revolution. We're in the midst of a communication revolution. It's motion-media that dominate this revolution—video, film, multimedia, and all their spin-offs. We're in the cyberspace world of interactive, digital communications. Kinetic photography, with sound and its attendant distribution to mass audiences, is the root of our current communication revolution. Over the years, kinetic photography has evolved into today's motion-media, which will soon include other rapidly evolving media like virtual reality and three-dimensional holography. Today, motion-media is our primary information source. We send and receive many of our motion-media messages through the ubiquitous Internet.

As does the written word, motion-media has many forms and uses, ranging from theatrical extravaganza to lyric poem, from hard-hitting documentary to the fluff of a television situation comedy, from training aviators to experiencing the abstractions of Norman McLaren (see photo, appendix 2).

People communicate by talking and listening, by writing and reading, by broadcasting and viewing, and by acknowledging. These processes of transmitting, receiving, and acknowledging require considerable skill. Currently, more printed matter is available than ever before, and the people who are reading are reading more intently. However, most of the population is reading less. They're watching television and exploring the Internet.

In today's high-energy motion-media environment, we are inundated with myriad miscellaneous and multifaceted messages, all competing for our time, energy, and attention. The barrage never ceases.

Alvin Toffler puts it this way: "The waves of coded information turn into violent breakers and come at a faster and faster clip, pounding at us, seeking entry, as it were, into our nervous systems."[1]

Information comes in waves of the spoken word, the written word, the electronic word, and the photographic and graphic-art word in infinite variations and combinations. These are the obvious media, the ones over which we as communicators have direct and creative control. Consider also the host of other communication media that make up the bulk of the waves: a color, a signpost, an abstract painting, a scrawl, a whiff of perfume, a uniform, a traffic signal—every sensation that our five senses can receive. And each sensation contributes to the barrage of communication symbols and messages that our audiences receive every day, each with its own influence on their daily lives, their attitudes, their mores. Some are concise, some are subtle, but each demands some attention. Each sensation is ignored or acknowledged, either consciously or subconsciously. If acknowledged, the message must be assimilated, associated, evaluated, collated, and stored.

In such a message-intensive environment, it's difficult for most of us to make the split-second choices needed to acknowledge messages and act appropriately. Often, it's easier to ignore the messages, especially the more demanding ones that require us to think for ourselves. Instead, we wait for someone to show us the way— "they" will analyze what we're supposed to think and do.

I suspect that we've become too passive in this media-rich environment. It's difficult for many of us to sort and evaluate information, to visualize or conceptualize ideas and philosophies, to reason. We are beclouded in communication fog and static. For instance, Everett L. Jones of the University of California, Los Angeles, found that in steadily increasing numbers, beginning college students cannot write a simple declarative sentence. They must be enrolled in remedial, noncredit writing classes, with many taking the class several times to earn a passing grade.[2]

This complex problem is summarized succinctly by Mike Wallace of CBS who wonders "if we all aren't vastly overcommunicated, if words [and television pictures] haven't become a kind of Muzak for us, a background hum that fills the silent gaps of time in which, otherwise, we might just sit and think."[3]

Our task is to ensure that the messages we transmit via motion-media shows are not Muzak and do not numb the senses. Rather, our shows must communicate as intended. When "the lights come on" after our audiences have seen our motion-media show, we want them to be inspired to accomplish the goals or solve the problems set forth for the show.

Communication Business

It's the communication business we're in, not the film, video, or multimedia business. Understand this precept to the depth of your being. Actually, if we strip our profession to its essence, we're in the psychology business. We manipulate the minds of our audiences so that they will do, say, act, or think according to the goals we set forth in our motion-media shows.

As the most powerful mass-communication tool available, motion-media communicates with diverse audiences to arouse, document, educate, indoctrinate, influence, inform, inspire, motivate, orient, persuade, propagandize, report, recruit, seduce, teach, train, or sell. Let's explore this power by defining motion-media's general characteristics as a mass-communication tool. A motion-media show:

- communicates messages to large, heterogeneous, and anonymous audiences[4]
- communicates the same message to mass audiences simultaneously, sometimes in public, other times in private
- embodies messages that are usually impersonal and transitory
- is multisensory in that the audience's sight and hearing are stimulated in concert. Such a combination of sensory stimuli forms a complex synergism that can significantly enhance communication. This powerful double-barreled combination of dual-sense stimulation contributes in large measure to the compelling influence of motion-media
- is a formal, authoritative channel of communication. Accordingly, its power in informing and entertaining lies in the communicator's ability to control visual and aural stimuli[5]
- is instrumental in behavior and attitude modification—that is, attitude formation, change, conservation, and canalization (directing a preformed attitude to a new direction)
- confers status upon issues, persons, organizations, or social movements[6]

Kinetic-Visual Communication

We are a visual species. Television, motion pictures, graphic novels, picture magazines, multimedia, and the World Wide Web are just some examples of the visual media that we're exposed to. It's common to find information on computer menus, restaurant menus, and traffic signs conveyed not through words but through icons.

The point is, we don't think much in words per se. Words are too linear and too slow. Admittedly, words create visual images, but it's only by convention that they represent their referents. Vision is our primary medium of thought, and graphic images are the most powerful way of enhancing our perceptual thinking.[7] Unfortunately, we often don't communicate effectively in this communication age because we don't understand how to use motion-media to maximum advantage. Marshall McLuhan's adage "The medium is the message" prevails.[8] I disagree. I'm convinced that "The message is the message"!

Viewing is the key. The human visual system is an incredibly powerful information-processing device. For most of us, audible words play a strictly subordinate role in the reception of information.[9] And audible words should play a similarly subordinate role in our films, videos, and multimedia shows. Some of the best shows I've seen over the years—those that engender maximum communication and win top awards in competitions—are those with no, or only minimal, narration or dialogue.

I'll admit up front that such shows are the most difficult to design and produce. Sometimes the subject matter may not be conducive to such a filmic design's *mise en scène*. For instance, sociological themes like alcoholism, drug abuse, and sexual harassment usually require a dramatic setting with actors. However, with lots of concentration, imagination, and kinetic-visual thinking, we can design and produce *visual* shows that optimize our power to communicate.

Because every show is unique, there is no optimal mix of visual and aural information. However, an extensive series of psychological studies at Pennsylvania State University has given some empirical evidence that aural information should not exceed 20 to 30 percent of the total information content of a show.[10] Thus, shows that encode the vast majority of their information in the visuals have the best potential to be highly effective communication tools.

If we are to maximize the communication power of motion-media, we must use words (narration or dialogue) only to tell the audience information they cannot perceive from the kinetic visuals. Hence, our task as script designers is to blend information into the right mix of kinetic images and narration or dialogue.

Education, Educators, and Advanced Technology

Film and video just aren't the same anymore, and some older sight-and-sound media are fading fast. Filmstrips are old-fashioned, best suited for the ol'-time rural one-room schoolhouse. Slide/tape with its single picture-frames and wall-to-wall talk is at best illustrated radio. The technological explosion in electronics and computers has transformed our profession. It's not out of the ordinary to do photography in one medium, edit in another, record and dub sound in another, and release in yet another or in several.

A while ago, a friend of mine, a professor of cinema/television at a prestigious university, asked me the following questions: "How can educators best teach advanced technology in film and television production? How can educators develop their own expertise in this technology?" From my perspective, the professor asked the wrong questions. His emphasis is on first learning and then teaching how to use advanced technology. Inherent in his question was another: What equipment is the industry using now? Which buttons do we push and what levers do we pull to get the "XYZ" effect? How do we integrate such technology to produce motion-media shows: film, video, multimedia programs, and the host of other such media sure to follow?

While these questions and the ideas posed in the initial premise are valid, they are secondary. Such a perspective puts the cart before the horse. The professor's emphasis was on the technology rather than on the more fundamental aspects of communication. The question ought to be: How do we teach our students to encode information into coherent messages effectively and efficiently with the new communication technologies? How are such messages transmitted so that ideas are firmly implanted in the target audiences' minds? And how do we affect audiences' behavior so that they speak, act, or think in a manner that meets our communication objective? *All else is irrelevant.*

I understand what's happening. We are easily seduced by an advancing technology that apparently makes our jobs easier, faster, and more creative. Good enough! But all too often we lose sight of what we are up to: communicating ideas. We're bedazzled by the razzmatazz. Technology, per se, overwhelms us, and its use becomes our primary goal. Communication becomes secondary.

I'm convinced that today's educators, students, and media professionals have lost sight of their primary goal: to use motion-media to communicate ideas. In fact, I'm certain that many don't understand that a motion-media show is a communication tool and not an end unto itself. Often, creativity becomes just noise that hinders communication. There are more-important factors involved in the communication process. For instance, there are message importance, urgency, currency, motivation, anticipation, relevance, and, most important, empathy. We need to understand to the depth of our souls that "The message is the message."

If we focus our endeavors on teaching university students the technical aspects of our profession, we've become a technical training school instead of an academic institution. The university is where ideas, concepts, and rational thinking must be paramount. It's far more important that motion-media students have an understanding of communication theory, psychology, logic, research, communication skills, and system analysis.

It's of minor significance that students know which buttons to push and levers to pull. Besides, technology is changing so rapidly that it's impossible to train our students in the *latest*. It's through on-the-job-training that former students become proficient in using ever-changing and client-specific advanced technology.

Our goal is to have technology enhance communication value, not overwhelm it. The prime factors we consider when deciding just what technology to use are: the difficulty of the communication task, quality needed, cost, schedule, and distribution scheme. The compelling need for fast, accurate, and cogent information at reasonable cost is the driving force of our burgeoning information age.

3

Motion-Media in the Communication Society

Communications in the Twenty-First Century

It will soon be commonplace to conduct our business, education, entertainment, banking, and a host of other activities through hybrid communication centers that integrate into one instrument (with multiple substations) our television, personal computer, telephone (voice and picture), facsimile, and a host of other communication devices sure to come. Already, from the comfort of home, we meet colleagues, make deals overseas, plan our vacations, play games with associates in distant locations, and carry out myriad everyday affairs. Information networks transmit, via an array of telecommunication systems, telephonic, videographic, computer, and all manner of electronically encoded signals to our offices, homes, factories, classrooms, hospitals, and universities.

What role are we going to have in this communication revolution? How will we contribute? What kinetic-visual communication skills do we need to meet our profession's demands now and in the near future? Our challenge remains to produce and distribute "mind-bending" motion-media shows for information purposes—to communicate all manner of ideas to our audiences.

The technology has developed so rapidly—due in large measure to the design of powerful algorithms and the proliferation of powerful personal computers—that we can develop complicated motion-media shows with our computers that just a few years ago required a multimillion-dollar studio to produce. It's almost too easy.

Has technology seduced us to forgo our basic communication skills? Are our shows technically excellent but communication poor? Has technology exceeded our ability to use it to communicate effectively?

It's beyond my imagination to envision the advanced communication technologies that we'll have as this twenty-first century develops, but they are on the way, and we need to be prepared to understand and work with them. One such technology that I understand is currently in research and development is kinetic holograms. Nicholas Negroponte, director of Massachusetts Institute of Technology's media lab, envisions the reproduction of a real-time, three-dimensional, high-fidelity, surround-sound kinetic hologram of exceptionally high quality. We could experience the Super Bowl being played from end to end in our media room—the ultimate telepresence scenario.[1]

And so it goes. Communication in our information society focuses not so much on mass media but rather on interactive, personalized requirements. It's diversified and tailored, and it appeals to those of us with a singular interest. It's niche communications. There are dozens of niche cable-television channels available today, each targeting its own specific audience in a vast variety of special interests. We'll not have a problem filling the five hundred- to thousand-channel interactive television (or whatever) system with programming. Significantly, much of this programming is based on film, video, and multimedia filmic design and technology. And herein lies our opportunity and challenge: to be twenty-first-century communicators.

Where We Are Today

Oftentimes, we're mentally numbed in this hyperkinetic world we live in. It's too difficult to reason for ourselves or to seek other sources and opinions. It's easier to let "them" think for us. Thus, because of the power of motion-media and our acquiescence to it, it becomes the unquestioned authority. According to one nationwide poll, people believe that news on television is more reliable than that of newspapers. Because motion-media is society's primary source of information, it is the integral instrument in informing citizens about their government. Therefore, there is a heightened importance on these functions of motion-media:

- reporting (straight news and features)
- making editorial comment and disseminating propaganda

- helping society cope with the environment (natural, economic, political, etc.)
- communicating the social heritage (information, values, mores)
- educating the populace
- entertaining the masses[2]

Considering these powerful functions of motion-media, it's incumbent on those in control of the media to exercise moral judgment, accuracy, and fairness. They have an ethical responsibility to the public and to their profession.[3] Unfortunately, each stratum of society has its cadre of communicators and opinion leaders who bias mass-media communications with their own beliefs, agendas, and interpretations.

Should a communicator or opinion leader control the mass media to the degree that the populace has no access to alternative information, the communicator has monopolization. Monopolization results in effective control of the social and political environment through manipulation of the behavior and thoughts of the masses. Significantly, my late, longtime friend Father Louis Reile, Society of Mary, professor of film at St. Mary's University in San Antonio, said, "The prophet has a new tool, the cinema, that graphic art of reality caught on celluloid and shot through a magic lantern to simulate life."[4] Is the prophet ethical or immoral? To what end is this "magic lantern" used?

Commercial television is the dominant medium in our culture, pervasive throughout society. We can put a book-sized antenna outside our bedroom window and tune in dozens of worldwide television channels beamed down to us from an array of satellites. We can even broadcast our own special event over private satellite networks.

But to what end? To make a buck for the broadcasters and to be entertained? Let's not short-change television's ability to communicate ideas, to inspire, and to motivate. Oftentimes, we're just not using this powerful and ubiquitous medium to its full potential. Our society needs and feeds on information. Information-processing and communication are now dominant forces in the economy of our planet. It's up to us, the motion-media professionals, to make our media worthwhile—educational, motivational, inspirational.

The Communication Challenge

Graphic images are the most powerful way of enhancing our perceptual thinking. As Rudolf Arnheim says, "Perceptual and pictorial shapes are not only translations of thought products, but they are the very flesh and blood of thinking itself."[5]

I'm not sure how much real thinking takes place while we watch a soap opera, but what if we used motion-media for information purposes—to communicate science, geography, language, history, and ideas of all types? Let's produce and distribute mind-challenging film, television, and multimedia shows. It's been done before and most effectively by the masters of our profession. For example, Leni Riefenstahl used film with telling effect in promoting the German National Socialist (Nazi) Party in the 1930s, in *Triumph of the Will* and *Olympiad* (see photo, appendix 2). Conversely, Frank Capra used film with striking power in the *Why We Fight* series to rally American morale and efforts during World War II—yes, the same Frank Capra who produced *It Happened One Night*, *It's a Wonderful Life*, *Mr. Smith Goes to Washington*, and a host of other people-oriented films (see photo, appendix 2).

In the future, it matters not what communication tool we work with—medium, media, multimedia, hypermedia, supermedia, or something else. What matters is that we use our communication skills and technology to design and produce shows that communicate our messages to the target audiences readily, efficiently, and economically.

4

Information, Communication, and Meaning

If we agree that we're in the communication business rather than the film, video, or multimedia business—and if you don't agree, put this book down and watch a rerun of *Gilligan's Island*—let's now define terms, explore concepts, and develop an understanding of what this profession of ours is about. We'll explore briefly a few fundamentals. We'll look at Claude Shannon's information theory, and I'll discuss Shelton's theory of communication. An appreciation of such fundamentals (even if not in depth) is essential to the comprehensive understanding of this book.

Message, in the broad sense, is whatever stimulates our senses. David K. Berlo defines messages as "ordered selection of symbols intended to communicate information."[1] Accordingly, it's how we integrate (or encode) messages into filmic design that defines scripting. In order to communicate with the target audience, we must encode our messages into filmic design that engenders empathy. It's the audience's perception of our messages that's relevant.

Unfortunately, audience perception is tenuous. Some possible audience perceptions of the messages in our shows are: real or fiction, objective or biased, believable or incredible, informative or abstruse, artistic or base, stimulating or dull. These perceptions coupled with the show's filmic design define motion-media's effectiveness.

Meaning is a psychological function that involves cultural, social, and environmental factors. Though meaning is contained in the messages, it's the sender and receiver who give meaning to messages through their common understanding.[2] Areas of concern regarding meaning lie in the ambiguity of the messages themselves. At a minimum, there are three interpretations of a message:

- *intended message:* what the sender meant to communicate
- *transmitted message:* what was actually sent and received
- *understood message:* what the audience perceived the sender sent

There is a reasonable probability that the audience will not understand precisely any message we send via motion-media. All too frequently, the discrepancy between what we mean and what our audiences understand is frightening. No matter how well-planned, well-structured, and well-produced our motion-media shows, we are assured that we'll never be totally successful in our communication.

Communication Theory

Communication theory evolved from classical information theory developed by Claude E. Shannon of Bell Laboratories in the 1940s. Shannon, with Warren Weaver, devised a general communication system to explain the special problems of information processing, transmission, and reception attendant with electric and electronic systems such as telegraph and telephone and with the newly burgeoning electronic data-processing machines.

Shannon's theory was published in a 1948 Bell Laboratories paper entitled "A Mathematical Theory of Communication." In his theory, the term *information* has a mathematical definition specifying the probability that any given bit of information will be transmitted and received undistorted. He said, "The fundamental problem of communication is that of reproducing at one point either exactly or approximately a message selected at another point."[3]

Shannon defined communication as the encoding of information into electronic signals or messages, transmitting and receiving the messages, and decoding the messages back into information that is error free or nearly so. In broad terms, Shannon's definition is valid for any general communication system.

The General Communication System

Let's explore how information theory applies to all communication systems. First, we need to establish the framework. Information theory is built on several elementary components. Here are three primary ones:

Noise is anything that interferes with the reception and understanding of the signals. Because noise distorts the signals, it also distorts meaning. Noise is either mechanical or semantic: static on the radio or misinterpretation of the signals because of referent differences.

Noise has another face. Too many messages cause communication "static" that overloads the channel and the audience. Research indicates that as we pack more and more information into our shows, our audiences set up interferences—mental or physical defense mechanisms that result in less-efficient communication. This is especially true if the density of the factual content is contained in the narration or dialogue.

Channel is the means by which messages in signal form are transmitted from sender to receiver. For face-to-face speech, the channel is vibrating energy traveling in air (sound waves); for printed words, it's inked signs on paper; for video, it's electromagnetic signals traveling through the air or over cable; for motion pictures, it's images and sound recorded on film; and for multimedia, it's all manner of information stored on digital disk and in the computer.

Feedback is the receiver's acknowledgment to the sender that authenticates receipt of the message, confirms that the message is understood, and indicates that the action item, coded in the sender's messages, is (or will be) underway. Ideally, feedback ought to be in real time, but except for one-on-one communication (face-to-face, telephone, etc.), it seldom is. Feedback in film and video is usually

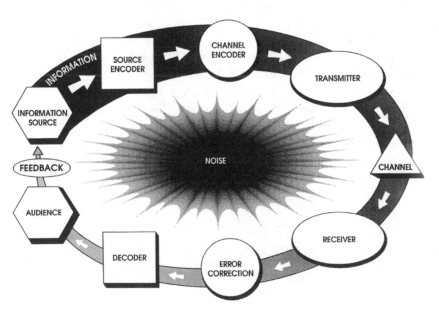

Fig. 1. Generic communication system

very low. However, in multimedia, feedback is a salient point. I would suggest that feedback is perhaps the most important characteristic of the entire communication process.

Let's see how these concepts integrate into Shannon's general communication system. Figure 1 illustrates the complete information flow from information source to audience and back to the source as feedback. In exploring this generic communication system, assume that we've completed our communication analysis, have clear goals, know our audience, and have our production plan in operation. I've chosen the video medium for an example.

- *information source:* the show's sponsor, research material, or interviews with the intended audience; with whom and how we do our research to determine what a show is all about
- *source encoder:* translation of the relevant information into a script and storyboard that detail the filmic design
- *channel encoder:* video camera that converts visual and aural messages into electronic signals
- *transmitter:* device that sends the electronic signals into the channel—for example, broadcast electronic boxes or the TV tower
- *channel:* atmosphere, cable, tape, digital disk, etc.
- *receiver:* antenna, black box, etc., that picks up the electromagnetic signals
- *error correction:* devices or algorithms that reduce noise that has gotten into the system; sometimes, the correction is a code introduced to prevent unauthorized receivers from receiving the messages *en clair*
- *decoder:* component that translates the error-corrected electronic signals into usable visual and aural information. Such signals may be re-recorded and transmitted to another receiver, such as a communication satellite
- *audience:* folks whose minds we're trying to manipulate
- *feedback:* element that closes the communication process; ideally, the audience acknowledges that the information has been received and understood, and appropriate action follows: "Aye, aye, sir," "Will do," "Okay," "I understand," "Ten-four," for example, or conversely, "Say again," "I don't understand," "Please rephrase"
- *noise:* bugaboo about which we need have most concern. Mechanical noise can destroy our communication system. However, it's semantic noise over which we have most control. Controlling semantic noise is in a sense what this book is about.

In any communication system with this degree of complexity, the probability of introducing error is high, through system failure, noise, or human frailty—barriers that make effective communication tenuous even under ideal conditions.

Information Theory

Shannon based his information theory on a mathematical model that resembles the second law of thermodynamics developed by Ludwig Boltzmann in 1894. Boltzmann avers that any closed system inexorably increases its disorder—that is, entropy increases. In essence, Shannon's theory deals with three primary and interrelated concepts: *uncertainty, entropy,* and *redundancy.*

Uncertainty is the amount of information the receiver does not have about the incoming information. Shannon notes that all information we receive is a combination of what we know and don't know. The incoming information is a blend of the probability of the expected and the unexpected, the certain and the uncertain. The more information the receiver has about the incoming message, the less communication is achieved. Thus, a message whose contents are known to the receiver before it's sent conveys no information. Conversely, some degree of information is conveyed if an unexpected message is received.

In other words, if a person knows that the first thing the boss says each day is "Good morning," and, sure enough, that's exactly what the boss says on Monday morning, no verbal communication is achieved because the person (receiver) knows in advance what the boss's incoming message is going to be. The boss has transmitted no new information. (We're assuming that no, or minimal, noise interferes with the communication channel.)

If, on the other hand, the boss says "You're fired!" then information received is optimum. It's the unexpected (what we do not know), the newness or surprise, that influences the amount of useful information we receive. Thus, *communication is the resolution of uncertainty.* Such resolution is the inverse measure of entropy. That is, maximum uncertainty corresponds to minimum entropy.

Entropy is a universal law that applies to communication, thermodynamics, and all other systems in this universe. The higher the disorder, the greater the entropy.[4] Entropy is an index of the uncertainty of a system. Put in another way, the higher the entropy of a message, the less work it can do and the less communication it can accomplish. The energy is there, but it's inaccessible.

Boltzmann posited that the tendency of any closed system is to become less orderly when left alone: Entropy increases to irreversible disorder. Or, things go from good to bad, maximum potential to minimum potential, order to disorder. It's easier for a system to migrate to disorder than to order. Order, on the other hand, is usually temporary and requires external energy to maintain itself once the migration to disorder has begun.

Let's suppose, for example, that we have a perfectly insulated container with a divider splitting its volume in half. Our container is totally free from any outside influence (a closed system). One side contains hot water. The other side has cold water. This thermodynamic system is orderly, and its entropy is low. The system's energy is available to do work. Unfortunately, our divider is water-soluble. Soon the divider dissolves, and the hot and cold water mix. Eventually, all the water in the container is at the same temperature, thoroughly mixed. The hot and cold water "system" is now disorderly, and entropy is at the maximum. The system can do no work or accomplish anything. Consider, then, that all worthwhile accomplishment results in an irreversible increase in entropy.[5]

You may well ask "What's this got to do with communications?" Excellent question. Before transmitting a message by speaking, writing, or projecting, the communication system has the ability to expend energy to send a message. Consider our example regarding the boss's Monday morning utterance. In the first instance, entropy is high. No communication is accomplished because the person knew in advance exactly what the incoming message was. In the second instance, entropy is low. Maximum communication is achieved because the person had no clue that "You're fired!" was the incoming message.

The higher the entropy, the lower the communication potential, and the lower the entropy, the higher the communication potential. That is because all possible messages are equally probable of being sent. Of course, after the person receives the message and the message is understood, entropy is high again. Nothing more regarding the communication can be accomplished. In effect, noise prevails.[6]

Redundancy is the transmission of more messages than are needed to ensure communication; it's the predictable or conventional in a message. In almost all transmissions, some redundancy is necessary for feasible communication. In the broad sense, redundancy is the set of rules by which we encode the information we are transmitting. We use redundancy to achieve a high probability of precision communication.

For instance, our English language has unnecessary letters in many words. Because we are knowledgeable about English, we most likely would understand the word *letter* if it were written *ltr.* This is because we know the rules of the language and know that certain sequences of letters are more probable than others. In aviation and military communication, we achieve redundancy by using words such as *Alpha* for the letter *A* and *Zulu* for the letter *Z.*

Another reason we use redundancy is to open channels of communication. For example, we might say on meeting our friend for the first time today, "Hi, Joe! I met Sam last night." "Hi, Joe!" is phatic communication. It's the opening gambit. It contains minimal communication, but it's important because it alerts our receiver to pay attention, because the primary or content message is coming. I call this phatic function the "heads-up." The content message is "I met Sam last night." We must assume that meeting Sam last night has significant meaning to both parties. Sender and receiver have a common referent, and communication is accomplished.

Our task as communicators is to keep entropy low, to reduce our audience's uncertainty by sending, in the appropriate channel, properly encoded messages that are meaningful, understandable, and, on the whole, new. We'll discuss these concepts in some detail in later chapters.

Shelton's Theory of Communication

We'll wrap up this chapter with a discussion of some ideas I have regarding communication. After much reflection over the forty-plus years I've been in this profession, I've developed a set of interrelated criteria that influences all *human* communication systems. These criteria define the ease or complexity of any communication task. I've codified these criteria in Shelton's Theory of Communication. Listed in descending order of relevance, these criteria are:

- *importance:* How important is the information to the audience? Its relevance? What's their advantage to know the information? The more important the information, the easier the communication. For instance, if the audience members know that to get promoted they must demonstrate skill in operating the Acme Thingamajig, they'll probably work to a fare-thee-well our multimedia program that deals with the Acme Thingamajig.
- *urgency:* When must the audience use the information? When must they take the required action? The more urgent the infor-

mation, the easier our communication task—a hurricane warning, for instance

- *currency:* When does the value of the information expire, become nearly worthless, or become historical? The more current the message, the easier the communication task
- *motivation:* Why is the audience interacting with the media: viewing, listening, reading? Is their interaction voluntary or compelled? Are they bored or interested in the subject matter?
- *anticipation:* Is there a heads-up that alerts the audience that a message is coming? What is the lead time before the communication process begins? Does the audience do preparatory work?
- *distribution:* What media do we use to transmit the information to the audience: speech, newspaper, motion-media, radio? Some of the factors affecting the distribution medium's influence on the audience are their familiarity with the medium, preference, access, and trust.
- *environment:* Is the ambience of the environment conducive to communications? What are the effects of the physical surroundings: ambient noise and light, climate, décor, and furniture?

With these criteria optimized, and if all other communicator factors are favorable, we've an excellent opportunity to engender empathy in our target audience. On the whole, the higher the empathy, the greater the communication.

I fully realize that the concepts in this chapter are extensive and complicated. However, they are the essence of our communication profession and apply equally well to all media: speech, video, newspaper, and motion-media. It's imperative, therefore, to understand these concepts and to know how to apply them in our script-designing and motion-media production efforts.

5

Creativity May Not
Equal Communication

The Alchemical Elixir

Our goal must be to design and produce eminently successful and highly acclaimed motion-media shows, but few of us ever do it, certainly not on a continuing basis. Our shows are often less successful and acclaimed than we've intended because we've deduced erroneously that a great show is a natural result of our application of creativity. To many of us in the communication profession, "creativity" has become a magical potion that ensures a successful show. It's a panacea that solves all communication problems. All too often, I've heard folks in our profession discuss creativity with a reverence that approaches idol worship—it's the alchemical elixir that cures all communication problems. We seem to be enraptured with the ever-expanding palette of advanced technology that enables us to produce shows with a dazzling degree of sophistication. Such sophistication makes a "great" show, I've heard. Such sophistry seduces us. Creativity becomes the *raison d'être* of many of our shows—communication fades to a secondary purpose. Our clients and audiences are disappointed because communication goals are not realized. The reason is that we didn't understand what creativity is—we misconstrued its worth in the motion-media process.

One example of this pervasive and misconstrued attitude that infects our profession was in our federal government's audiovisual (motion-media) standards, as published a few years ago.[1] To qualify to bid on government audiovisual contracts, prospective producers must submit a sample of their shows for evaluation by a panel of "experts." On several occasions, I served as one of the experts on such review panels. The shows we reviewed, on the whole, were inept—void, or nearly so, of communication values and technical prowess. Significantly, many of the experts on these panels did not know the difference between a sprocket hole and an f-stop. Trying times, indeed!

Out of a total possible score of one hundred (seventy is the qualifying score), a show can earn up to twenty points for "creativity." And creativity is divided into two subcategories: (1) Was the show fresh and innovative? (zero to fifteen points) and (2) Was the manner of presentation appropriate? (zero to five points).

Our federal bureaucrats tried to define creativity, but they missed. Neither of the subcategories defines *why* creativity enhances communication, which is the only valid criterion. Rather, the bureaucrats concentrated on the format of the shows rather than on their intrinsic communication power. This example pinpoints exactly the way we've distorted this concept of creativity. Twenty percent of the qualifying score is for something we don't understand, which is an inordinate weight to assign to such an ill-defined concept.

Is Creativity Essential?

Many people earnestly believe that creativity is essential to communication, but they fail to define their concept of creativity. Most dictionary definitions of creativity are truly elusive. Creativity is uniformly defined as "the quality of being creative," which doesn't tell us much. Let's hear what two professionals contend. Ed Gray, a scriptwriter, discussed creativity in terms of art: "The very nature of the audiovisual [motion-media] business is art. . . . By utilizing the artistic skills inherent in an audiovisual production house, we are attempting to transfer information in the most effective way." But we're not sure what he means by *artistic skills,* and note the word *attempting.*[2]

David MacLeod, an audiovisual producer, said, "In communications, creativity is the essence of packaging ideas and conveying them most effectively. It is not an add-on; it is not a peripheral. It's a foundation of our business, and it shines brightly through the lens . . . of projectors."[3] His assertion seems to echo McLuhan's maxim "The medium is the message."

As we see, some designers and producers tend to define creativity in terms of production value—a dramatic storyline replete with actors and actresses speaking well-rehearsed lines on elaborate sets and exotic locations, "clever" scenarios, special effects, and lots of other "neat" stuff. Wonderful! Hope you have a great time. To these designers and producers, resources are expended on the razzle-dazzle, and cleverness (i.e., creativity) becomes the critical element that makes a "great" show. Does the show accomplish the communication goals set for it? What audience feedback do you have? Are the show's goals fitting, realistic, and worthwhile? Is the show worth the client's money, time, and other resources?

Here's a contrary opinion. One of my longtime friends Charles "Cap" Palmer, pioneer in information films, avers that "creativity is a vastly misunderstood and misused value, whose effectiveness in forwarding the sponsor's objective often is in inverse ratio to its noticeability. True creativity (effectiveness) is seldom tricky, bizarre, spectacular, or obviously 'clever'—in fact, *it is more often basic and deliberately concealed*" (emphasis added).[4] Palmer's philosophy established the basic tenet of just what creativity is in our information motion-media profession. If our shows are to be successful, we must embrace this philosophy and integrate it into our shows.

Communication Fundamentals Often Ignored

What frequently warps the perspective of script designers and producers in the information motion-media profession is a hidden agenda that clouds their reasoning and jumbles their priorities. In essence, they've been bitten by the Hollywood bug and want to produce "movies," to create, and to be recognized and accepted by the film industry. They're wanna-bes.

To illustrate how inane this mind-set can become, I'll cite one classic example. Some years ago, the U.S. Air Force produced a training film on the C-10 aircraft for Strategic Air Command crews. To grab the audience's attention, the opening scene shows the well-endowed actress Bo Derek in a scene from the film *10* (1979), wearing a form-fitting swimsuit and her cornrow hairstyle, gliding along a beach. The scene fades into the outline of a C-10 aircraft. Such a scene may well grab the audience's attention, but I'm not sure where. An air force lieutenant colonel's comment on the justification for this opening sequence was, "We try to make it interesting . . . you can't just throw schlock at them."[5] Do you mean to say, colonel, that a Bo-10 begets a C-10?

Though this example may be at the extreme fringe of creativity gone awry, it's not atypical. I've seen all too many of this kind of gratuitous scene in shows over the years. It's the high-tech equivalent of third-grade refrigerator art. What's "interesting" is a show that motivates the target audience to action. It communicates.

Perhaps the most profound statement on creativity in motion-media comes for Jean O'Neal, producer/designer of multi-image shows. She has earned widespread recognition from her peers, winning a number of best-of-show and other top-notch awards. In a letter to me, she stated, "I still feel that it's much more difficult to do a one-projector show well than it is to do a 12-projector razzle-dazzle number. *You simply cannot cheat on a one-projector show and pull it off*" (emphasis added).[6]

Interesting = Communication

No matter how uninteresting the information is to us—the motion-media designers and producers—it will be interesting to the target audience if it is important to them and if they can realize benefit from the information.

Communication via motion-media is dependent on many factors. Notwithstanding any cinematic design or other considerations, communication is a primary function of audience receptivity to the information: The degree of communication achieved is directly related to the intensity of audience desire or need for the information. For the audience, communication involves factors of message importance, urgency, currency, motivation, anticipation, distribution, and environment. (See Shelton's Theory of Communication in chapter 4.)

In relation to information motion-media, most of our audiences are mentally prepared for our communication—they are receptive because they want the information. With neutral or hostile audiences, our communication task is more demanding; a touch of persuasion is needed to heighten or precipitate these audiences' desire or need for the information.

If our audiences have a receptive frame of mind, they are ready to receive our messages. On the whole, it's not necessary to sugar-coat these messages with entertainment and gimmicks. We don't need epic productions, sexist stories, moronic jokes, or technical perfection.

John Grierson, the acclaimed documentary film pioneer, commented on these points in 1942 when discussing the great influence his documentary films have had on a host of audiences throughout the British Empire (and on the rest of the world). He said, "It is not the technical perfection of the film that matters, nor even the vanity of its maker, but what happens to the public mind."[7]

Information motion-media shows should have an inherent dignity with a clear-cut purpose. Usually a simple, straightforward presentation with voice-over narration, keeping the message in plain view, is appropriate for most situations. We use fundamentals of persuasion and learning to lead the audience to a conclusion or decision that we've made obvious or inevitable. Gimmicks simply introduce noise into the communication process and should be avoided.[8]

Creativity Defined

We can consider creativity to be a function of two primary factors for which we can establish criteria for evaluation: communication value and technical achievement. Even though they are closely interrelated, each has distinct characteristics that set the tone and style of the motion-media show. Below some of the more important factors of communication value and technical achievement. There are many more. It's their totality that defines the grammar and syntax of the motion-media show.

Communication value is a measure of the effectiveness of the motion-media show. To what extent are the stated objectives accomplished? The evaluation criteria are:

Appropriateness. Considering the target audience and subject matter, the motion-media show is the appropriate communication tool to achieve the show's goals—goals that are fitting, realistic, and worthwhile.

Information. The essential elements of information are developed logically, clearly, and succinctly and are in the proper tone. The bulk of the information is encoded in the visuals. Audio elements reinforce the visuals, thus enhancing communication to full measure.

Empathy. The show gains and holds the target audience's attention and involvement. It generates peak empathy. Communication is engendered to maximum effectiveness.

Approach. There is a fresh, imaginative, and pertinent approach that facilitates information flow. Information is couched in a tone and form that are relevant to the audience's needs.

Cinematography. It's technically excellent and aesthetically pleasing. Composition facilitates communication by highlighting key points of the essential elements of information. Lighting sets an appropriate mood and has continuity throughout individual scenes.

Sound. It is crisp and clear; words are pronounced for proper emphasis and spoken at the appropriate pace and style. Music and sound effects help set mood and pace. All sound elements are blended to achieve a harmonious whole.

Editing. Relevant visuals are sequenced to achieve optimum communication. The pace is appropriate, moving easily from one point to the next, using smooth transitions that reinforce audience interest and commitment. Screen direction is used effectively to create filmic continuity (harmony) or dissonance. Plasticity of the medium (manipulation of time and space) is optimized to maintain orientation and to accomplish an appropriate flow of information that reinforces communication objectives. This plasticity is one of the most important elements of motion-media.

Art. The art is pleasing and appropriate. Its style fits with the tenor of the show. Art elements use spatial relationships to accentuate important points. Perspective is true. Shading and highlighting are used to create depth and emphasis. Form, mass, and color are arranged in compositions that heighten communication.

Thus, by my definition, a creative motion-media show fulfills to the maximum the criteria that constitute communication value and meets an acceptable threshold of technical achievement commensurate with the communication task at hand—and not much more.

We're professionals in this motion-media communication profession. We achieve success not with the technology we use but with the creative use of our communication and technical skills. Such creative prowess is basic and deliberately concealed. We need to understand to the depth of our souls that "The message is the message." Creativity then may well equal communication.

I conclude this chapter with quotes from two educational giants in our profession.

Charles F. Hoban Jr., communication theorist, pioneer in communication research, and emeritus professor of communication at the University of Pennsylvania, casts the problem in its true perspective when discussing sophistication in the technology of filmmaking. In some of the new film genera, he maintains, hedonism is transparently triumphant. The gimmickry is great, but the message is lost or, worse, the wrong lesson is taught.[9]

Robert Davis, professor of communications at Florida State University and a visual scholar, notes, "Although technology is a wonderful thing, it is all too easy to become seduced by the hardware in audiovisual [motion-media] production, and forget the true goal of getting ideas across to the audience. True, you can dazzle them with special effects, but did anyone get the message?"[10]

Part Two

Motion-Media

6

Information Motion-Media

Communication objectives for our shows are extensive and diverse. They range from teaching psychomotor-skill development to cognitive learning, from attitude and behavior modification (work safely or stop smoking) to persuasion (buy Acme automobiles or vote for Samantha Smythe-Farthingale). Other objectives include correcting widespread misconceptions, improving morale, increasing awareness and sensitivity, informing, inspiring, instructing, introducing a new product or service, motivating, reporting on scientific progress, and training.

As a mass communication instrument, information motion-media has brought the world to the school-bound student and to all of us at our work and in our homes through television and the World Wide Web. Information motion-media is wonderfully effective in exploring the invisible, such as electron flow in digital circuits; describing the immovable or unreachable, such as the moons of Saturn; reporting a current event—for example, the Nobel Prize awards; or selling an intangible product, such as group life insurance.

Unfortunately, sometimes such goals are masked as commercials for the sponsor of the show. Commercial messages ought not to infect other types of information motion-media. I recognize, however, that if the Acme Computer Company sponsors a show for senior citizens on how to use the Internet, it's okay to show seniors using Acme computers. Obviously, commercials are okay if the show is, in fact, a commercial. I, for one, consider the television commercial to be the definitive information motion-media show, but when we're not producing a commercial, we need to be certain that the message we are trying to communicate is not confused by embedded competing messages.

More troubling, all too often I see information motion-media shows couched in a narrative (entertainment) filmic milieu. I'm convinced that entertainment per se should never be the underlying basis or style of an information motion-media show. Over the years, I've seen too many of these shows. Universally, they fail in their primary communication objectives. They may entertain the audience, and they may boost the script designer's and producer's egos, but more often than not the entertainment elements engender noise that hinders communication.

Power of the Information Motion-Media

Why is it that information motion-media is so powerful in communicating ideas? How are we using it to shape minds? John Grierson, founder of the documentary film movement in England, speaking of information and documentary films on the eve of World War II, said, "Like the radio and the newspaper, film is one of the keys to men's will, and information is as necessary a line of defence as the army."[1]

Grierson was one of the first to realize the medium's persuasive power—the overt and subliminal intrusion of ideas and emotions into a person's psyche. In 1935, he said, "Cinema is neither an art nor an entertainment, it is a form of publication, and may be published in a hundred different ways for a hundred different audiences. . . . [However,] the most important field is propaganda."[2] If we define propaganda to mean marketing, his perceptions were uncanny—note the surfeit of highly effective television commercials that hawk everything from army recruitment to zinfandel wine.

Background

In the early days, information film was called sponsored film because industrial organizations first used it as a marketing tool. According to the curator of Eastman House in Rochester, New York, sponsored films were produced shortly after the invention of motion pictures, the first appearing in the early 1890s. Film historian and information film producer J. Walter Klein said in his book *The Sponsored Film* that the Standard Oil Company of Indiana sponsored a film in the early 1900s. General Electric produced one in 1907, National Cash Register in 1911, and the International Harvester Company sponsored *Back to the Old Farm* in 1911. By 1930, there were only about thirty films that could be called "educational."[3]

During World War II, the use of information film exploded as a powerful communication tool to train our military. Significantly, it was our archenemy Field Marshall Wilhelm Keitel (1882–1946), chief of the High Command of the German Armed Forces, who commented prophetically, (and I'm paraphrasing), "We cannot win this war because of the way the Americans use film to train their soldiers."

Factors Affecting Influence

We can identify five major variable factors that apply to all information motion-media:

Motivation. The audience must be motivated in order for communication to occur. Each one has to be convinced that it is to his or her advantage to be in the viewing environment and to pay attention.

Credibility. If a persuasive information motion-media show is to be successful, the audience must hold the film designer, sponsor, and the medium itself in high esteem in terms of credibility and prestige.

Audience profile. Audiences come in all sizes and compositions. Individual temperament, background, understanding, and values are singularly diverse. Yet, if we are to communicate effectively with the target audience, we must know who they are. That is, we need to know the audience's composition—the audience profile. Optimum communication occurs when the messages are couched in a tone and a *mise en scène* that are familiar, relevant, and sympathetic to the audience. Such messages engender understanding, acceptance, involvement, and empathy. And without empathy, there's little or no communication.

Content. There is a host of content factors that apply. I've found the following general points to be crucial for most of our shows (I recognize that exceptions exist for special applications):

- The messages need be short and to the point. Too many details cause a mental "short circuit" in our audience.
- Cute gimmicks often backfire and become noise that obscures the primary message.
- Most messages should be visual. About 70 to 80 percent of the information should be in the pictorial content.
- Auditory messages must be secondary and used sparingly only to reinforce the visuals.

Structure. How the messages unfold is critically important. The following abbreviated list contains ideas on filmic structure that I've found particularly useful:

- Anticipation heightens audience awareness for a coming event.
- A "heads-up" alerts the audience to the incoming message; requirements tell the audience what is expected from them after the viewing and explains why.
- Repetition is more than simple duplicative iteration; it is the varied presentation of the major points, concepts, and meanings.
- The optimum development rate allows the audience time to assimilate the new information or concepts and allows time for reflection.
- Participation involves overt sharing in the communication process, exemplified by interactive multimedia.
- In shows with sociological themes, narrative (dramatic) structure can generate empathy if the audience can identify with the elements of background, characters, and plot.
- Summation reviews key points and presents a cohesive survey of their relevance.

Cinematic Techniques

In addition to the influence factors that we've discussed so far, we need to explore the various cinematic techniques that influence audiences. Such techniques are detailed masterfully in Joseph V. Mascelli's (a member of the American Society of Cinematographers) landmark book, *The Five C's of Cinematography*.[4] I urge you to study Mascelli's book in detail. Here is my summary of Mascelli's "Five C's":

1. *Camera angle*. Determines the audience's viewpoint, engenders emotion, and sets the scope and perspective of the shot. The basic camera angles are extreme long shot, long shot, medium shot, two shot, close-up, and other specialized angles. Additionally, Mascelli classifies shots as:

- *Objective*. Audience sees the action through the eyes of an unseen observer, as if eavesdropping. This is the basic cinematic shot.
- *Subjective* (sometimes dubbed zero-degree camera angle). Subjective camera is that camera angle that shows the action from the eye position of the audience. Audience sees the scenes as if they are seeing them through their own eyes. This angle is preferred in detailing procedures in close-up shots.
- *Point-of-view*. Audience sees the scene from the point-of-view of an off-screen player. Puts the audience cheek-to-cheek with this off-screen player.

2. *Close-up*. Eliminates all nonessentials in the scene and focuses on the critical element of information. Engenders dramatic impact and visual clarity, involves audience in details of the scene, and concentrates on key points. (Even though close-up usually is included in camera angle, Mascelli separates close-up as one of the Five-C elements.)

3. *Composition*. Arranges all pictorial elements in a shot with the goal of forming a unified, harmonious milieu that forces the eye to the center of interest and stimulates the audience to the appropriate mood. Lighting is a prime factor in setting mood.

4. *Continuity*. Makes a smooth, logical flow of visual imagery from shot to shot and from scene to scene. Establishes coherence; defines the path in the plastic medium. There are exceptions for special considerations. Nowadays, discontinuous cutting between sequences is in vogue. Sometimes, sound continuity is the thread of coherence.

5. *Cutting* (editing). Editing is the function that in large measure manipulates the plasticity of the medium. Editing determines the measure of coherence and tells the story. Editing is largely responsible for capturing and holding audience interest through scene selection, sequencing, tempo, screen direction, interplay of scenes, and selection of optical and electronic effects. Superior editing is essential to a successful motion-media show.

Mascelli's Five C's define the basic tenets of filmic design—the grammar and syntax of motion-media. It's with filmic design that we script the kinetic visuals and produce our shows.

If We Can Do It in Five, Why Take Ten?

Most linear information motion-media shows are too long, saturated with too much information and too many concepts. I've seen far too many shows that ramble incessantly, pounding the audience into catatonia with a barrage of overwhelming and gratuitous trivia that obscures the essential points and significantly reduces communication. In essence, too many messages confuse and bore the audience.

Our information motion-media shows are competing with a host of other interests and distractions for the valued time and minds of our audiences, yet we continually ignore this fundamental fact. We make our shows too long and ponderous. We pack them with too much information—information that is beyond the comprehension, concerns, and retention of our audiences. Some of this information overload is due to our own ineptness. But all too often, I suspect, it results from our kowtowing to the sponsor's whims to include this, that, and everything else, regardless of what we know to be best. And candidly, sometimes, information-overloaded shows result from our financial needs—that is, longer shows command larger budgets.

Some designers and producers contend that a show must contain many subtle points to achieve its goals. Two examples often cited are motivational and attitude-modification shows. The reasoning is that sufficient time is needed to set the stage, fully develop the rationale, array the inferences, and cinch the conclusion. Perhaps, but not always. I tend to agree with this reasoning for shows dealing with sociological problems, such as drug abuse, alcoholism, and sexual harassment. Such shows usually have the key points couched in a narrative or storytelling milieu. We need to develop these points carefully and logically, and this takes screen time. How much? Unknown. Each show is unique. But my maxim still holds: the shorter the better.

Most topics with which we deal ought to be developed quickly. For instance, the five-minute motivational film *The Man from LOX,* with its sharply focused communication thrust, was eminently successful and became a standard in its field.

Several researchers have conducted empirical investigations into the problem of communication overload. In the aggregate, their conclusions are much the same: As more and more information is presented, interference (noise) is induced in our audience and results in reduced empathy and thus less-efficient communication. It's an inverse proportional ratio: As we increase the information content, there's a proportional decrease in the amount of communication accomplished.[5] Most audiences can comprehend only a discrete amount of information in a viewing because of the linearity of film and video.

Communication Advantage

The liability of linearity argues well for short motion-media shows—five to seven minutes—designed with a rapier-like communication thrust aimed directly at the target audience. In such shows, there's no tedium, preaching, or ennui.

Today, we're dealing with sophisticated audiences who are experienced in receiving messages in fifteen- and thirty-second blasts (e.g., television commercials). Thus, in today's communications environment, successful information motion-media shows need to transmit information in highly concentrated, relatively small doses to select, well-defined audiences. All other factors being equal, such shows gain the communication advantage by:

- using a memory aid to reinforce what the audience already knows about the topic
- highlighting three or four key points of one central theme
- setting these points in relevant perspective in terms of background and related facts or concepts
- tying the points together in a related chain
- reinforcing critical points
- getting "The End" title on quickly

The memory aid is an excellent device to save lots of screen time. It enables us to get our show off to a running start and to keep it at a fast pace.

Television Commercials

In many ways, the television commercial and information motion-media are akin. The television commercial's primary goal is to sell. There are other goals, of course, such as persuading us to vote for ——, make contributions to ——, or deposit our recyclables. But in the grand scheme of things, these types of commercials are secondary. Perhaps, then, a slight digression is in order to explore the basics of why the television commercial is so successful.

Producers of television commercials, forced by the constraints of having to get their messages across in just a few seconds and driven by intense pressure to succeed, pioneered a metamorphosis in our profession. Using linearity to advantage, they developed a neo-Orwellian communication tool, engineered with the latest high technology, populated with glamorous people, and laced with seductive messages. The messages are singular in purpose, rapid-fire, repetitive, and largely inescapable. The television commercial molds minds and shapes lifestyles effectively, quickly, and categorically. There are four fundamental psychological keys to television commercials:

- send short messages to realize effective communication
- blur the boundary between reality and fantasy
- stimulate the self-gratification libido
- reinforce impulsiveness and selfishness[6]

Though it may be awkward to admit, we need to realize that these same four principles apply to the entire genre of information motion-media, albeit perhaps not always so flagrantly or intensely.

Nonetheless, they are fundamental to our profession. No matter how we rationalize or what we call it, our task is to manipulate the minds of our audiences. We influence the behavior and thoughts of others, whether they want to be influenced or not.

In essence, the television commercial is a single-concept information film—a hybrid, perhaps, in that it is much shorter, more sophisticated in production values, and carries a deeper psychological punch. Of utmost significance, it's in the television commercial that many new, often radical, production concepts and techniques are first used. From my perspective, the television commercial is the research, development, test, and evaluation function of our profession. As such, there is much we can learn from these highly effective, single-concept communication tools—if we would only heed the example.

The Prophesy

Fortunately, some in our profession did understand and heed. Taking his cue from the early television commercials of the 1960s, Charles "Cap" Palmer, a missionary for the short, single-concept information film, prophetically said, "The educational film we have known is doomed . . . tomorrow's audiovisual will be single concept, from thirty seconds to a few minutes long."[7] The important point is that Palmer's prophecy of doom was based on the general ineffectiveness of the traditional, long-winded, overbearing training films of the day. He saw the compelling need for the short, single-concept film to break through the traditional barriers of cost and clutter and to open up new worlds of effective communication.

Short, Single-Concept Motion-Media

The short, single-concept presentation is in ascendancy. It is becoming the most critically important communication tool we have, a tool that readily engenders communication. Sometimes dubbed *chapter film, trigger film, film bit,* or *film clip,* this maturing medium is inherently simple, direct, cogent, and succinct. In other words, every second counts. Every frame counts. The audience instantly engages. The show gains momentum all the way to the final credits. The audience should leave a little wiser, a little sadder or happier, a little different.[8]

Communication in concentrated bursts is the intrinsic elixir of the short, single-concept, linear information motion-media show. Ideally, the screening of such a show should be backed up with liberally illustrated printed material. To encompass a total communications environment, there ought to be participatory discussions before and after a screening. From such an environment, the audience should have the show's information embedded in their brains, ready to use.

In addition to facilitating communication, other advantages realized by the short, single-concept shows are:

- moderate production, duplication, and distribution costs
- production values are usually high
- valued time of the audience is used sparingly
- facilitator has more time for direct audience interaction
- time is available for repeat screenings/viewings

Not a Panacea

The short, single-concept information motion-media show isn't the ultimate answer to all persuasive communication tasks. Nothing is. In some instances, the topics, goals, and audiences are not suited to this type of show. To get our communication task done right, we need to consider the full repertoire of communication alternatives— different forms of motion-media (multimedia or slide/tape for example), or some other media. Or perhaps some combination of media is appropriate. I've found that combining media is exceedingly successful in communicating many types of complex messages.

Remarkably improved over those training films that Palmer decried, some of today's single-concept shows are crisp, creative, and powerful. Perhaps it is the short, single-concept show that we should consider as the primary solution for some of today's persuasive communication problems.

7

Film and Video

As communication media, there is no difference between film and video. Both develop information linearly, one point at a time in sequence. The principal differences are technical: the way information is captured, stored, manipulated, and distributed, chemically or electronically. Nowadays, even this difference is melding. For instance, a show may be shot on film, edited in video, and distributed in film, video, or in a variety of digital formats.

Film and video are excellent motion-media to solve communication problems that require strong, animated visuals and whose goals tend toward altering the mind. (Multimedia is best for most cognitive teaching and psychomotor-skill training.) Mind-altering suggests general goals such as informing, motivating, imparting broad-based concepts, heightening awareness, and other "soft" goals. A simple, straightforward approach is usually best for communicating these sorts of goals. Sociological themes are sometimes communicated effectively in a photoplay *mise en scène,* using actors in authentic locations to create a realistic scenario that engenders empathy in our audiences.

Sometimes linear film/video is effective in tackling cognitive-teaching goals. Such a film/video is short, has no more than five or six key points, and is narrowly focused. If a film/video with cognitive goals exceeds these maximum criteria, it's almost always ineffective. Our audience just can't remember all the details, gets bored, and loses interest. For instance, a few years ago I critiqued a film/video that was intended to teach sales personnel about the products that the sponsor manufactured and sold. The show was fifty-eight minutes long and had about fifty key points. The ultimate blow to communication was that the show's *mise en scène* was the classic stilted scenario of the "old guy talking to the young guy." In this case, it was the store manager (male) talking to the sales associate (female). This super-expensive show was a total failure. Admittedly, some of the audience might remember a few of the key points, but how could they put these points in context? I suspect that boredom and resentment in the audience negated whatever minute positive communication value the show had.

Unfortunately, film/video's tinsel glamour seduces too many of us, and we end up producing "movies" rather than communication shows. We couch our messages in entertainment. I've seen far too many of these sorts of shows. They always fail. They're too complicated, long, expensive, and tedious. Wake up the audience when the lights come on!

Advantages of Film/Video

Film/video offers a host of unique advantages as a communication medium. Conversely, it has serious disadvantages. Let's focus first on the advantages. I've listed several in descending order of importance. Also, in this section we begin to explore the grammar and syntax of the media.

Visual medium. Film/video's most important characteristic is that it's a visual medium. Each photographic scene is a faithful reproduction of the images and movements of events (real or simulated). Of course, we can distort the scene with optical and digital manipulation. The power of film/video as a communication tool is illustrated by the old maxim "A picture is worth more than ten thousand words." Results of a study conducted by the National Audiovisual Association a few years ago found that in a motion-media show 83 percent of learning comes from the visuals. Audiences remember *long-term* 30 percent of what they see, and 50 percent of what they see and hear simultaneously.[1]

These remarkably high learning and retention figures result from an audience's ability to assimilate visual information at an extraordinarily rapid rate. Wilson Bryan Key, professor at the University of Nevada, Reno, (author of *Subliminal Seduction*), conducted studies that found that, on average, a person can grasp, process, and store visual information in as little as 1/3,000 of a second.[2] Also, the more familiar the audience is with the visuals, the more there is a progressively nonlinear, almost exponential, increase in assimilation and understanding. Key indicates that all our sensory equipment operates simultaneously and continuously and that the upper limit of our reception ability has not yet been determined.

Thus, as a kinetic visual-medium and with the camera in deft hands, film/video's power is projected exponentially. Camera moves such as pan, tilt, zoom, dolly, truck, and crab change visual perspective. Long shots give orientation and perspective to the scene. Medium shots show comparisons. Close-ups give detailed examination. Deft use of the camera attracts the audience's attention to objects and movements that are only marginally perceptible in a scene. Transference of attention occurs in a scene by a movement (perhaps ever so slight), a light shift, a change in composition or perspective.

Multisensory. The visual primacy of film/video is reinforced by its multisensory features. Both sight and hearing are stimulated in concert. This multisensory quality, with the right mix of sight and sound, has a powerful synergistic effect on audience comprehension, assimilation, and retention. Such a right mix of sight and sound portends maximum opportunity for optimizing communications and engendering empathy in our audiences.

There's no absolute formula for the right mix of sight and sound. The mix depends on the show's goals, audience, and *mise en scène.* Studies conducted by Charles F. Hoban Jr. and Edward Van Ormer at Pennsylvania State University in the 1950s found that, on average, maximum communication effectiveness is achieved when the sight and sound mix is about 70/30—that is, when about 70 percent of the information is in the visuals and about 30 percent is in the commentary (narration or dialogue).[3] We don't consider music and sound effects in this mix unless they convey critical information. Of course, there are lots of exceptions, but some of the best motion-media shows I've seen over the years have no commentary whatsoever. Three examples are Albert Lamorisse's narrative film *Le Ballon Rouge,* awarded the Palme d'Or at the Cannes Film Festival; Frédéric Back's *Crac!,* which received an Academy Award; and Bob Rogers's *Ballet Robotique,* which was named best of show by the Information Film Producers of America.

The auditory information, conveyed by narration or dialogue, must not introduce communication static. To be effective, auditory information must complement the visual information. *Auditory information must be used only to explain or amplify what the audience cannot perceive from the visuals yet must know for a complete understanding.* For instance, in the award-winning ten-minute show *299 Foxtrot,* there's minimal narration, perhaps only a minute's worth if it were spoken continuously.

On the other hand, in shows that deal with sociological themes, dialogue and narration are important factors in the communication process. Such is the case because we're using actors who speak lines, so the pace of the show is slower and usually there's minimal requirement for fast-paced montages. For example, in a show that depicts the effects of gambling addiction on family life, the scene is the final confrontation between the husband and his chronic-gambler wife, who abuses the children and is destroying the marriage. The objective is to communicate the destructive effect her gambling addiction has on this family. The film designer might conclude that there's no effective way we can communicate this bit of sociological information into the visuals. We need to hear (and see) the anger and frustration of the husband and the denial of the wife. Facial expressions and staging help to communicate, but they can't do the task alone. Therefore, we've had to put much of this information in the dialogue. The auditory information must have absolute coherence with the visuals. These elements must show and tell the same message; otherwise, we're sending mixed messages and confusing our audience. We must avoid that old saw found too often in scripts that describes the visual information as "a variety of scenes to complement the narration."

Karel Reisz of the British Film Academy put it this way when discussing the robbery sequence in Carol Reed's 1946 film *Odd Man Out:* "The dialogue track does not anchor the visuals by conveying important information, but adds to the total effect on a contributory rather than a primary level."[4]

If the audio consists of music, sound effects, or background prattle (or a combination of these), it must be unobtrusive to the degree that its presence is not noticed. These sound elements set moods, add the dimension of reality, and amplify the pacing established by the visuals. Interference is established quickly when these aural elements become preeminent (in volume or importance), or incongruous, or not germane.

The primary interference, however, usually emanates from a commentary in the form of an incessant harangue of drivel or from a mélange of technical trivia that dulls the senses. Attempting to comprehend what is being said, most audiences will concentrate on the commentary to the exclusion of the visuals. Since there's no time for reflective thought in this linear medium, our audience falls further and further behind. Eventually, they'll give up by escaping mentally or physically to a more comfortable environment.

Sometimes, music or dance is the major theme in film/video. Such shows fall into the enrichment genre and are not strictly informational. Two examples are Norman McLaren's *Ballet Adagio* (which won a Bronze Plaque at the Columbus Film Festival) and Allan Miller and William Fertik's *Bolero* (which won an Academy Award).

Mass media. Another major advantage of film/video is its ability to reach the populace simultaneously or sequentially over time. The show is transmitted over and over again in a myriad of locations, each time sending the *identical message* to new audiences. Even though all audiences receive the same message, it's important to understand that a message's influence will vary with individuals and kindred groups within the audiences. For repeat audiences, the message may be reinforced. In terms of overall audience influence, sometimes reinforcement can be a powerful communication factor. The total audience is limited only by the show's distribution scheme. The cost per screening/viewing per person, over the long term, is usually the most economical of all media for a given message.

Visually sophisticated audiences. As a result of many years of incessant bombardment by the mass media of film/video, today's audiences are attuned to receiving copious amounts of kinetic sight-and-sound information quickly. In our fast-forward society, our audiences expect to get much, if not most, of their daily dose of information through linear motion-media. Capitalizing on this audience expectation, we can design film/video shows to be shorter, faster paced, and more cogent—all with overall economy of production and distribution resources.

Empathy. Empathy is that close identification or emotional commitment that audiences have with a person, place, or event depicted in a show. Unless a show is a total botch, some degree of empathy is engendered in our audience. *Our goal is to optimize the empathy.* I've found that the more intense and enduring the empathy, the more immersed and involved our audiences become. It follows that there is a significantly higher probability that our audience will receive, process, and store the show's messages and take appropriate action.

Message factors to consider in engendering empathy in audiences are:

- Are the messages relevant?
- Are the messages couched in familiar terms and settings?
- Are the messages believable (no matter how false they may be)?
- Does the show have an asking, sharing, and involving tone rather than a talking-down-to or a telling tone?
- Is the audience motivated to understand and accept the messages?

Should a film/video not generate empathy, no matter how skillfully produced it is or how invitingly real or fictional its theme, communication will usually fail. The communication power of a film/video is a direct function of how well its messages relate to the audience and the intensity of the empathy generated and, thus, audience acceptance. It's "the willing suspension of disbelief."

Our task as film designers is to exploit this willing suspension of disbelief in our audiences to engender empathy. In the preproduction process, we must conduct a comprehensive audience analysis. We need to know exactly who is this audience that we intend to influence, manipulate, motivate, or train. Among the host of questions we must ask and answer are: What are the audience's motives in viewing our show? What are their education, intelligence, age? What are their interests, mores, and attitudes? What is the viewing environment? There are no pat answers to these questions. Each show is unique and requires a distinct set of questions and answers for a valid audience analysis.

From this analysis, we can design and produce the show to fit the audience profile—a show with which they can empathize. Generally, I've found that the shows that engender the most intense empathy are not patronizing or abstruse; they present just enough challenge to pique interest. Admittedly, this is a fine line.

Plastic medium. We distort reality by manipulating time and space. We can extend or compress time. We can visit any location near-instantaneously and make remote locations congruent with our theme. With such manipulation of time and space, we incite intense emotional reaction in our audiences by using rapid movement, contrast, comparison, pace, and warping of familiar forms.

We manipulate time and space through various editing techniques. For instance, with a simple editorial cut, we could jump from outer space to the interior of the Oval Office in the White House. Or we insert a close-up (CU) shot or a cutaway shot into a master scene to either expand or compress time. (In motion-media parlance, abbreviated shot descriptions are capitalized.)

By juxtaposition of scenes and sound, we combine individual, unrelated elements into a new relationship that they do not inherently have, thus creating dramatic, powerful psychological effects "to explode ideas in the heads of our audiences," as John Grierson said.[5] These unique capabilities result from editing shots into a cinematic rhythm that manipulates relationships in an infinity of unnatural combinations of connotations and associations. Emotions and ideas are juggled and interpreted in unusual ways that evoke audience responses to different perspectives, which may be real, distorted, or false.

Sergei Eisenstein noted, "Two film pieces of any kind, placed together, inevitably combine into a new concept, a new quality, arising out of that juxtaposition."[6] For example, if I were to edit a three-shot sequence consisting of a close-up (CU) of a computer screen (photographed in Baltimore), followed by a close-up of the hands of a person working a keyboard or mouse (photographed in Dallas), followed by an extreme close-up (ECU) showing changes on the monitor—assuming backgrounds and lighting are similar—our audience would conclude that this person is causing the changes on the monitor.

Also, scenes that are dissimilar, unrelated, or nonsequential can be joined into a pregnant relationship by juxtaposition and adroit screen-direction manipulation. This technique is prevalent in historical documentaries composed of stock and news footage. *Victory at Sea* is an excellent example.

We use time and space manipulation for detailed study of fast-happening events, for scientific analysis, for understanding of natural phenomena, or simply for artistic purposes. Time-lapse photography compresses into a few seconds the hours or days that some events take to complete—cumulus clouds building or flowers blooming. Conversely, high-speed photography expands near-instantaneous events into seconds, minutes, or hours—for example, an explosion or a staged automobile crash shown in slow-motion.

Also, we distort time by digital and optical processes. For example, in duplication, we expand time by repeating frames. And we compress time by skipping frames.

Designer selection. Designer selection is the artistic and scientific blending of the psychological and technical elements to design and produce the show—the synthesizing of major filmic-design elements into a total communication package. It's the control we have in what imagery is shown to the audience, how it's shown, and where in the show it's shown.

One elemental advantage of designer selection is that we show the audience precisely what we want them to see and when we want them to see it. With scene selection, the film designer has total visual and audio control. In a live stage play, the audience can choose by concentration and selective viewing what they see, be it the entire scope of the stage or just the face of a speaking actor. In film/video, the audience can see only what we show them. Recognize that the audience has some selective viewing decisions in certain types of scenes—a long shot, for example—but this is severely limited in terms of the total viewing experience in motion-media.

How information is shown, in terms of scene types—long shot (LS), medium shot (MS), close-up (CU), and extreme close-up (ECU)—determines in large measure its relative importance. The more full-frame an action is, the more emphasis it has. It's in the close-up and the extreme close-up, and to some extent the medium shot, that the essential elements of information (key points) are successfully transmitted. Additionally, a series of CUs or ECUs edited into a montage sequence significantly enhances the importance of an action.

Another element that gives import to information is simply the amount of time it's on the screen or monitor. Generally, the longer the screen-time an action has, the greater its importance. *Caution:* Such is the case only so long as the audience continues to get new information from the scene. If we dally, our audience's saturation point is quickly reached. They get eye exhaustion and mentally focus on something else—dinner, for instance.

How information is shown is another factor influencing emphasis and importance. Some of the techniques used for this purpose are split screen, rack focus, multiple image, zoom, soft focus, perspective distortion, solarization, and color shifting. All are image-controlling devices that distort or enhance the audience's visual perspective.

The juxtaposition of information within a show influences greatly its relevance and importance. Juxtaposition defines where information is shown in terms of internal sequencing. For example, consider this fundamental filmic-design sequence: LS, MS, CU, ECU, CU, CU. All shots depict related and sequential action. If the essential elements of information are contained primarily in the CUs and the ECU, the audience should immediately comprehend the information's meaning and importance. And they'll understand its relationship to the preceding background information established in the LS and MS.

In summary, designer selection is the psychological strategies and technical means we use to influence our audiences to ensure that they receive our show's message completely and correctly.

Captive audience. In most viewing environments, our audience is captive. If we've designed and produced our show correctly, audience members look at the screen or monitor to see what we want them to see, and they hear only what we want them to hear. We've established near-total control of their sensory environment. The only options for our audience are to adapt to the environment and follow the show, to mentally turn off, and switch channels, or to leave the room.

Passive audience. In most cases, our audience is passive in shows with soft communication goals, such as informing, attitude changing, or motivating. (This element is a concomitant factor of the captive-audience advantage.) Audience members don't have to do anything. Physically, they settle in their chairs, relax, and are ready to receive information. They follow along as we, the film designers, visually lead them through every facet and nuance of information. Ideally, sometime after the show is over, they'll think of the show's message. This can happen within seconds, several days, or even later. Some particularly well-designed and well-produced shows of the attitude-changing or motivational type can exert their influence for many years. This is especially true in shows that cause the audience to become intensely emotionally involved—to have empathy.

Abstract visualization. Film/video is an excellent medium to visualize abstract concepts. Through a short animation sequence, the economic concept of gold in international finance or the effect of oil on the world's economy could be made understandable to tenth-graders.

Remote location. Film/video takes the audience to realms far removed from the screening/viewing site. Our cameras go anywhere on the earth's surface, under the oceans, and into space. This advantage is not limited to geographical locations; it encompasses the total range of possibilities, including microphotography of bacteria, macrophotography of molecular structures, or astrophotography of a distant nebula. With fiber-optic photography, we can see the aortic valve functioning. Through animation, we can visualize something that is inaccessible by reason of size or nonavailability. For instance, we can explore the inner workings of the human circulatory system or look inside a transistor to see the electron flow. With specialized cameras, we record microwave, infrared, and radar images.

Tailor-made. Every show is unique. We design each show especially to resolve a particular communication problem. (A few very specialized shows have multipurpose applications.) The precision-communication thrust of the show is concentrated on the essence of the problem for the specific target audience. If we design and produce our shows with filmic-design professionalism, we'll engender empathy in our audience, and the probability is high that tailor-made shows will be successful in achieving the communication goals we've set.

Silver-screen magic. All factors considered, I've found that audiences generally tend to be receptive to messages contained in information film/video. Such acceptance stems from some sort of silver-screen magic that I've not been able to identify clearly. This magic comes from an arcane and inherent authority attendant on all well-produced shows. Simply said, it springs from the perception that if the show was made, it must be important. I've found that our audiences usually are receptive to an upcoming show and bring lots of goodwill and anticipation. They're willing to be open and follow our development as long as we keep their interest piqued.

These advantages of film/video I've noted make motion-media a powerful tool in solving many communication problems. It's not infallible, however.

Disadvantages of Film/Video

The many advantages of information film/video ought not to cloud our reasoning in motion-media selection. Information film/video has serious disadvantages that make it unsuitable for many communication scenarios and tenuous for others. As professional communicators, we need to examine the specific communication problem at hand. Our final media selection results from a trenchant analysis of all favorable and unfavorable factors. Let's look at the most germane disadvantages of film/video. Again, I've listed them in descending order of importance.

Linearity. The prime disadvantage of film/video in its traditional format is that it must be seen continuously from start to finish. Because the medium is a time-based product, its information must be developed sequentially. Perhaps more important, the show must be seen sequentially. Our audiences can't skip, freeze-frame to concentrate, or peruse at random. There's no time for reflective thought, for review of difficult sequences, for detailed scrutiny of complex visuals, or for discussion. Too much information is lost and cannot be retrieved. (A book has no such disadvantages.)

Multiple screenings alleviate the problem only marginally if such screenings can be arranged at all. It's important to note that with today's audiences, we run a risk with multiple screenings: Audiences get bored quickly, causing negative attitudes resulting in reduced communication. Film/video's linearity reduces significantly its overall effectiveness in teaching cognitive and perceptual motor skills.

Linearity also poses serious problems for those who do not have the need, time, or inclination to see the whole show—at least to see it the way the film designer intended it to be seen.

Transitory nature. Information in film/video is evanescent. The messages, though stored on the film/video medium, evaporate the instant they've been projected and seen. Generally, our audience has no residual material for perusal or for review. If our audience didn't get the messages, or most of them, the first time they saw the show, they're out of luck. Unless they get a copy of the show, odds are that they'll not have another chance to see it.

Except in very few instances, this fleeting nature of the medium, coupled with linearity, significantly negates most long-term retention of hard information. Specifically, I'm referring to depicting a complex, sequential, motor-skill operation, listing exact numbers or items or showing a complex drawing or detailed technical information. Usually, after a few months, our audience remembers only a few impressive highlights of such shows. Detailed information is lost so quickly that, if it's not reinforced in some other way, it has only marginal validity for inclusion in a show. (A handout, such as a liberally illustrated printed-word document, is an excellent reinforcement medium.)

Alien perspective. In terms of information content, development, and pace, motion-media shows have the perspective formed by the subjective judgments of the film designer. Such a perspective may well be alien to some of our audiences. Careful preproduction audience-analysis will alleviate some of this problem, but we can never completely eliminate it because of the uniqueness of each individual in our audience. The easiest show we can produce is designed for one person. Our audience analysis enables us to draw an accurate psychological profile of this individual. Accordingly, we tailor the show in precise terms of this profile to optimize communications.

Alien perspective can negate an opportunity for audience members to find or evaluate the truth, relevance, import, propriety, and perspective of each element of information. Also, it can negate the totality of the show's overall message. Other problems arise for those who cannot or do not want to follow the development we've set as to what's seen, how it's seen, and where it's seen. For some, the pace of the film may not be to their liking or need—either too fast or too slow for their individual comprehension rates. (Multimedia is not encumbered by these properties.)

Inflexibility. Sooner than most of us expect, our films and videos become obsolete. This is especially the case with shows that deal with topical subjects. Because the medium is an inflexible composite of sight-and-sound messages, no message element can be changed without affecting all others. Any updating or revising is nigh impossible without substantial expenditure of resources: time, energy, and money. As a result, there are far too many obsolete shows in circulation.

Logistics. To screen/view a film or video, we need lots of sophisticated equipment and suitable electric power. In the Western world, viewing video (in all its releasing media) usually is not a problem. Most facilities have power, video-playback devices, and monitors.

Film screening is a more difficult scenario. In addition to power, we need a projector, loudspeaker, speaker cable, screen, take-up reel, darkened room with chairs, a projectionist, and, if possible, a host to introduce the topic and lead the discussion. The logistics of putting all these parts together are decidedly complex. All this equipment, the technical personnel, and the audience must assemble in near-perfect harmony at the appointed time and place.

Should all this film equipment and personnel not come together as planned, negative attitudes are generated in our audience, which seriously impede receptivity. Additionally, the audience should be motivated to realize that it is to their advantage to view the show then and there. One research study found that the nearer the goal for using the show's information, the greater the communication.

Under all but ideal conditions, release prints and videotapes deteriorate rapidly. Scratches, torn sprocket holes, missing sections, dirt (especially on the sound track), burned-out lamps, and incorrect projection all contribute to the degradation of the film screening and to a negative ambiance among the audience members.

The screening/viewing environment should be conducive to audience reception of the show's messages to provide enough isolation from outside influences and enough comfort so that the audience is not distracted. Ideally, the screening/viewing room ought to have light and acoustic controls and be insulated from outside glare and noise. The seating arrangement should provide clear viewing for all audience members.

In both film screening and video viewing, the equipment is heavy, expensive, in constant need of cleaning and preventive maintenance, and prone to breakdown. (Digital distribution media have long lifetimes.)

Cost. It's expensive to design, produce, and distribute film/video and multimedia. Considering all the communication tools available to us, motion-media is probably the most expensive in terms of cost per show. However, over the long term, with many screenings and viewings of the same release print, tape, or disk, I suspect that motion-media is the least expensive in cost per person per screening/viewing.

Of all the disadvantages, cost is the one that needs a most careful evaluation. We must determine clearly that the expected communication achieved by the prospective audience is worth the cost. (Flip charts, viewgraphs, slide tape, and audiotape are comparatively inexpensive.)

Lead time. It takes a relatively long time to produce a communication-effective information motion-media show and to get it distributed. If there are no other compelling reasons, this disadvantage alone seriously erodes the justification to produce shows dealing with fast-developing topical subjects and communication problems that can be effectively tackled by other media. (Live radio and television are faster.)

No room for error. Effective motion-media by its inherent authority commands attention and, I believe, respect. Therefore, one absolute guarantee of failure in a show is to be dishonest or inaccurate in any way. Today's audiences are too sophisticated to be deceived. A show's total credibility is lost quickly if the audience detects any misstatement of fact or visual distortion that's intended to deceive. On the other hand, deception is the norm in propaganda shows. Such deception doesn't necessarily have to be overt; deception can be subtle, ingratiating, effective, and dangerous.

Within my experience, I've found that one way to have a visual or aural distortion accepted is to tell the audience unabashedly that the scene is a fake, for whatever reason. For example, our narrator might say, "We are using a model now (instead of a real airplane) because it's easier to control in this demonstration of approach procedure." In such circumstances, the audience usually will empathize and, by being more receptive, join the film designer in the communication process.

When to Use Film/Video

Linearity and the medium's other disadvantages augur well for short films/videos—five to seven minutes—with pinpoint communication thrust. I've found this type of show to be significantly more effective than those that laboriously drag on, and on, and on. The short film/video is a more efficient use of design and production resources. Such films spare our audiences the tedium of watching material they won't remember.

Frequently, I've found that there is no one best communication medium. Film/video is excellent for some types of messages—for example, general information, sales, motivation, orientation, and some limited kinds of teaching. The film/video medium is not effective usually for communications that require detailed, long-term retention of specific facts or procedures. Nonetheless, film/video is a powerful communication tool that influences vast audiences every day.

8

The False Reality of Motion-Media

The Filmic Genres

As does the written word, motion-media has many filmic forms and uses ranging from theatrical extravaganza to lyric poem, from hard-hitting exposé to the fluff of a television situation comedy, from army training film to the abstractions of Norman McLaren. Whatever its chameleon form, motion-media is vitally effective in influencing vast audiences through its inherent power to evoke intellectual and emotional stimulation.

To categorize the various filmic forms, I've defined five genres that encompass the gamut of motion-media production. The filmic genres discussed apply primarily to film and video, though to some extent they also apply to multimedia. (From this point on in this chapter, I'm using *film* to encompass all motion-media).

Suffused throughout the various genres is an aura of reality that ranges from intense to shallow. When we view a show, there are always factual and psychological distances from reality. In point of fact, there is no reality in film—there's only the illusion of reality.

Reality per se has only moderate influence on film's effectiveness as a communication tool. Rather, it's the audience's perception of reality that engenders involvement and empathy—the acceptance of the show's message—and thus communication.

Because motion-media usually is a formal, authoritative channel of communication, our audience's perception of reality in our shows is a critically important factor in script design and production. Any deviance from honesty, relevance, and actuality will quickly subvert our audience's acceptance of our message.

Reality in Film

If we acknowledge that reality per se can never be achieved in film, it follows that realism is a function of audience perception of the medium's encoded messages. Are the messages real or not real? What matters is whether the audience believes the messages to be real and accepts them in the context presented. Nevertheless, the credibility of the sender is a compelling factor in audience acceptance.

Film's physical form is real (motion-picture film, tape, or disk). Images on the screen and monitor and sound from the amplifier are real, albeit transitory. Thus, film and its images and sound are all tangible reality—they are signal messages. However, the film's content (information coding) is almost always in the form of sign messages—representations of reality, similar to photographs and recordings. Sometimes, message coding is in symbols, that is, abstract representations of reality—mathematical or graphic symbols, for example.

Perhaps the closest that film can come to true reality is to use the camera and microphone as factual recording instruments. An example would be to record an event such as a medical operation—say, brain surgery—in continuous real time with a fixed camera having a prime lens chosen for undistorted perspective and using color-reversal film. Although not artistic, the resulting film would be a faithful reproduction of the operation and would have value to medical personnel for training. Use of film in this way does not exploit a farthing of film's potential, and it flies in the face of any filmic design or artistic achievement. However, we recognize this use of film as a valid application of the medium.

Even though the film in this example of medical documentation is realistic and true, it does not begin to approach reality. The camera and sound-recording equipment that substitute for our eyes and ears fail to create an all-encompassing multisensory experience. The fixed camera prohibits our natural propensity for selective viewing—such as long shots, medium shots, and close-ups of the central action and scanning of the operating room to understand the environment, background, and reactions of the participants. It fails to use the fundamental essence of film: the plasticity of the medium. Missing also are the tactile, olfactory, and taste sensations that would be stimulated in a real situation.

Some contemporary narrative films, attempting to intensify and broaden stimulation of the senses, use techniques such as wide-screen or three-dimensional photography, and there have been attempts to stimulate the audience's olfactory and tactile senses. Usually, these techniques do not significantly enhance reality or, for that matter, artistic merit or communication effectiveness.

In film, reality is the film designer's interpretation of actuality. Using technical devices and filmic techniques, the film designer transforms actuality into a media form that reflects his or her personal aesthetic to solve the communication or entertainment problem at hand. The feeling or sense of reality is the foundation of film's effectiveness. This is particularly true for the information film. Yet because of film's plastic nature, real time, space, and form remain infinitely distorted.

Clearly, then, the camera and the microphone are much more than recording instruments. When properly directed, these mechanical tools become creative instruments that stir the emotions, generating audience involvement and empathy.

Theories of Film Reality

There are several theories and concepts of reality in classical film study. Of these, five find historical and philosophical perspective for the concept of reality in film:

Part-whole theory. As expounded by Sergei Eisenstein and V. I. Pudovkin, this theory contends that individual scenes in themselves are unfilmic and only fragments of reality. Only by editing scenes into coherent montage sequences does film become art, and reality emerge. (*Battleship Potemkin* is an example.)[1]

Relation to the real theory. This theory, developed by André Bazin and Siegfried Kracauer, rejects the idea that film art and reality result from creative editing. Rather, Bazin asserts that if individual scenes are faithful reproductions of reality, only a simple assembly of scenes is needed to make the total film art and an accurate replication of reality. He notes, "We are forced to accept as real the existence of the objects reproduced, actually represented, set before us [in film], that is to say, in time and space"(the medical film, for instance).[2]

Kino-eye theory. A forerunner of the current-day cinema-verité, this theory propounded by Dziga Vertov asserts that the camera, as an extension of the human eye, has the ability to penetrate every detail of contemporary life.[3] Essential to this theory is the concept that the film designer must never stage a scene or interfere with a spontaneous action among people or in nature. The film designer's only job is to record events as they happen naturally. Through use of technical devices and montage editing, film evolves as a mirror of reality (Barbara Koppel's *Harlan County, USA,* for instance).

Creative actuality. John Grierson, founder of the documentary film tradition, defined documentary film as "the creative treatment of actuality." Grierson illustrated his concept with comments on the film *Moana: A Romance of the Golden Age:* "Being a visual account of events in the daily life of a Polynesian youth, [it] has documentary value. . . . It became an absolute principle that the story must be taken from the location, and that it should be the essential story of the location."[4] (An excellent example is Grierson's *Night Mail.)*

Paul Rotha, one of Grierson's associates, amplifies and explains Grierson's thesis: "The film is photographed from real life and is, in fact, recorded 'reality' by the selection of images, brought about by an intimate understanding of their presence. The film becomes an interpretation, a special dramatization of reality, and not mere recorded description." Some years later, Rotha restated Grierson's definition of the documentary film as "the use of the film medium to interpret creatively and in social terms the life of the people as it exists in reality." Rotha's comments recognized the focus of documentary film as it was evolving in the mid- and late-1930s. Hardened through time, his definition precisely describes documentary film as we know it today. Significantly, Grierson first became interested in film as a medium for reaching the public, not as an art form.[5]

Psychological distance. In 1933, Allardyce Nicoll discussed the concept of the "willing suspension of disbelief" in his essay "Film Reality: The Cinema and the Theatre." He contends that dramatic illusion is never an illusion of reality; rather, it is always make-believe. For aesthetic appreciation, the audience asserts a measure of psychological distance so they may "believe" (accept) what they see, even though they know it to be a dramatization.[6] (An example is G. T. Rogers's film *My Father's Son.)*

An apparent realism in characters, costumes, sets, objects, and forms creates an environment conducive to shortening the psychological distance. Conversely, in a surrealistic film, such as Jean Cocteau's 1930 *Sang d'un Poète (Blood of a Poet),* where the nightmare is realism played in fantasy sets, the audience increases the distance, never "believing," just being entertained or mystified from afar, having minimal or no empathy.[7] Significantly, some audiences who understand the nature of such a film will accept it for what it is and have an appreciation of it as artistic achievement.

Appearing to be intrinsically at variance on first glance, these five principal concepts of reality in film are mutually reinforcing. Each has a valid premise, and each makes a cogent point.

Film Reality Scale

Film, as the powerful mass communication tool it is, encompasses a broad continuum of genres, ranging from hard information that approaches absolute reality to symbolic surrealism that approaches complete abstraction. Within this continuum of film as a medium, I define five general film genres:

- information
- documentary
- narrative
- enrichment
- experimental

Each genre has its own set of distinguishing characteristics and representations or distortions of reality. We can make a grid of these five genres on a Film Reality Scale (fig. 2) to illustrate the concept of reality in film.

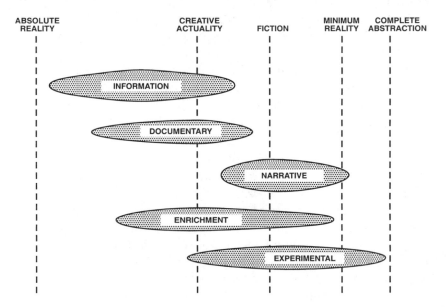

Fig. 2. Film Reality Scale

Here's my rationale for the genres' nonsymmetrical forms. If I were to place a dot on the Film Reality Scale to classify and plot every film ever made, the resultant scatter-diagram might look like figure 2. Admittedly, there would be some dots scattered throughout the diagram, because not all films fall into discrete groupings. However, the bulk falls along the spectrum as shown.

As you can see, there is considerable overlap among the film genres because each type, by its nature, spans a broad spectrum on the Film Reality Scale. The termini for the film types are based on limits inherent in the definitions of the types.

The Film Reality Scale ranges from absolute reality to complete abstraction on a nonlinear continuum. Interim measures on this graduated scale indicate cardinal points defined in accordance with my interpretation of the film reality concept. These cardinal points should be considered representative concepts that illustrate the gradual evolution of change along the reality continuum, rather than as definitive points that have a pragmatic measure. Scanning the scale from left to right in figure 2, these points are:

- absolute reality
- creative actuality
- fiction
- minimum reality
- complete abstraction

Absolute reality. In the categorical meaning, reality can never be achieved in film. However, through cinematic techniques, some films have a sense of reality that approaches the absolute. Increasingly, as interpretations are introduced and the plastic elements of the medium are utilized, the film becomes more illusory and thus less real, though it may appear to be more real to the audience through the willing suspension of disbelief and other psychological factors.

Creative actuality. Located slightly to the left of midpoint is Grierson's concept of "creative treatment of actuality."[8] In creative actuality, the filmmaker has restaged (or staged) many of the scenes in the film. Much of the restaging reflects the filmmaker's bent to emphasize the goals of the film. As fanciful elements are introduced, the film drifts increasingly toward the fictional.

Fiction. As with absolute reality, there cannot be total fiction in film except perhaps in some bizarre fantasy film. Even in fiction films, the actors themselves are real people speaking a recognizable language. The definition of fiction used here is that the film's major dramaturgical elements of plot, events, and characters are fictitious, while ancillary dramaturgical elements, such as props, costumes, locales, sets, and background, are actual, or nearly so, and the historical setting is reasonably accurate. As reality wanes in the major elements, the tenor of the film approaches the outlandish and, concurrently, as the ancillary elements become less real, the film drifts toward the phantasm of minimum reality.

Minimum reality. At the point of minimum reality, communication, by its standard definition, becomes insignificant. The film becomes more an exercise in artistic achievement than a carrier of messages. It's a statement of self-expression. Surrealism with bizarre or incongruous symbols in unnatural juxtapositions prevails. As these characteristics intensify, the film evolves quickly to nonsense and complete abstraction.

Complete abstraction. By definition, no film can be completely abstract, though some approach it closely. Near this point on the Film Reality Scale, the film has no meaning except perhaps to the filmmaker. The film is aesthetic gibberish, a fantasy of unrecognizable images linked by a totally random process of no significance.

Classifying Films by Genre

The critical elements I use in classifying film by genre are:

- purpose of the film
- primary audience
- production design (the *mise en scène*)
- scope of the show
- filmic techniques
- plausibility of the plot
- credibility of the characterizations
- actuality of the events
- distribution scheme

With these elements as our guiding influence, we can evaluate a film as a totality in order to classify its genre. The five film genres are defined with the following general properties:

Information film is a mass communication tool produced to communicate messages to mass audiences. The general goal is to influence audience members so that they will act or think in a way to accomplish the goals established for the film—that is, what to do or think, how to do it, or why to do it. Usually, a client sponsors the film, and it is produced conventionally with a moderate to low budget, using standard filmic techniques. Occasionally, the film shows a sparkle of artistic merit. A nonpaying audience views information films on private and public channels—for example, in classrooms, training centers, and on television.

Documentary film is produced to enlighten the masses about a contemporary topic, a social idea, or an editorial position through the technique of creative treatment of actuality: a restaging or re-creating of events according to the filmmaker's interpretation of some facet of life and the world in which we live. That is, the film is a representation without introducing consequential, fictional story interest. Production values are higher, on average, than those of the information film. Some such films are aesthetically accomplished. Generally, a nonpaying audience views documentary film on the public channels of television. However, it is not uncommon for this film type to be seen in a classroom or in a commercial theater (especially in Europe) where admission is charged, as it was in the beginning of the documentary film movement.

Narrative (entertainment) film is an entrepreneurial venture, produced to make a profit. Almost always, narrative film is a drama based on human emotions, experience, and conflicts, and many of the dramaturgical elements are fictional. Narrative film has very high production values compared with the other genres. We view narrative film in theaters, on commercial television, and in private settings through rentals. Narrative film provides enjoyment, pleasure, diversion, etc., to very large, heterogeneous audiences. Profit is realized by selling air time and collecting admissions, rental fees, and royalties.

Enrichment film is difficult to classify because it's usually produced for aesthetic enjoyment and peer recognition. Generally, this film has no specific communication goal to achieve except in the broadest terms of a central theme. Frequently, profit, realized from film sales, rentals, or public screenings, is a strong underlying motive. Often, the theme is chimerical, production techniques are unorthodox, and the budget is limited. Usually the enrichment film is privately funded or financed by grants. Enrichment film is screened at film festivals and in museums, cine clubs, classrooms, and other private channels for cineasts and other selected audiences. The cognoscenti savor the show's artistry. At times, enrichment film may be seen on television and even more rarely in commercial theaters.

Experimental film includes several subtypes, such as abstract, avant-garde, fantasy, implausible, impressionist, surreal, and underground. In experimental film, anything goes, and it should. The imagination has free rein and is bounded only by the limits of the filmmaker's skill and of the production budget. An experimental film is the filmmaker's statement of some inner compulsion—an interpretation of a dream, for example—expressed by a collage of imaginary images distorted in time and space, a grotesque illusion. Often, visual, abstract patterns prevail in a fantasy of artistic experimentation not bound by any tradition and not produced to accepted norms. Nowadays, the experimental film is frequently privately funded, sometimes by grants. Often, experimental film is seen (and appreciated) by elitist film buffs and jaded aficionados in private or semiprivate screenings. Experimental film also is screened in art houses and noncommercial theaters for discriminating audiences. Film students write papers about the experimental films they screen and try to emulate the producer, usually without much success.

Of all the film types, it's the experimental film that performs the aesthetic research-and-development function of the medium—revolutionary ideas are tried, new cinema techniques are innovated and introduced, and old ideas and techniques are rediscovered, modified, and honed. Music videos are an excellent example.

In this discussion of film genres, many other features could be considered and evaluated. Therefore, this treatment is not to be construed as limiting or pragmatic but reflects my concept of this complex and amorphous topic. It also illustrates the extreme differences in film as a mass communication medium, circumscribes the spectrum of each film genre, and lets us zero in on how the films are classified. Since the concept of reality, in terms of plausibility and credibility, is integral to a film's classification, the reality continuum of the Film Reality Scale also needs to be developed.

I admit that the classification of all films into these five types and their placement on the Film Reality Scale are subjective and reflect my own predilections. I recognize as equally valid a host of other classifications and placements that would reflect another author's unique perspective. Rotha, for example, classifies film into twelve categories, including abstract, cine-poem, cine-surrealistic, fantasy, cartoon, and documentary or interest. Interestingly, Rotha does not recognize the information film. At best, he defines the film type he designates the cine-record "as a representation of modern fact, without the introduction of story interest . . . to be found in current newsreels." Another writer and filmmaker, J. Walter Klein, notes that there are "three general categories of nontheatrical films shown to the public: television commercials, sponsored film, [and] education films."[9] He does not specifically mention these as belonging to the information film type as I define it.

There are, of course, films that cannot be easily classified. These exceptions defy pragmatic classification because they span a large segment of the Film Reality Scale, having substantial elements of several types or because they appear to be something they inherently are not. With minimal justification, these films could be placed in any one of several categories. For example, there probably is some entertainment value in all films, but not all films are produced for entertainment. In addition, almost all films have some informational value, though clearly all are not information films.

In the final analysis, it is the individual in the audience who makes the decisive and important categorization and placement, either consciously or, more likely, unconsciously. According to the social-categories theory, these determinations are based on the individual's unique value of what is real and what is fantasy—that is, what is plausible and what is sophistry.[10]

Let's explore this audience-perspective thesis with a real-life example. A film with a religious theme justifiably can be placed in any type; it depends on who in the audience makes the decision. A devoutly religious person might classify the film as information and plot it near absolute reality. An agnostic might classify it as entertainment. An atheist might classify the film as experimental, approaching complete abstraction.

The possibilities of viewer perspective and reaction are endless and reflect the plastic and three-dimensional nature of the Film Reality Scale. To develop this idea of the variable nature of film, we can explore the five film genres and plot representative films on the scale. Specifically, we are interested in the ability of film to convey information and arouse emotions as a function of audience perception of reality and their acceptance of the film for what it is, real or not.

Plotting Films on the Film Reality Scale

To see how this scale works, I've plotted a few films on the information and documentary spectrums. With a spectrum ranging from near absolute reality to a spot somewhere between creative actuality and fiction, the information film encompasses an extremely large region on the Film Reality Scale, reflecting the broad spectrum of this type of film as a communication tool. To repeat: Information film is produced specifically to communicate messages to audiences with the prospect that at some time in the future, audience mem-

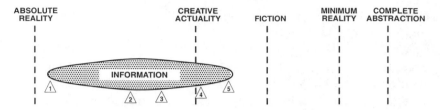

Fig. 3. Information film spectrum on the film reality scale

bers will think or act to the predefined level of satisfaction necessary to solve the communication objectives defined for the film.

Figure 3 shows a plot of five films along the information film spectrum on the Film Reality Scale. The films are representative of the
gamut of information film; each has a different communication goal:
to instruct, to sell, to motivate, etc. I have plotted these films according to my own perception to demonstrate the scope of the genre along
the information film spectrum. I encourage you, the reader, to plot
your own selection of information films along the spectrum and
perhaps to rearrange the ones I have selected according to your own
perception. I suspect the difference may be substantial.

Near absolute reality, at point 1, lies our hypothetical film on
brain surgery. This kind of film is the least functional of all and
appeals to the most narrow of audiences. Nevertheless, it is an accurate record of a real event, with its messages having value to
medical personnel.

At the opposite end at point 5 is the nonconformist *Man from
LOX*. I produced this six-minute motivational film in 1971 to motivate Navy liquid-oxygen (LOX) handlers to work safely. Reality is
tossed aside within the first few seconds of the opening scene. In a
series of chimerical scenarios, played in stylized yet simple settings,
with a chameleon-like, know-it-all lead character, the film unfolds
in a fantasy world of improbability punctuated by hard-hitting, real
scenes of LOX at its worst. The film was highly successful and became the standard LOX training film for all the U.S. armed services,
most NATO countries, and several Latin American countries.

At point 2 are television news broadcasts. (Nearby but not shown
would be a host of films such as Louis de Rochemont's 1935–1954
The March of Time series.) Since news broadcasts cannot be just
factual reporting of the day's events, several factors combine to
reduce the reality of this sort of film. Of these factors, most important is the interpretation that includes what events are or are not
covered, as well as what is said and shown and how it is said and

shown. This raises a serious question: Does television news report the news or make the news so it can be reported? The *what* is typified nowadays by the advocacy and exposé themes that are laced throughout news broadcasts and the editorializing and interpretation of the news. Another factor is that news broadcasts have become presentations—staged productions with a show-business–like atmosphere—and the news readers are beautiful personalities who generate ratings. Further reducing reality and credibility is the practice of using news broadcasts to tout upcoming network or local entertainment shows.

Spotted at point 3 is the delightfully innovative film *Powers of Ten,* produced by Charles Eames and Ray Eames. The goal of this nine-minute film is to inform the audience about the relative size of things in our universe. It's a classic example of cognitive learning through use of the highly practical technique of comparison. Using animation and special techniques, the film begins with a full-frame scene of a one-meter-square picnic blanket. The camera zooms outward. Image size and time accelerate in logarithmical increments of ten until the camera is at the edge of the universe. Zooming quickly back to the starting point at the blanket, the camera then continues inward to explore the microcosm of the human cell and the world of atomic particles. Executed with fanciful imagination and artistic skill, this highly successful film substantiates the point that it is the audience's perception of reality and acceptance that engenders communication.

Even though there is much fiction in television commercials and some that touch on the abstract, they are included in the information film genre because they inform about a product or service with the purpose of selling. Creative and often successful, television commercials as a genre are spotted at point 4, on the abstract side of creative actuality.

Documentary Film

The documentary film spectrum encompasses only slightly less range than does the information film. Documentary film's spectrum skews to the right on the continuum, toward fiction, as illustrated in figure 4. The maximum cluster of films centers around creative actuality, in consonance with the definition of documentary film. To explore the scope of the documentary film in terms of reality and acceptance, I have plotted four representative films along the documentary spectrum.

At the far left end (toward absolute reality) at point 6 is Michael

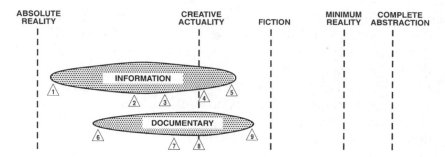

Fig. 4. Documentary film spectrum on the film reality scale

Wadleigh's 1970, Academy Award–winning film *Woodstock,* a factual documentation of the music of the times and a microcosm of
human emotions of the era. One of the few documentary films to
be released commercially, *Woodstock* was one of Warner Brothers'
top-grossing films of 1970. Using twelve cameras and approximately a third of a million feet of 16mm film (about 154 hours'
screen time), Wadleigh and his crew recorded a three-day rock-
music festival that occurred at a farm near Bethel, New York. Much
of the photography was centered on the enthusiastic young audience, estimated to be about a third of a million. Few if any scenes
were staged or reshot. All action and sound were recorded as they
happened. Through creative editing and split-screen techniques, the
film was cut to two hours for its theatrical release.[11] *Woodstock* is
placed nearest to absolute reality because of the high order of the
factual recording of the event. Interpretations in editing introduce
the fanciful elements, small though they may be.

Set at point 7 is the classic war-propaganda film *Memphis Belle.*
Produced in 1944 by Lt. Col. William Wyler of U.S. Army Pictorial Service, the film tells the story of the B-17 bomber dubbed *Memphis Belle* and her crew on their twenty-fifth mission over the
heavily defended industrial port city of Wilhelmshaven, Germany.
Because the toll on our aircraft and their crews was incredibly high,
crews that survived twenty-five missions were allowed to return to
the United States. Built around strikingly real documentary footage of the Eighth Air Force's war in Europe, *Memphis Belle* is edged
closer to creative actuality because some of the scenes were restaged.
The singularly real aerial-combat sequence was edited into coherence through montage editing. The crew's voices recorded from the
plane's intercom during combat were of such poor technical quality that the identical words were dubbed by professional actors in

a sound stage. Through a general theatrical film release, the film was seen by much of the American public. Done most professionally by a master craftsman, *Memphis Belle,* according to Richard Dyer MacCann, "unquestionably did more to bring home the realities of aerial combat to the American public than all the tons of newsprint which verbally described them."[12]

Astride creative actuality at point 8 is the classic documentary *Song of Ceylon.* Basil Wright of the England's Empire Marketing Board directed this film in 1934 for the Ceylon Tea Propaganda Board. Beautifully photographed with an unorthodox and poetic sound track blending an original score and an imaginative narrative, *Song of Ceylon* is a remarkably sensitive film that captures the beauty and remoteness of Ceylon and the Ceylonese heritage. This film had a wide theatrical distribution, won enthusiastic praise, and was one of the most important documentary films of the 1930s. *Song of Ceylon* was the hallmark documentary that set the standard and, by and large, solidified the documentary film as a recognized and accepted film genre. By staging much of the film, Wright photographed life in Ceylon to his artistic bent, creatively interpreting actuality without introducing significant fictional elements.[13]

At the far right on the spectrum at point 9, approaching fiction, is the epic film *Man of Aran,* set in the bleak Aran Islands off the coast of Ireland. Produced by Robert Flaherty in 1934, this feature-length film has as its theme man's struggle for survival against the raging sea. Flaherty took great liberties with the truth to develop reality. For example, he contrived a hunt for basking sharks, something the islanders had not done for many decades and had long forgotten how to do; they had to be taught by an imported expert. Dialogue was postsynchronized, as were sound effects, to add realism. *Man of Aran* was severely criticized by the Griersonian purists as being dramatically sensational and socially irrelevant, because Flaherty did not expose the social evils of absentee landlordism that dominated the islands. Though imbued with liberal interpretations of the actual scene of the Aran Islands, recreating reality as Flaherty saw it, this classic documentary remains a definitive statement of man's fight against nature and his endurance and survival. *Man of Aran* had a large theatrical film release and garnered enthusiastic praise, much as it does today. By opting to develop the story along more typical entertainment film lines rather than the traditional documentary ones and by using entertainment film techniques, Flaherty captured the essence of this human story in a real portrayal that appealed to vast audiences, engendering their empathy and acceptance.[14]

Reality in film is a nebulous concept that is perceived differently by individual members of the audience from their own unique perspectives. The function of reality in film has several interrelated and yet independent factors in the communication process. Factors of particular importance for information film, which has specific objectives to accomplish, are:

- the truth or fiction inherent in the film's messages
- the credibility of the sender or the channel
- what the audience believes to be true—their perceptions of reality
- what "non-sense" (fiction, absurdity, and technical shortcomings) an audience will accept through their willing suspension of disbelief

As a function of audience background and motivation to view a film, the net psychological effect of these factors determines the film's effectiveness. That is, effectiveness is determined by the degree to which the audience becomes involved in experiencing vicarious identification with the characters, events, and places depicted in the film. Effectiveness also reflects the degree to which the audience reacts in accordance with the communication goals of the film.

Film with a high reality factor has communication appeal and effectiveness, on average, only for specialized audiences. Perhaps the same conclusion can be made for film that approaches the abstract. Thus, for most audiences, film that falls at about the center of the Film Reality Scale tends to be more effective in communicating messages (and in entertaining). The point is, a faithfully real film, including information film, probably is not as effective a communication or entertainment tool as it could be because the advantages of the medium are not utilized—time, space, and image manipulation, for example. By exploiting film's compelling and unique technological and psychological factors in terms of audience background, needs, and understanding, we can fully utilize film's inherent persuasive power to evoke intellectual stimulation and emotional commitment, generating empathy and thus communication.

That's enough plotting. I suggest that you carefully plot films that you know on all five of the film genres. Such an exercise gives in-depth understanding into the fundamental nature of the plotted film.

9

Documentary Film:
A Learning Tool

If we are to excel as information motion-media designers and producers, we must have a deep and broad-based understanding of our profession—its theory, history, and philosophy. Such background knowledge, coupled with hands-on skills, engenders professionalism. The hallmark of a professional is the insatiable desire to learn, to constantly expand and improve our knowledge and skills.

One of the best ways to gain understanding and to increase our script-designing and producing skills is to learn from the masters, those filmmakers who designed and produced the classic documentary films and videos. If we're fortunate, after we've completed our education, we'll serve an apprenticeship under the tutelage of a master—the hard and sure way to learn our profession. Under such tutelage, one of the most important skills we'll develop is the critical eye, that uncompromising perspective that keenly discriminates between effective and ineffective motion-media, between communication craftsmanship and schlock.

Unfortunately, most of us don't have the advantage of serving an apprenticeship. Instead, we're plunged into the motion-media profession with potential but lacking a well-developed reference base. We lack in-depth understanding, essential skills, and most important, the critical-eye perspective. Thus, we don't discriminate as well as we ought. The quality of our shows suffers in a blur of personal and professional compromises. Some of us are convinced that the "medium is the message" and that "creativity" supersedes basic communication value.

I understand what's happening. We have little time for reflection as we respond to today's compelling demand to design and produce our motion-media shows economically and quickly. We're seduced by new technologies that make our designing and producing tasks easier, faster, and cheaper but not necessarily better. "Better" is strictly a measure of audience reaction.

Screening Classic Documentary Films

An excellent way to develop the critical eye is to screen the documentary films of the master filmmakers. Screening is not enough, however; we must analyze and critique them with our developing critical eye. Analyzing and critiquing need to be directed toward understanding how the masters accomplished the communication task at hand through relevant filmic design. Points to look for are:

- Does the film have a clear vision and tone that communicate a strong central theme?
- Does the film generate empathy in the target audience?
- What filmic-design techniques are used, and why are they effective?
- Is most of the information carried in the visuals?
- Do audio elements *reinforce* the visuals, thereby enhancing communication to full measure?
- Is there coherence between the narration/dialogue and the visuals?
- Is the pace appropriate?
- Does cinematography facilitate communication?
- Do music and sound effects contribute to communication?
- Is the plasticity of the medium (manipulation of time and space) used optimally to maintain orientation and to facilitate information flow?
- Are spatial relationships and art elements used to accentuate important points?

In appendix 1, "Evaluating Information Motion-Media," I've included my Motion-Media Evaluation scoring form, a few comments, and instructions. I recommend that you use this form to evaluate motion-media shows for their communication effectiveness and to develop the critical eye.

During your critique, it's best not to concentrate on negatives. Too often, such activity degenerates into time-wasting, nitpicking exercises of no real import, and the essential goal of understanding is lost. No filmmaker ever made a perfect film, and no filmmaker is totally satisfied with his or her film.

Documentary Film Defined

If we are to appreciate documentary films to full measure and make relevant analyses, it's important that we have some background on the documentary film. This discussion will not be an in-depth review of the history and significance of this genre. Rather, what follows is a brief discussion of what a documentary is, both to gain understanding of the medium and to help understand why the documentary film is espoused as the keystone to learning and to developing the critical eye. Documentary film pioneers such as John Grierson, Paul Rotha, Erik Barnouw, Lewis Jacobs, Roger Manvell, and Pare Lorentz have written in-depth commentaries. Modern-day authors include Rachel Low, Elizabeth Sussex, Eva Orbanz, and Forsyth Hardy. (Please see the bibliography for a complete listing.)

Most of us in the information motion-media profession consider John Grierson, Commander of the British Empire, (1898–1972), to be the founder of the documentary film movement (see photo, appendix 2). In 1927, under the aegis of Sir Stephen Tallents (1884–1958), secretary of England's Empire Marketing Board, Grierson founded the EMB Film Unit.[1] Under his tutelage, the group developed and refined the documentary film to a fine art, producing a host of classic documentaries over the years. I've included several of these documentaries in the list in appendix 2, "101 Classic Documentary Films."

It was Grierson who first applied the term *documentary* to a film. In an article in the *New York Sun* in 1926, Grierson reviewed Robert Flaherty's film *Moana: A Romance of the Golden Age:* "Of course *Moana* being a visual account of events in the daily life of Polynesian youth, has documentary value."[2] Grierson defined the documentary film as "the creative treatment of actuality," which acknowledges that in documentary filmmaking of "the living article, there is also opportunity to perform creative work."[3] Roger Manvell amplified this concept as the filmmaker's interpretation of a factual subject as the filmmaker sees it.[4]

Complementing Grierson's definition, Paul Rotha, a sometime associate of Grierson in the General Post Office Film Unit (the successor of the Empire Marketing Board Film Unit), postulated that the origin of documentary film lies in Flaherty's *Nanook of the North.*[5] Produced in 1921 for Revillon Frères of New York, the film tells the human story of Eskimos in the far northern climes of Hudson Bay. Much of the cinematography was staged for dramatic impact or reconstructed to introduce creative art into the recording of Inuit life on film.

Grierson developed the documentary film's first principles:

- Documentary would photograph the living scene and the living story.
- We believe that the original (or native) actor and the original (or native) scene are better guides to a screen interpretation of the modern world.
- We believe that the material and the stories thus taken from the raw can be finer (more real in the philosophic sense) than the acted article.[6]

The documentary tag stuck. In the intervening years, *documentary* was applied to a host of realistic-type films—indeed, to almost anything that was nontheatrical, that is, narrative film.

Significantly, Grierson insisted that the primary aims of documentary film are national education and public information and that the documentary should strive for sociological rather than aesthetic goals. He insisted that within the documentary film, "There must be power of poetry or of prophecy. Failing either or both . . . there must be at least the sociological sense implicit in poetry and prophecy."[7] It is important that Grierson did not pooh-pooh aesthetics. During the 1939–1945 war, Grierson's former documentary film group (later the Crown Film Unit) fine-tuned the documentary film into a propaganda medium of a high order with such classic films as *Target for Tonight* and *Listen to Britain*.

Through the years, other documentary filmmakers have augmented Grierson's definition and philosophy with their own perspectives. Rotha said of the cine-record documentary film, "The representation of past fact, without the introduction of fictional story-interest, is an attempt to put on record the actual happenings of some past event."[8]

Ivor Montagu, film director, critic, historian, and pamphleteer, tended to de-emphasize human interaction in documentary film. His is a more pragmatic approach in which the nonhuman objects in the scene are of primary importance. He said, "Documentary deals with nonhuman objects and processes, or processes in which, if human beings are included, this is only in relation to their offices and functions and not in respect to their qualities and interrelationships as individuals." What impressed Montagu was "the cinema's capacity to present a plain scientific record [of man]. . . . No other medium can portray real man in motion in his real surroundings."[9]

Perhaps it was Pare Lorentz whose simple yet elegant definition is the most profound. He described the documentary film as "factual film which is dramatic."[10] Such a definition is reflected in his Depression-era films, such as *The Plow That Broke the Plains* and *The River,* which set the documentary standard on this continent.

Over the years, documentary film has been a key element in influencing mass audiences, particularly about social themes. Today, the genre has been refined to a hard-hitting communication art form that, on occasion, can take a position of extreme advocacy or exposé that is blatantly nonobjective. Two-time Academy Award–winner Robert Richter produced documentary films in this style. One example is his film *Pesticides and Pills: For Export Only.* He makes serious charges against several multinational corporations for knowingly selling dangerous pesticides and pills in Third World countries where consumers lack the sophistication to know what they are buying or how to cope with it if they do know. Other current-day documentary filmmakers take a less-extreme position, following more traditional lines—Ken Burns's *The Civil War,* for example. However, social themes are common to all in varying degrees of intensity and importance.

Documentary Film List

Without formal education or extensive background, it's difficult to know who the documentary film masters are and to know their work. To this end, I've compiled a list of 101 classic documentary films in appendix 2. They're listed in alphabetical order. I've listed films with non-English names by their original titles.

Some readers may note that I've omitted important films and filmmakers. Others may question my choices, preferring a different selection. Admittedly, the list I've compiled is incomplete; my subjective preference and space limitations dictate the list's content. Yet the list is a representative sample of classic work that spans a broad spectrum of styles, goals, and milieu. The films are cosmopolitan, reflect varied political ideologies, and range from contemporary to *vaunt-courier.*

Not all of the films on the list are, strictly speaking, documentary. Some are information films. A few others are enrichment films. A couple are experimental. The common thread in all the films is that none is narrative. In the broad context, therefore, all of them can be considered a part of the documentary genre. Such a conclusion is especially valid when considering Grierson's support for inclusion of a host of film types within the documentary genre. He wrote, "Think of all the different categories of documentary productions, e.g., public reporting, scientific films, technical films, instructional films, etc."[11]

Many of the early documentaries may well appear crude by today's standards. Contributing to this perception are technical inadequacies, unsophisticated filmic techniques, and film's natural deterioration over time. Don't be fooled! Look through these superficialities to see the real worth of these films—their poignant power. Focus on flaws, and you'll miss gaining the basic understanding of the origins of the documentary genre and an appreciation of the pioneers who produced these films. Discover the filmic-design techniques of the masters. Hone your perspective of this powerful communication medium, nurture that developing critical eye—our key to professional success. But most of all, enjoy.

Unfortunately, some of the films on this list may not be in distribution. Some research and hunting will be necessary; of those that are in circulation, viewing copies are available in many university and public libraries, museums, and film-archival institutions.

10

Introduction to Multimedia

Multimedia is the vanguard of the media revolution: It's powerful, nonlinear, and most important, it's interactive. Differing from film and video, multimedia is the computer-based medium. And it's the computer that begot the media revolution.

Visuals are transmitted to remote locations where they can be enhanced, manipulated, or turned into hard copy. Sound is heard in stereophonic high-fidelity. Satellite and fiber-optic networks carry telephonic, videographic, computer, and all manner of electronically encoded signals to our office, factory floor, classroom, and living room.[1] The ability to relay information via direct-broadcast satellite to almost any receiver in the world offers near-unlimited communication opportunities. Fiber-optics offer two-way communication. A single fiber-optic cable, using digital-compression technology, has the capacity to carry five hundred television channels and lots more electronic data. Imagine how much data a *bundle* of fiber-optic cable carries!

Definition

Technology is developing so rapidly that we can't pin down a definitive description of multimedia. By the time you read this, no doubt that some of what I've said here will be obsolete, and some new multimedia technology will have evolved. That's one reason I don't discuss tools. Accordingly, this chapter necessarily treats this complex subject somewhat superficially. Nonetheless, here's my tentative definition:

Multimedia is an umbrella term that describes an evolving host of processes under synchronous computer control that consolidate in real time various external visual and audio inputs with computer-generated text, graphics, animation, and audio into integrated sight-and-sound, nonlinear shows. Such nonlinear or interactive shows mimic the viewer's associative thought and cognitive learning processes. Multimedia requires the viewer to select and respond. In essence, multimedia is a computer-designed, computer-controlled, interactive medium that's viewer-controlled, coherent, and network-branching.

In figure 5, I've drawn a generic composite of the various elements that constitute multimedia. The figure is not intended to be all-inclusive or detailed. Rather, it's a broad overview of the media inputs, computer functions, and program outputs.

Fig. 5. Generic multimedia system

Interactivity is the key to the communicational power of multi-media. It allows for one-on-one training between the audience and the computer—the instruction. Students assimilate information at their own pace and need. They can browse, review, scan, freeze-frame, fast-forward, or reverse. A number of studies prove that multimedia significantly improves learning (communications) in the short and long terms for all audiences. In chapter 11, I discuss a simple multimedia flowchart.

Background

I am not sure when multimedia was born, neither the term nor the process. I suspect, however, that it began in the late-1970s with the rise of computer-aided instruction and the multi-image medium. Back then, the technology supporting multi-image shows consisted of an array of 35mm slide projectors, stereophonic reel-to-reel or cassette tape-recorders/players, and maybe some 16mm motion-picture film. All elements of the show were controlled by various electronic "black boxes." I've seen shows with twenty-five projectors and have heard of shows with more than forty. As you might imagine, multi-image shows were plagued with technical snags—stuck slides, burned-out projector bulbs, loss of sound synchronization, etc. Multi-image had a meteoric rise and decline because the medium could not overcome the technical complexities and distribution logistics.

Soon the black box became the personal computer. Advancing digital-compression technology enabled video and audio information to be stored in a minute fraction of the space once required. A new generation of external and internal plug-in devices further expanded computing capabilities. Now, the personal computer could generate complex 3-D graphics, animation, and all manner of visual effects. Concurrently, multimedia-authoring programs became more generic and powerful. Such programs integrated a host of visual and aural inputs with computer-generated information into one medium. For the first time, a broad spectrum of our audience had access to an interactive medium that was practical, cost effective, and readily available.[2]

The Multimedia Team

We're now at the point where technology has made it possible for just about anyone who is computer literate to produce a multimedia show. The question is, does the "anyone" have the wherewithal to make such multimedia communications effective? The tough part is mental: reasoning, researching, planning, and accomplishing. It takes in-depth knowledge, superior filmic-design skills, artistic achievement, and panache. In aggregate, such attributes are best found in the multimedia team.

The multimedia team is composed of people with expert knowledge and learned-the-hard-way experience in one or more of the multimedia processes. Often one multi-talented person fulfills several tasks in multimedia production. But be cautious: Should one person be responsible for too many tasks, there could be problems unless he or she is a super-industrious, committed team player with a plethora of in-depth skills. Regrettably, there's a paucity of these folks.

Here is my concept of a multimedia team. I've listed just the key personnel. Some of these personnel may have multifunction responsibilities, which frequently is the case. Obviously, there are other people who work under the supervision of these key personnel.

Producer. Has overall fiscal, communicative, and creative responsibility for the show. In many training and educational shows, the producer is an instructional designer with expert teaching skills. It's the producer who designs the educational approach and validates testing of the program.

Communication analyst. Conducts the communication analysis (i.e., the needs assessment). Such an assessment includes determining the profile of the target audience, communication goals, essential elements of information, and overall strategy.

Subject-matter expert. Sometimes dubbed the technical advisor. Has in-depth knowledge of the topic of the multimedia show. Advises the team on content (information) accuracy and appropriateness and on political and security considerations.

Script designer. Working with the producer, communication analyst, and subject-matter expert, develops a comprehensive plan for accomplishing the goals for the program. This mini-team develops the show's architecture as expressed in the structure of the flowchart. Included are branching, chapters, and stops, as well as the content of the live action, animation, text, and graphics sequences. Should narration or dialogue be needed, the script designer develops this aural information in concert with the overall communication plan. (See chapter 11 for a simple flowchart.)

Art director. Plans and executes animation, overlays, and graphics, either by hand or computer generation.

Live-action director. Responsible for live-action film and video sequences in the program. Working with a team composed of cinematographers or videographers, sound recordists, grips, gaffers, and others, records on film or tape the program's live action. Supervises the editing of this footage into meaningful filmic-design montage sequences.

Audio engineer. Supervises the recording of narration and dialogue, their editing, and the integration of all the various sound tracks (music, sound effects, etc.) into one master-mixed track that is in synchronization with the visual elements of the program.

When no appropriate over-the-counter (general) authoring program exists, it used to be customary to employ a computer specialist to devise the needed programming. With the proliferation of generic authoring programs, today we use a computer programmer only when we require very specialized applications.[3]

Advantages of Multimedia

Interactivity enhances communication. We think associatively and in pictures. Such self-paced activity is the basic strength of multimedia. Our audiences learn more and learn more quickly. A 1987 study indicates that students using interactive programs learn and retain 25 percent more of the information presented and learn it 50 percent faster than those who use traditional learning methods.[4] A series of six studies conducted from 1990 to 1992 shows that students have a 55 percent learning gain over traditional classroom teaching. They learn the material 60 percent faster and their long-term (thirty-day) retention ranges from 25 percent to 50 percent higher.[5]

Let's highlight some specific advantages:

- Viewer-controlled, almost-immediate access to any part of the show allows for individualized, self-paced progress.
- Viewer performance and accountability can be collected for automatic recordkeeping. Such data is used to determine user accomplishment, program strengths and weaknesses, frequency of repeat viewing, and times of use, for example.
- Viewers' questions are answered in near–real time through internal communication networks or the Internet.
- Hazardous training situations can be simulated—for example, bomb-disposal training.
- Expenses for training-related travel are reduced. Send the multimedia show via Internet/intranet, satellite, or commercial carrier.
- Expensive classroom setups are eliminated.
- Training (viewing) can be scheduled to meet the needs of individual viewers.
- Multimedia combines the power of self-study media with computer management into one medium.

- In many multimedia training and education scenarios, an on-site instructor is not needed.
- Program content, through branching networks and feedback, is individualized to meet the viewers' identification factors: demographic, socioeconomic, and psychological profiles.
- Narration and dialogue can be heard in multiple languages.
- Complex concepts are explained via animation, motion video, still photographs and drawings, freeze-frame, forward and reverse, and step motion—for instance, to see the inner workings of the classic electronic "black box."
- Proprietary authoring programs enable nonsystem analysts to individually tailor multimedia programs.

Disadvantages

In making our medium choice, we need to evaluate carefully all factors involved. Multimedia is not the perfect medium for all communication goals for the following reasons:

- Notwithstanding all the hype, *communication-effective* multimedia programs are expensive to produce. Authoring programs can be expensive. Labor and production-equipment costs are high. Beta testing is expensive. Reworks blow most budgets.[6]
- Viewing equipment is specialized and expensive, and it's carried as capital equipment on most inventories. Since most multimedia programs are intended for individual viewing, lots of equipment is needed for mass viewing. If not in constant use, downtime on capital equipment is costly.
- Maintenance and repair of sophisticated multimedia equipment are expensive and time consuming. To maintain scheduled multimedia training, backup equipment is needed.
- Multimedia shows produced for one proprietary system may not be interchangeable with another system.
- For many multimedia shows, change is extremely difficult and expensive in terms of money, time, and expertise.
- Some of our audiences are intimidated by the hardware, don't like to work alone in a self-directed manner, and need hard copy to mull over.
- Finally, maybe I'm old-fashioned, but it seems to me that no matter what the training environment, an on-site instructor is essential, and instructors cost money.

Despite these disadvantages, multimedia is becoming pervasive in all facets of our communication society. Fortune 500 corporations are investing heavily to maintain currency in a global marketplace where instant communication and feedback are the cardinal principles.[7] For the novice and motion-media communicator, opportunities in multimedia abound. If we are to grab these new opportunities, we'll have to reorient our thinking, learn new communication skills, and adapt to a different way of doing business to meet client and audience requirements. We need to master the intricacies of multimedia production and communication if we are to be proficient catholic communicators in this communication age.

The Future

I consider virtual reality, not often thought of as multimedia, to be the next-generation multimedia medium. Virtual reality is that technology that creates a multisensory, computer-modeled environment of three-dimensional holographic images, realistic multiphonic sound, and lifelike tactical sensations. It allows for near-total sensory immersion in a realistic, 360-degree world of stereo-optic vision, sound, and touch. When we are absorbed in virtual reality, it's easy for us to lose conscious perception of the real world.[8]

Current and future applications for virtual reality abound—for instance, sports training, surgery, medical diagnosis, flight simulation, war gaming, engineering design, 3-D layout for building design and furnishings, and perceptual motor-skill training of all sorts. We're in a new communication age where the old "ride the wave to the beach" lincarity of traditional film/video is passé. Interactivity is key.

11

Multimedia Flowchart

If, instead of film or video, we choose to use multimedia to fulfill our communication objective, we'll need to create a flowchart. A flowchart is somewhat like a script or storyboard in that it's the specialized map we design to develop the branching network for our program. I've included a sample of a very simple multimedia flowchart in figure 6.

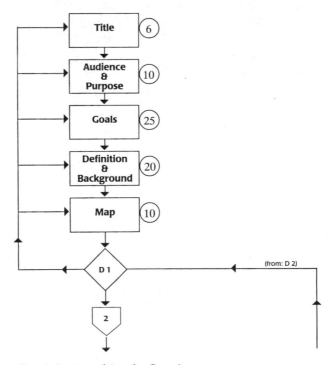

Fig. 6. Basic multimedia flowchart

Simple as it is, this flowchart is not complete. It could quickly become much more complicated. However, the flowchart is flexible, and as we explore it, we can suggest additions or deletions. To keep the flowchart easier to follow, I've left off the all-important escape button that ought to be on each page.

Flowcharting doesn't get much more basic than this. What's important is that you see a sample flowchart to understand its layout, follow the network branching, and learn what the several symbols mean. With just a little effort, we could expand this flowchart to fill a dozen or so feet of butcher paper pasted around our room.

This particular show's goal is to introduce junior-high and high-school students to four Florentine Renaissance artists and samples of their work. Figure 6 is the first page of the flowchart; and note the linear progression from the show's title to the map of Europe. The arrowhead lines indicate the direction of information flow and the network-branching options available to the student. Rectangles indicate a scene. Here, the scenes are text and graphics. The numbers inside the circles attached to the rectangles indicate the number of seconds the scene is on the screen. However, the student does have the option to freeze the scene to peruse it longer. Note that when the show opens, the student has no decision options until after the map scene quits. A diamond with the notation *D1* is the first decision point. The student can choose to continue into the show or go back to any one of the opening graphics. (See fig. 7 for the script of this opening sequence.)

Figure 8 shows page 2 of the flowchart. Note the many decision points and the complex branching networks in this simple flowchart. Actually, we could incorporate many more. I recommend that you trace it through to see all the options available to the student.

Note the quiz at the bottom. If students complete the quiz successfully, they might have the option to quit or to go back into the show to review a section. Should students fail, we can force them back into the show at any point of our choosing. We might base our decision on the specific questions that were answered incorrectly to force a review of this area of the show. In point of fact, we could insert quizzes at any part of the show.

At the bottom of the flowchart is "Quit," which gets the students completely out of the show. In an actual show, we need to have an escape or help icon that always remains on the screen. This is necessary because students easily get lost in the complex network branching. Clicking on this icon provides directions and answers questions.

We can easily see how complicated we can make the flowchart for this show. For example, we could set up the requirement that

Visuals	Audio
(*Title*)	
(Pop on the title)	(Music in)
A Sample of Florentine Renaissance Art	(Appropriate chamber music of the fifteenth century)
(*Audience and purpose*)	(Music down)
Montage of junior high and high school students in class room studying Florentine art. We see photographs of the sculpture. Students interacting.	(Narrator)
	This show is an introduction to Florentine Renaissance art in the fifteenth and sixteenth centuries with a focus on sculpture.
(On cue superimpose the title)	
15th and 16th Centuries	
(*Goals*)	(Continue music softly)
(Pop on the titles in sequence)	(Narrator)
• Define Renaissance art	Listed are the minimum goals you are expected to achieve upon completion of this multimedia show.
• Identify the centuries in which Florentine Renaissance art flourished	
• Identify four artists	
• Name two works by each of the four artists	
(*Definition*)	(Continue music softly)
Build a montage of examples of classic Roman and Greek sculpture. Use close-ups and extreme close-ups to emphasize the texture and form of the art.	(Narrator)
	Renaissance art represented a rediscovery of the form and aesthetics of classic Greek and Roman art.
(*Background*)	(Segue music to modern upbeat)
Build a montage of modern-day Florence—city scenes—Ponte Vecchio and Piazza della Signoria, etc. Cut to montage of museums: include Palazzo degli Uffizi, and Galleria dell'Accademia (show Michelangelo's *David* and *Slaves*)	(Narrator)
	Renaissance art began in Florence in the early fifteenth century. It flourished under the patronage of Florentine nobles who were interested in pre-Christian cultures.
(*Map*)	(Continue music softly)
Pop on a map of Europe: Italy is highlighted. Pop on a dot for the location of Florence, and pop on the title "Florence." Superimpose street scenes of Florence. Fade out the title and let the street scene play for a couple of beats.	(The narrator may be quiet. Or we may develop narration that tells about Florence. You, the reader, try writing a line or two of narration for this scene.)

Fig. 7. Opening sequence for the multimedia show: A sample of Florentine Renaissance art

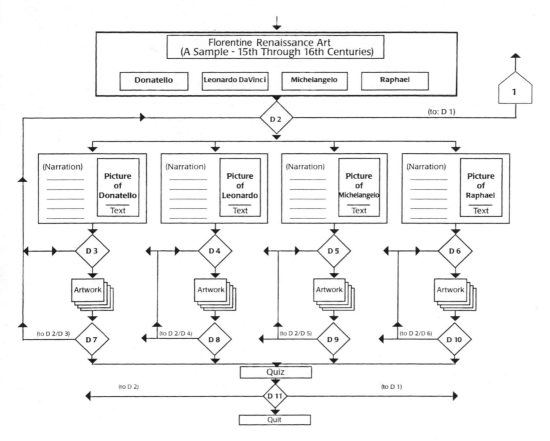

Fig. 8. Sample of a multimedia flowchart

the student make side-by-side comparisons of the artwork of the different artists. Insert a quiz: Pass or fail leads to another set of networks, etc. Here's my golden rule: Make your flowcharts (and the resulting show) as simple and direct as possible—just enough to meet the show's goal.

Thoughts on Copyrights

It's easy to take kinetic images, still pictures, animation, and music of all types from the Internet for use in our multimedia shows. *Don't!* Almost all of these images and music are copyrighted. If you use them without permission, you're stealing another person's property. You're in violation of federal copyright law, and you may be prosecuted in federal court. Also, you're committing a tort. It's a sure bet that the copyright holder will sue you and your organization. It's not worth it. (In chapter 21, "The Sound Track," I highlight a few aspects of music copyrights.)

Copyright law is beyond the scope of this book and of my expertise. Suffice it to say, you should consult expert legal advisors to ensure that you have legal permission to use all images and sounds you use in your shows. *No exceptions!*

Part Three

Communication Analysis

12

Stating Your Objectives, or What's This Show About?

When the room lights come on after a motion-media screening/viewing, the audience should think or act in a way that accomplishes the objectives (or goals) we've established for the show. If such objectives are achieved, our show is successful. But designing and producing a successful show is a complicated task. The necessary first step in producing a successful information motion-media show is to detail the communication goal in specific terms. In this chapter, we'll work on goals. In the next chapter, we'll study audience analysis.

What's the Real Goal?

Defining the show's goal is a task that's not as easy as it sounds. We can't just take at face value what our client says is the goal. Sometimes, I've found that my client's idea of the goal is, for whatever reason, faulty or misbegotten. After conducting an in-depth analysis of the problem the show is supposed to solve, we might conclude that the actual goal for the show ought to be something other than the client's notion, or it ought to be a modification of the client's ideas. Accordingly, before we begin designing the script for any show, we need to comprehend fully the actual problem the show is to solve and dig to uncover the root of the problem. We must be absolutely certain that we understand completely just what the proposed show is supposed to do.

For instance, some years ago a client of mine, the owner of a small prototype machine shop, asked me to produce a show that would motivate his machinists to work more safely—a practical goal. Over the years, a number of the machinists had accidents. Easy enough, right? Not so! After I visited the shop and talked with the workers, I concluded that the problem was not with the workers but with the industrial layout and the lighting. My client should have consulted an industrial or safety engineer first. This problem didn't need a motion-media show to fix it. It's imperative that we conduct a thorough analysis of the situation to understand the exact nature of the communication problem we're asked to solve.

Once we fully and accurately understand the problem that the proposed motion-media show is to solve, we must state the show's goal in terms that are fitting, realistic, and worthwhile:

- *fitting:* the goal is appropriate for the problem at hand and the medium chosen
- *realistic:* the show has a reasonable chance to achieve the goal
- *worthwhile:* the goal serves a useful purpose and is worth the time and effort spent to design and produce the show, and it's worth the audience's time, energy, and concern to view the show

Also included within our goal statement is the minimum rate of achievement, or level of performance, required from the audience in the near term and in the long term. Our show is a success if the audience performs at the established minimum level. The degree of success is a measure of audience performance above the minimum level. Unfortunately, except for some multimedia shows that score audience achievement in real time, we don't get much feedback on how our shows fare. If the show fails, we can count on our client letting us know. However, success usually begets silence from our clients. Ideally, we'd want a statistical measure of audience performance obtained through testing, because it's only through such testing that we and our clients know for sure how the show did.

Goal and Audience

A statement of a show's communication goal is not complete until we couple it with the sociological analysis of the target audience. Exactly who is our audience, and why do they need to view this proposed show?

To illustrate, I'll describe a motion-media communication problem I worked on some years ago. There were several serious accidents aboard the navy's aircraft carriers operating in Southeast Asia because of the unsafe work habits of personnel handling liquid oxygen (LOX) on the flight deck. My navy client wanted a show that would "train" the LOX handlers to work safely. LOX handlers typically are eighteen-to-twenty-year-old males. After conducting extensive research, we found that the problem was not lack of training. Rather, it was one of motivation. All LOX handlers had attended a special school with rigorous standards and had received follow-up on-the-job training on the "how" of their jobs. Some of the LOX handlers had become inured to the hazards in handling this highly dangerous, volatile, and erratic cryogenic liquid. They "knew their jobs backward" and carelessly concluded that nothing would ever happen to them. Contributing to the unsafe work habits of the LOX handlers was the ennui resulting from long and exceptionally hazardous hours working the carrier's flight deck under the most demanding conditions.

My task was to motivate LOX handlers to work with LOX precisely as described in the operator's manual and as they had been taught. The goal was to reduce hazardous activities to zero. The solution to this problem was the highly effective six-minute motivational film, *The Man from LOX,* which met its objectives to a fare-thee-well. LOX accidents dropped to zero and remained there for years afterward.

Once the problem to be solved and the goal are defined, the purpose of the communication can be stated in positive, concrete-action terms. It is not sufficient to make general statements such as: to inform the public of pending legislation, to improve morale among employees, to increase sales, or to teach sailors how to handle LOX. The purpose must be specific and must pose a precise solution to the problem, as did the motivational film on LOX handling. Inherent in this statement of purpose is the key element that describes the target audience. With these factors established precisely, we've completed the first step in designing a successful show.

Essential Elements of Information

Now that we've defined exactly the problem our motion-media show is to solve, we need to establish precisely what information our audiences must know to accomplish the show's objectives—the essential elements of information (EEI). The EEI is the key information our audience must know—and must know in context with all other EEIs. These EEIs are the foundation of our script. In a linear show, we ought to limit our EEIs to three or four. If there are more than five EEIs, the show probably is too ambitious and will not be successful. In a multimedia show, where viewers have control of the show's rate of development, there can be several more EEIs, especially if the show is backed up with take-home material.

As an example, let's look at the EEIs for *The Man from* LOX:

- Stay intensely focused on your job no matter how tired you are. Mishandled LOX can kill you and your shipmates.
- LOX-impregnated clothing must be changed immediately and properly destroyed.
- Grease and LOX make an extremely volatile and dangerous combination. Instantly notify the safety officer of any such interaction.
- After use, immediately return LOX equipment to its safe storage space.

Goal Statements and Successful/Unsuccessful Shows

Let's rework the goal-statement scenario from another perspective: motion-media competitions and festivals. It's here that we see what sort of shows our peers are producing and what success (or not) they're having.

I managed a major international motion-media competition for twelve years, served on a host of local and blue-ribbon juries for several other national and international festivals and competitions, and I screen as many information shows as I can. In almost all festivals and competitions, a large part of a show's total score is based on the judges' subjective evaluation of how well the show achieves its communication objective with the target audience. In some competitions, the scoring weight of achievement of objectives (and related criteria) can be as high as 50 percent of the total score. (See appendix 1, the Motion-Media Evaluation sheet.)

Time and again, I've seen "well-produced" shows score poorly because the statement of objectives is inadequate—although not inadequate in terms of brevity (if it were only so!). Rather, an inadequate statement of objectives fails to tell precisely and succinctly what the goal of the show is and who the target audience is. Such an inadequate statement of objectives guarantees that the judges (and most likely the target audience) won't know what a show is all about—a fatal flaw.

An inadequate or inept goals statement almost always reflects incompetent communication analysis: lack of clear understanding of the problem the show is designed to solve, the target audience, and the filmic design needed to solve the problem. The resultant show almost always fails. (It may be aesthetically pleasing, however.)

Let's get personal. It's challenging to enter our motion-media shows in festivals and competitions. It's fun to win an award. It's even more fun when the show successfully communicates with the target audience. Peer recognition, publicity, and kudos are what it's all about. Such recognition gives us a sense of self-worth and accomplishment—makes our jobs worthwhile. Management and clients take pride when one of their own films/videos earns recognition. Festival and competition awards are evidence of your (and your department's) talent and importance—a kind of built-in job security, as it were.

Is it possible that your great shows haven't fared as well as they ought to in competitions because of the inadequate-statement-of-objectives syndrome? If so, you'll have to improve your communication with the judges if you're going to improve your success rate. For the judges to evaluate your show properly—to make relevant judgments based on meaningful information—they must know exactly what the show's objectives are. To this end, the statement of objectives must pinpoint precisely who the target audience is and what the audience is supposed to do, say, think, or learn. The statement must state when the action item is required. The statement of objectives is a precise description of the level of achievement expected from the audience. You've got to communicate the show's goal/goals.

Unfortunately, I see far too many shows entered in competitions (perhaps as many as 80 percent) with statements of objectives that fail to communicate. On the whole, such inadequate statements of objectives tend to be ambiguous, irrelevant, or rambling. Such a statement really doesn't say much about what the show is supposed to accomplish and with whom.

The inadequate statement of objectives comes couched in many guises: some obviously fatuous, some deceptively void of any real goals. The following potpourri includes some of the most common ones; many of the examples are quoted verbatim, others are modified slightly to illustrate the point.

Ambiguous: "We hope this film does everything for our client that she expects of it. So far, she has been very pleased because the audiences seem to like it. . . ."

Irrelevant: "I'm so thrilled to enter my 'wonderful' video in your swell competition. Watch for . . . and see how we accomplished . . . and we tried so hard to . . . and our budget was so small . . . and I just know you'll love my wonderful video, and . . . " (quoted verbatim, unfortunately.)

Worthless: "I'm concerned about how you fellows judge my shows. Here's my new film to let you know just what a great film-maker I am." (Folks, I kid you not. This is an almost exact quote without the invectives.)

Rambling; "We had this kind of problem at work, and our public relations director thought we in the Communications Division could help. So she called us . . . and we produced this show. . . ."

Ad nauseam: A few years ago, I read a statement of objectives that rambled on for three typed, single-spaced pages! I couldn't figure out if buried somewhere in this tome was the reason to communicate, who the target audience was, and what they were supposed to do. Frankly, I gave up, as did the other judges.

Synoptic: "This show is about how Jane and Jim cope with and overcome the problems of. . . ." This sort of statement of objectives is nothing more than a capsule summary of the show. The judges don't need a synopsis; they need to know what's supposed to happen when the lights come on after the target audience views the show.

Incomplete: "This film explains how a high-powered laser will be used to produce an unlimited supply of affordable energy." Or another one: "To provide an overview of the integrated-services digital network." Generally, these kinds of statements of objectives are okay as far as they go, but they don't go far enough. They don't pinpoint the target audience and what the producer expects from the audience. They are incomplete.

Litany: "In this video, we tell the audience about the details of processes *A* through *Z*, how to integrate the processes, why the processes need to be integrated, what the results of such an integration are, etc., etc., etc." The key to the failure of the litany is "tell the audience." Again, the judges usually can figure out what the producer is trying to "tell" the audience simply by screening the show. What the judges want to know is who is the target audience and what are the target audience's action items—what does the producer expect the target audience to do? What the producer did is either evident or irrelevant. Another irritating factor about this statement of objectives that foretells the outcome of the judging is use of the word *tell.* That's exactly what the show did: It told and told and told. Kinetic visuals were irrelevant; almost all of the information was contained in the sound track. *Ugh!*

Gobbledygook: "To explain in simple and nontechnical terms the key ideas and benefits of object-oriented programming, a new programming technique used in artificial-intelligence applications. The main challenge of the program was to visualize highly abstract technical concepts by analogy with everyday life experiences." Frankly, I don't have a clue what the producer is trying to communicate—nor am I much motivated to find out. The negative mind-set generated by such a gobbledygook statement of objectives is tough to overcome—and almost never is.

The list of deficient statements of objectives goes on and on, but the point is made. A deficient statement of objectives usually indicates inadequate communication analysis during the show's concept and planning stages, resulting in ill-defined goals for the show. Consequently, the show's communication effectiveness suffers from lack of focus. This kind of show tends to wander, is often badly overwritten (to cover all contingencies), and usually doesn't do much for anyone in the audience. The technical razzle-dazzle may be great, but on reflection the judges wonder what the show was all about.

Sometimes a statement of objectives is well written, succinct, precise, etc., yet is still inadequate in that it reflects unattainable goals for the show. The producer attempts too much and almost always fails. Two examples are:

Unrealistic: "This ten-minute video will teach aspiring medical students how to perform brain surgery." (I fabricated this one to illustrate my point, although it's not too far from some I've seen.) This kind of show struggles to accomplish an impossible task. It usually deals with perceptual motor-skill development that requires precise actions performed in an exacting sequence. This type of skill is the most difficult to teach with linear motion-media even when the goals are realistic. However, such perceptual motor-skill training is ideal for interactive multimedia.

Too ambitious: "This film will recruit electronic engineers, give the annual report to the stockholders, convince the buying public that our corporation is interested in human concerns and the environment, and persuade Congress that $750 is a fair price for a toilet seat." (I made this one up also.) Here's a classic case of moving heaven and earth for everybody, ready or not. Clearly, this sort of show tries to do too much for too many audiences and does nothing for anyone—except, perhaps, put some to sleep. It's a prime example of preordained failure.

Writing a Strong Statement of Objectives

So far, we've emphasized the negative aspects of the statement of objectives. Let's explore the positive side to see what the judges expect, which is a precise statement of objectives that communicates exactly what the show is all about.

A precise statement of objectives should be composed of three parts. It should begin with the overall intent of the show, best expressed with the infinitive verb form beginning with the word *to*. Examples are *to train, to motivate, to inform, to persuade, to sell,* etc.

Next, there's a description of the target audience. This description should be expressed as specifically as possible. Some examples are:

- eighteen-to-twenty-year-old sailors who handle liquid-oxygen (LOX) on the flight deck of aircraft carriers
- visitors to our corporate office who are executives in other corporations or in the federal government and who are concerned with oil production and allocation
- retired senior citizens with fixed or limited incomes

The possibilities are endless, but the goal is to define the target audience as narrowly as possible. On the whole, the narrower the audience, the easier the communication task. Communication objectives for shows intended for the general public tend to be harder to accomplish.

Sometimes the audience description is requested as a separate item on the entry form. If so, there's no need to repeat it in the statement of objectives—we can simply use the phrase "the target audience."

Lastly, a statement of what the audience is supposed to do, say, or think is needed—the action clause. Inherent in this clause should be the level of achievement expected and when it is expected. Some examples that tie into the audience examples listed above are:

- to work safely, reducing LOX accidents to zero now and in the future
- to press for and to support legislation in line with corporation policy (lifting all federal controls on oil production and allocation) in the upcoming congressional session
- to stretch food dollars to realize a 10 percent gain in purchasing power now and a 30 percent gain within a year

Note that the action clauses in these examples also begin with the infinitive verb form.

It's not easy to develop a precise statement of objectives. What's needed is a careful analysis of the problem at hand—the reason to produce the show. Most important, this analysis must be completed prior to scripting, not when completing the entry form—which I suspect is often the case. No manner of eloquence can overcome the built-in fatal flaws in a show that resulted from lack of preplanning. It's just too late!

Of course, there are exceptions to the model statement of objectives detailed here. Adapt the model to suit your particular needs, ensuring that it communicates what the judges need to know to evaluate your show properly.

Should a show be produced for one's pure artistic satisfaction, a form of self-expression with no action goals in mind, the ideas discussed here are not applicable; with these shows, anything goes and should. Of course, we don't see many of these kinds of shows in information motion-media competitions.

More could be said about the statement of objectives, but the point is made. If we've defined the show's goal clearly and concisely, we've made an excellent start in designing a successful show. And the judges won't wonder, "What's this show all about?"

13

Who's Our Audience?

Audience Analysis

The most difficult of the pre-scripting analytical functions is determining just who is our audience. We must define our audience as a group and have insight into individuals within the group. We need to know precisely whom we are attempting to influence. If our motion-media communications are to be successful, the messages encoded in the medium must be structured to fit the format of the show and couched in symbols and terms relevant to audience understanding and acceptance, based in large measure on audience background, attitude, comprehension, motivation, need, and approval. We must engender empathy.

Empathy is that close identification an individual has with a person, place, event, institution, or combination of these. It's the psychological and emotional involvement the individual has with a stimulating situation. Skillfully designed motion-media shows are especially adept in engendering intense empathy. A number of researchers have verified the thesis that empathy is the primary constituent of communication in information motion-media; in general, the more intense the involvement, the more effective the motion-media show.

There is a caution, however: Some research indicates that should the empathy be too intense for some individuals, communication effectiveness can decrease markedly. Because of the intense emotional involvement generated in some individuals, they can make a near-total projection into the "reality" of the screen, especially if the scene mimics a phase of their lives or is threatening. The audience may lose perspective and not receive many of the persuasive messages being presented.

Social-Categories Theory

The social-categories theory of mass communication proposes that people with similar social and psychological characteristics will be influenced and behave in much the same way when exposed to mass-communication products. A number of researchers have substantiated this theory to a high level of statistical significance.[1]

Information motion-media shows made for the general public or large heterogeneous audiences are the most difficult to produce and often are not as successful in influencing most of the audience. Nonetheless, there are many notable general-public shows that were quite successful. For example:

- *Battle of Britain* from the *Why We Fight* series by Frank Capra
- *Night Mail* by Basil Wright
- *Triumph of the Will* by Leni Riefenstahl
- *The Plow That Broke the Plains* by Pare Lorentz
- *Harlan County, USA* by Barbara Koppel

These shows are more properly categorized as documentary rather than informational; however, they contain much information that is communicated very well indeed, and they have been instrumental in altering mass-audience attitudes.

Frequently, the designer of a mass-communication show tries to strike a mean in style and content so that the show will not talk down to the more-informed in the audience or over the heads of the masses. Sometimes the result is pabulum that does not do much for anyone— except perhaps to put the audience to sleep. I've found it's best to decide on a style of approach and stick with it. We always lose some in our audience, but if we influence the majority, we've succeeded.

Individual-Differences Theory

Even when our audience is homogeneous in a very narrow range— navy LOX handlers, for example—all will not get the same message. Audience members are influenced differently and will react in diverse ways. The rationale for this nonuniform behavior is proposed by the individual-differences theory, which recognizes that an audience is composed of individuals who react to communication in their own ways rather than as duplicate automatons. Individual selectivity of exposure, perception, and retention is the salient point in this theory.[2] This theory is summarized in the maxim that no matter what message we intend to send, some in the audience will receive another.

Let's look at three salient points of the individual-differences theory:

- *exposure:* People tend to migrate toward communications whose scope, tone, and messages are in agreement with their own opinions and interests; they avoid communications with which they do not agree.[3] However, sometimes, unbeknown to the audience, they are fed a sugar-coated communication that really doesn't set so well on digestion. Such a communication appears to be something it is not—for example, subtly couching a political message in a show that's billed as something else or subliminal communication.
- *perception:* People tend to construe, or misconstrue, persuasive communications according to their own concepts and attitudes.[4]
- *retention:* Communication is enhanced for those who are in general agreement with the treatment, more so than for those who are not in agreement.[5]

Simply, different people select, distort, and interpret mass-communication messages in ways peculiar to their individual psyches—they get from the messages what they can and want. Yet, on average, the overall behavior of the group is predictable, and this is the basis for successful mass-media communication.

Sometimes, in extreme cases, a few individuals will act almost inversely to the behavior desired. On Wall Street, this effect is called the contrary-opinion rule. Generally, with all other factors being nearly equal, this effect reflects problems with the individual rather than with the information motion-media show. It's the there's-one-in-every-crowd syndrome. Such behavior probably should be discounted.

An audience profile for a small homogeneous group may be as difficult to develop as that for a large heterogeneous one. However, once the profile is developed to an acceptable level of certainty, we have a better chance of producing a successful information motion-media show. We're required to recognize and utilize the manipulative filmic devices and techniques that optimize the influence on the specific target audience.[6] Or, in general terms, we optimize communication by encoding messages into the medium in a manner that engenders maximum empathy in the particular audience.

Target Audience Profile

To define the audience within the scope of the social-categories theory, we develop a target-audience profile. We look at the total theoretical person to identify similarities and divergences. Many factors need to be considered in developing this audience profile. For convenience, I have broken these factors into three broad categories that are interdependent and interrelated. These categories are not intended to be definitive; they are illustrative of the complex problem of defining an audience. The primary audience identification factors are:

- *demographic:* age, gender, health and well-being, geographic location, and marital status
- *socioeconomic:* education, income, occupation, social status, race or ethnic background, and religion
- *psychological:* innate intelligence, sophistication, emotional profile, responsibility (mores, character, industry, etc.), motion-media literacy, experience with the subject

Audience Motivation Factors

Additionally, we need to determine our target audience's motivation factors. Why are they viewing our show, and what are their expectations? The motivation factors are directly related to Shelton's Theory of Communication, developed in chapter 4. Anticipation is one of the most critical of these factors, a state of readiness or expectation for a coming event to which the audience has been alerted. Anticipation is caused by prescreen activities or by an introductory sequence within the motion-media show. Motivation factors are:

Anticipation. Will the target audience be briefed on the show's central theme and be alerted to watch for specific points? How much background information does the target audience have on the essential elements of information? Previous experience with the topic? How much lead-time will they have to prepare emotionally and physically for the screening/viewing? What is their media experience?

Importance of goal achievement. Why is it important for the target audience to get the show's messages? What is the target audience's advantage? Is there a performance test? What's its significance? Does the audience know there's a test involved? What degree of communication is satisfactory? What impact does the show's information have on the audience? What benefit/detriment does the audience get from the information? To what degree? What are the short- and long-term implications should communication be only partially effective? If communication fails?

Information currency/obsolescence. How time-sensitive or perishable is the show's information? When is the information of little or no value to the target audience? What is the information-value decay rate? Is it timeless? When will the information become unimportant? Obsolete?

Urgency of communication. What is the exigency of the intended communication? How soon is the target-audience action preferred? Required? Demanded? What is the significance of meeting this time goal? Of failing?

Predisposition. What is the target audience's disposition toward the sponsor of the show? The communicator? Information? Medium? What are their prejudices? Are they sympathetic, neutral, or hostile? To what degree are these prejudices manifest? What is their medium preference?

Feedback. Does the target audience participate in the communication process through feedback? How important is audience feedback in accomplishing the show's communication goal? Required? Desired? To what extent? Not relevant? When is feedback required? In real time? Delayed? How long delayed?

Dramatic structure. In expertly produced shows that deal with sociological problems, we might use a dramatic structure to generate empathy in our target audience. The audience can identify with the dramatic elements of background, characters, situation, and so forth. Sometimes the empathy is intense, especially if the dramatization hits home.

Subjective camera. Subjective camera is the camera angle that shows the action from the eye position of the audience. The subject is seen in much the same way an individual would see it in reality. Subjective camera is especially effective in teaching perceptual motor skills.

Clearly, the task of developing a complete audience analysis is so complex that it would require a battery of psychiatrists, sociologists, and other experts, as well as time and finances beyond reason. Fortunately, if we can accept less than perfection in this development (and we must), we can formulate an audience profile that augurs well for success. Required of us are training, astute research, diligence, and intuition. When these factors are used properly, our shows are conducive to audience acceptance and understanding and thus to communication—ensuring a successful motion-media show.

Medium Versus Message

Frequently, a discussion on message encoding into medium format stirs the controversy of whether the medium or the message is the more important factor in communication. This question is timeless, much debated, and unresolved to any degree of satisfaction. Because the thrust of this question is germane to the coding techniques required to transform the essential elements of information into motion-media, a few comments are in order to establish a perspective.

Marshall McLuhan, when discussing the electric light as needed for activities such as night baseball and brain surgery, makes the point that "The medium is the message." He reasons that brain surgery and baseball could not be accomplished without light and, in some ways, are the "content" of the light because it is the medium that controls all human activity.[7] Also, the unsophisticated and unwary may be enchanted by a medium—the silver-screen magic of a film, for example. If a film is produced, some viewers will conclude, "It must be important."

Conversely, there are a number of researchers and communicators who espouse the concept that the message is the more important factor in communication. For instance, Charles F. Hoban Jr. and E. B. Van Ormer, after an exhaustive and scholarly review of the research literature, proposed that there is nothing in the medium of film per se that guarantees communication. Communication is a direct function of how well the messages relate to the audience.[8]

We have all seen terrific information motion-media shows that have dazzled us with their brilliance and showmanship, and we were much impressed. Yet, on reflection, we realized that the shows did not say much to us. Perhaps the shows entertained, but they did not communicate the intended messages. In these cases, the medium is the message, but entertainment is not the reason the audience viewed the shows. The simple fact is that too many of us have focused on the selling of media rather than on relevant messages. We are more concerned with the gadgetry, hardware, software, and glamour of it all than with concepts. This is not to discount these items; without them, we could not communicate via motion-media. Rather, we ought to de-emphasize their primary importance and concentrate on the manipulative filmic devices and techniques that we use to encode information into motion-media messages, zeroing in on those messages relevant to changing audience behavior.

Too frequently, we find that message coding is suited more to the sponsor or to the show's designer than to the audience—that is, it is geared to individual or corporate ego-massaging. Though this coding often applies to the motion-media show as a whole, individual elements can be treated this way also. Some examples include gratuitously holding a favorite scene beyond the point at which it can transmit new information, using complex animation when simple techniques would suffice, or building complex montages involving optical/computer effects when a few simple straight cuts would do as well. The processes and techniques available to us, the filmic designers, in structuring and producing our information motion-media show are many, varied, and powerful. They should be used judiciously toward accomplishment of communication goals.

14

Creating a Communication Analysis Plan

If our information motion-media show is to be successful, we must perform an in-depth communication analysis before we begin scripting. To this end, I've included at the end of this chapter the Communication Analysis Plan with instructions. This plan is designed to codify specific key points concerning the proposed information motion-media show and to channel our thinking into successfully resolving the questions posed. Each motion-media show has unique needs and requires an individual approach to communication analysis. The basic elements that I outline should be used as a guide. Modify it to meet the particulars of your communication problem at hand.

Communication Analysis

It is important that all of the information be completed as accurately as possible to ensure a clear understanding of what the motion-media show is about, what is expected from whom, and when the completed show is due. Obviously, not all of the data required will be known after the first meeting with the client. It probably will take several meetings and extensive research to uncover all the pertinent factors.

The following are the essential points you need to address in preparing your communication analysis:

Proposed title. List the title. If it is not finalized, put in a working title or several proposed titles.

Reason to produce this motion-media show. Pinpoint exactly why this show is being produced. What problem, function, or issue is it intended to solve or alleviate? Is the problem real or imagined? What is the impact of the problem?

Target audience. Define the target audience in as specific terms as possible. Some examples are tenth-grade students studying chemistry, the general public, professional engineers who visit our organization, or impoverished senior citizens.

Purpose. The purpose or statement of communications objectives should be in three parts:

1. Define the sponsor's and/or producer's intentions. Over the years, I have found that this part ought to begin with the infinitive verb form *to.* Complete the verb with one of the following words (or another appropriate one): *arouse, canalize* (modify an existing attitude), *indoctrinate, influence, inform, motivate, orient, propagandize, report, train, teach,* or *sell.*

2. Specify to whom the sponsor's and/or producer's intentions are directed—the target audience as defined earlier.

3. State the action clause. It also begins with an infinitive verb form. What is the target audience supposed to do, say, learn, understand, think, or feel? What is the target audience's action item? What level of achievement is expected, and when it is expected?

Target-audience profile. As carefully and completely as possible, describe the target audience in terms of the three profile factors listed. Obviously, it's almost impossible to develop an all-encompassing target-audience profile. However, it's essential that the salient characteristics be identified and listed, thereby forming a comprehensive profile of the target audience. (Please see chapter 12 for details on the target-audience profile.)

Secondary audience. Can other audiences benefit from the show? Who are they? It's important that the integrity of the motion-media show should not be compromised for the benefit of secondary audiences.

Essential elements of information (EEI). What are the main points and primary concepts the target audience must have if the goals for the motion-media show are to be achieved? What information must be communicated? Usually in the form of broad-based notions or general guidelines, these elements are the foundation for the script, and they direct the source of the research. Three or four elements are optimum. If there are more than five in a film or video, the show is probably too ambitious and will not be successful. In multimedia, the number of information elements depends on the show's goals and how the interaction is designed.

Technical quality. Considering the difficulties inherent in achieving the communication goal set for this show, as deduced from all the factors in the communication plan, what is the *minimum* level of technical sophistication required to achieve this goal?

Schedule. Pinpoint as accurately as possible the due dates for the cardinal phases as listed on the communication plan. Update the schedule to meet changing conditions.

Filmic approach. This is what the motion-media show is composed of—how all the artistic, psychological, and technical elements are integrated to form the final show:

- *tenor:* This is the overall personality of the show. Is it frank or subtle, serious or humorous, calm or excited, telling or asking, authoritative or dubitable? Perhaps it's some combination of these qualities.
- *milieu:* This deals with the setting or environment of the show. Where and under what conditions does the scenario occur? Is the atmosphere real, fictional, or surreal? Dramatic, documentary, or cinema verité?
- *characteristics:* These describe the production techniques. Will actors or real employees be used? Does photography include high-speed (slow-motion), time-lapse, microphotography, special effects, or computer-generated art? Regular art and animation? How about sound: synchronous dialogue, voice-over narration, theater of the mind, or stream of consciousness? Or some concoction of all of these? What language is spoken? Stock or original music? Stock footage or slides?
- *form:* This refers to the physical structure of the show—production and distribution: length, gauge, black-and-white or color, digital or analog formats. Is the show complete, or is it in several parts? Is it part of a total communication package that includes other media?

Communication surround describes the physical environment in which the motion-media show is viewed—the environment in which communication occurs. Some of its most salient characteristics are the following:

- *audience size:* How large is the audience at a typical screening/viewing? A group? Just one?

- *frequency of screening/viewing:* Will the audience view the show more than once? How many times? How far apart in time are the screenings/viewings expected to be?
- *physical environment:* Where will the audience view the show? What is the size of the screening site? What are the site's appointments and acoustics? Lighting? Ambient noise and light?
- *leader or proctor:* Does the show require a leader or proctor to coach and monitor the audience? What qualifications are required? What is the availability of leaders or proctors?
- *projection/viewing equipment:* What equipment is needed? Cite the exact types and quantities at each location (computers, projectors, screen, monitor, etc.)
- *projectionist:* Is a projectionist required to operate the equipment? Can the audience operate the equipment in a fail-safe manner?
- *power requirements:* What are the electrical power requirements at the screening site? What arrangements must be made to supply the needed power if it's not there now?
- *backup material and equipment:* What support material and equipment are needed for a successful screening/viewing? Consider such items as handouts, publications, photographs, charts, testing materials, models, chalk, blackboard, pointer, microphone, and speaker equipment.

Controlling factors are usually client-imposed conditions that are concerned with production and distribution. Some factors are budget, schedule, distribution scheme (where, when, how), technical constraints, and information obsolescence. Others include the following:

- *due date:* How much time is available to produce this show? When is the completed show due in the client's hands?
- *serialized:* Is this show part of a series? How many others are in the series? Are they sequential? Do they stand alone? How much background information is needed in this show to maintain continuity?
- *part of total communication package:* Are other communication media used to make up a total communication package to achieve overall communication goals? Detail the package and pinpoint the significance of this show as part of the total package. How is the show integrated into the total package? What is the nexus? Are the same or similar elements used in more than one medium? Do these elements build on each other? Do they refer to each other?

- *changes or updates:* Will this show need to be changed or updated after its initial release? Are both visuals and sound to be changed? Visuals only? Sound only? How important are these changes/updates? How frequently must they be made?
- *technical and political production considerations:* What concerns are anticipated during research, scripting, production, and distribution? Consider such factors as availability of key organization personnel, equipment, facilities, travel, locations, weather, contacts, shooting permits, and clearances.
- *hazards and safety considerations:* What hazards are likely to be encountered during production? What safety precautions need be taken? Special equipment? Clothing? Special insurance?

Client concerns. Clients zealously strive to project and maintain a positive image. For some, it may be their most important asset. They are particularly sensitive to images projected or perceived in mass communication media where negative interpretations can easily be made and are hard to rectify.

- *image projected:* What image does the client want the show to project? Is it to offset an existing negative image? What topics are sensitive? What are the pitfalls?
- *company/organization policy:* What management position has the client taken on the topics covered in this show? What is the client's standard practice? Procedure? Rules?
- *legal aspects:* What impact will this show have on any pending legal actions? Will it precipitate legal action? Are the statements made in the show defensible? Do they affect union contracts or negotiations? Consumer groups?
- *political impact:* Do objectives of the show enhance or compromise short- or long-term organization goals? What impact will the show have on other organizations? Governments? Employees? Consumer groups? Unions?
- *proprietary information:* Is company proprietary or sensitive information included in the show? If so, what safeguards are there to protect this information? What impact is there should such information be compromised?
- *classified information:* Is classified government information included in the show? If so, exactly which visuals and audio are classified? What is the level of classification? What markings are required? How is distribution controlled?

Budget. What will this show cost? How much is the client willing to invest? What compromises can be reached? Will the show still be viable after the compromise? A motion-media show's budget should be separated into three distinct parts: scripting, production, and distribution. Such a breakdown protects the client and producer and ensures, in the long run, that the best possible show is produced for the resources allotted.

Medium Selection

Nowadays, with technology rapidly developing new media, sometimes we forget that there are producing media and distribution media. In the ol' days, a show was produced and distributed on film. Later, shows were produced on film and distributed in video or the other way around. Today, we produce our shows electronically, incorporating such elements as film and video clips, computer-generated animation, art, text, and perhaps even voice. We distribute the show over the Internet or via any number of digital media. In other words, when we use digital production and distribution media, most any combination is viable.

Let's review some of the production and distribution options:

- *producing medium:* What medium has the best potential to accomplish the communication goal set for this show? Consider all the factors discussed on this form in relation to each medium's advantages and disadvantages. What medium has the communication advantage? What medium engenders optimum communication in the most cost-effective way? Deciding which medium to select is not an easy task. For a detailed analysis of medium selection, I recommend consulting *Selecting Media for Instruction* by Robert M. Gange.
- *primary distribution medium:* It is possible that, because of special considerations, it's best to produce the show in one medium (film, for example) and distribute it in another (videotape or digital disk). All factors considered, in what medium should this show be distributed to maximize communication in terms of quality, cost, timeliness, urgency, etc.?
- *secondary distribution medium:* Do extraordinary situations or audiences require that this show be distributed in a secondary medium to fulfill unusual needs? What medium would best accomplish the secondary distribution goals?
- *distribution scheme:* How many copies are needed in the primary distribution medium? Secondary distribution medium? Will there

be a foreign-language version? Will the organization distribute this show? A professional distribution organization? The government? Is a distribution circuit required? Do users keep the copies or do they return them? To whom?

Key Personnel

List all the important contacts involved in the production of this show. Such a detailed listing facilitates harmonious business dealings.

Communication Analysis Plan

Now that we've reviewed the fundamentals, let's see the plan and determine how we can use it on our next show. You may duplicate and use this plan as often as you like. However, please note on your plan that the form is used courtesy of Shelton Communications.

Communication Analysis Plan

Today's Date: _____

Proposed title: _____

Reason to produce this motion-media show:

    The problem is: _____

    _____

Target audience: _____

Purpose: To _____ the target audience to _____

_____

Target Audience Profile

Identification factors

    Demographic: _____

    Socioeconomic: _____

    Psychological: _____

Motivation factors

    Anticipation: _____

    Importance of goal achievement: _____

    Urgency of communication: _____

Predisposition factors

    Sponsor: _____

    Communicator: _____

    Information: _____

    Medium: _____

Feedback

    Feedback?   Yes   No

    Importance: _____

How accomplished: _____

       Testing: _____

       Performance: _____

       Direct communication: _____

    Real time or delayed: _____

Secondary audience: _____

Essential Elements of Information

1. _____

2. _____

3. _____

4. _____

5. _____

Technical Quality Needed: _____

Interaction: _____

Schedule

Research: _____	Production: _____
Treatment: _____	Postproduction: _____
1st draft of script: _____	1st answer print/master dub: _____
Final script draft: _____	Distribution: _____

Filmic Approach

Tenor: _____

Milieu: _____

Characteristics: _____

Form: _____

Communication Surround

Audience size at each screening: _____

Frequency of screening: _____

Physical environment of the screening site: _____

Leader or proctor: _____

Projection/viewing equipment: _____

Projectionist: _____

Power requirements: _____

Backup material and equipment: _____

Controlling Factors

Due date (time available): _____

Serialized: _____

Part of total communication package: _____

Changes or updates: _____

Technical and political production considerations: _____

_____

Hazards and safety considerations: _____

Client Concerns

Image projected: _____

Company/organization policy: _____

Legal aspects: _____

Political impact: _____

Proprietary information: _____

Classified information: _____

Budget

Script: _____

Production: _____

Distribution: _____

Medium Selection

Producing medium: _____

Primary distribution medium: _____

Secondary distribution medium: _____

Distribution scheme: _____

Key Personnel

Client/sponsor

Organization: _____

Name(s) of contact(s): _____

Job title: _____

Telephone number/e-mail/fax: _____

Address: _____

Technical advisor

Name: _____

Job title: _____

Organization: _____

Telephone number/e-mail/fax: _____

Address: _____

Client/sponsor approval authority

Name: _____

Job title: _____

Organization: _____

Telephone number/e-mail/fax: _____

Address: _____

Producer

Name: _____

Job title: _____

Organization: _____

Telephone number/e-mail/fax: _____

Address: _____

Script designer

Name: _____

Job title: _____

Organization: _____

Telephone number/e-mail/fax: _____

Address: _____

This form is courtesy of Shelton Communications.

15

Filmic Design

If we are to use motion-media to communicate effectively, we need to master and employ filmic design to optimize the plasticity of the media. Here's my definition: Filmic design is a nebulous concept that can't be defined with precision. It's the techniques we use to encode the messages we want to communicate into motion-media's visual and aural signals. In essence, filmic design is that concoction of psychological manipulation, artistic achievement, and technical prowess that we use to design and produce our shows. Each such concoction is unique, and the infinitely variable potential of filmic design allows us to meet the specific communication task of any show. When we integrate these three aspects of filmic design into scripting and producing our shows, we've defined our filmic-design technique.

How are we to accomplish these communication goals using filmic-design techniques? How do we best encode the messages that engender maximum empathy? What techniques do we use? To what extent? When? There are no easy solutions. Knowledge, experience, and a common-sense approach are the basic factors in successfully using filmic design to solve communication problems via the motion-media. Not an easy task! If we are to be successful, we need to learn how to exploit filmic design by understanding the *language, grammar,* and *syntax* of motion-media, much as we must learn the grammar, language, and syntax of any medium.

Filmic-Design Techniques

We can categorize filmic design into several broad (and perhaps overlapping) functions: filmic characteristics, milieu, tenor, approach, and execution. The specific items listed under each of these functions are some of the most common. Producers often combine several of these styles in a show for greater impact and audience involvement. Factors considered in determining filmic-design techniques are communications objectives, nature of the audience, budget, schedule, and predilections of the producer and client.

This list is not intended to be definitive. It's a general overview, and it's subjective.

Filmic characteristics. Refers to the *mise en scène,* the physical elements that define the media. Genre. Setting. Arrangement. Form. The primary genres of form are:

- information
- documentary (nonfiction)
- narrative (dramatic)
- enrichment (personal expression)
- avant-garde (experimental)

In chapter 8, "The False Reality of Motion-Media," I discuss these genres in detail.

Filmic milieu. Refers to the style in which motion-media images are captured and presented. It's the environment, condition, or element of the motion-media show. Some of the more popular, listed alphabetically, are:

- *documentation:* recording of uncontrolled actions, sporting, or scientific events
- *historic past:* actual or purported footage from the past
- *metaphor:* scene is something other than it is, an analogy
- *narrative:* dramatization or slice-of-life scenario
- *objective past:* past becomes present
- *past as memory:* character's memory is the past
- *show-and-tell:* traditional voice-over narration where picture and sound are in coherence, archetype report, technical, information, education

Filmic tenor. Refers to the tone of the motion-media show—its mode of expression. The "feel" of it. Tenor affects the emotional response of audiences and their willing suspension of disbelief. The show may be:

- authoritative or dubitable
- calm or excited

- frank or circumspect
- serious or humorous
- straightforward or subtle
- telling or asking

Filmic approach. Refers to the method of encoding information in the media. How the sight-and-sound images are recorded and presented.

- *cinematic continuity or discontinuity*
- *cinema verité* (literally "cinema truth"; sometimes dubbed "direct cinema"): unrehearsed recording of sight-and-sound of real people at work, play, etc.
- *flashback:* the show's in current time, the plot reveals a past event
- *kinestasis:* extremely fast montage of still images, photographs, drawings, etc.; an individual shot of one frame may be on the screen for only 0.025 second
- *players:* professional actors or "real" people
- *kino eye:* the camera penetrates every detail of an unstaged scene and doesn't interfere with spontaneous actions
- *self-reflexive cinema* (sometimes dubbed self-referential): on-screen actor turns to camera and speaks to the audience
- *stream of consciousness:* character's thoughts as voice-over narration or images
- *symbolic imagery:* visual metaphor
- *subjective camera:* zero-degree camera angle—audience's eye has the view of the camera lens; usually used as a close-up or extreme close-up shot
- *talking head:* synchronous sound–cinematography/videography of a person speaking and looking into the camera; the shot usually is a close-up or a medium close-up; further discussed in chapter 20
- *theater of the mind:* today's images with sounds of the past or future

Filmic execution. Refers to those technical, cinematic, and artistic components and procedures that craftsmen and artists use. There are far too many such items to list and explain here, and such a treatment is beyond the scope of this book.

Clearly, it'll be to our advantage to be technically proficient. We learn and hone technical prowess by hands-on experience and with academic study. Many excellent publications abound on this topic—

far too many for me to list. Because the technology is changing so rapidly, we ought to subscribe to the several trade magazines that highlight these developments.

There are many other factors in filmic-design technique that I've not included in this list. What's here is a representative sample of the filmic-design techniques available to us. With experience, we'll expand our palette to include many others and some of the newly evolving technologies. Most important, we'll learn how to use technology to achieve optimum communication in our shows.

I want to restate: Our shows must be produced with appropriate filmic design if we are to achieve our communication goals.

There are some exceptions. One is the little-green-men metaphor. First, recall my maxim "The message is the message." Here's the scenario: A flying saucer lands on the White House lawn. Little green men hop out, storm the White House, capture the president, and whisk the chief executive away in their saucer. If this event were captured on film or tape, no matter how technically incompetent (out of focus, overexposed, or scratched), it would be a record of incalculable value. A real-life example is the Zapruder film recording the assassination of President John F. Kennedy on 22 November 1963. In such a scenario, *the importance of the message overwhelms all else.*

Part Four

Script Design

16

An Information Motion-Media Writer Should Be a Script Designer

Script-Designer Concept

I use the term *script designer* to describe the motion-media communicator who is known traditionally as the scriptwriter or the film writer. Script designing is more than just a change in job title; it's a management and production strategy to enhance the effectiveness of our shows. The script designer's task is to develop a viable scheme for solving communication problems through the use of kinetic visuals supported by audio.

Consequently, the script designer has near-total responsibility and authority for conception and development of the information motion-media show. Such responsibilities encompass the full spectrum of communication analysis, interpretation, and production—the primary functions that encode information into filmic messages. It's best if directing and producing the show are included among these responsibilities. In effect, the script designer has the artistic, psychological, and technical wherewithal to affect the achievement of the show's goals.

Traditional View

The traditional view of what the scriptwriter does is narrow in scope and fails to recognize the realities of information motion-media production in today's communication environment. To be a successful script designer, writers of all stripes must overcome their natural tendency to use the written word as their primary communication medium. Rather, their task is to develop scripts that optimize the kinetic-visual efficiency of our sight-and-sound motion-medium. Such a script is a detailed storyboard. (See appendix 3 for a sample storyboard.)

Frequently, I hear expressed the notion that a competent writer of technical reports, press releases, or articles is equally adept at writing information motion-media scripts. Unfortunately, this erroneous concept is held even by some of the longtime professionals. All too often, important information motion-media script-designing assignments are made on the assumption that "a writer is a writer is a writer."

And it's true: A writer writes. To such a person, the written word is the end communication product and primary communication medium. This is as it should be. However, when the written-word writer is tasked to write an information motion-media script, he or she often is ill prepared for the task. Writing such a script is essentially a discipline in kinetic-visual communication. The script may be meticulously researched, well organized, geared to the audience, and skillfully written, but it probably is inadequate as an information motion-media script because it's *written* instead of *drawn* as a storyboard. It's a publication to be read. It's not a script.

Nonetheless, it's a fairly common convention among many writers that the commentary (narration or dialogue) is *the script*. In some instances, I have seen entire script pages that do not have a word, sketch, or thought of any kind that deals with kinetic-visual development. With some scripts, the visual development is dismissed summarily by a curt "show it" or by the flippant "appropriate scenes to complement the narration." The writers in these instances have ensured communication failure. Any writer who believes that words really are preeminent in information motion-media communication doesn't belong in our profession.

Oral and Visual Development

Communication inadequacy is an inevitable and natural consequence of a script that doesn't focus on the kinetic visuals. The writer, following the style that is comfortable, tends to concentrate on the development of the oral commentary—the narration or the dialogue—relegating the visual planning to limbo. By indirection, the writer has made the commentary the primary communication element. Thus, motion-media's most powerful communication element, kinetic visuals in related juxtapositions, is ill used or negated altogether.

Though a script is composed of words and pictures, it's not a document meant to be read. Rather, it's a flexible plan for the development of the end communication product—the motion-media show. A script that engenders a high order of communication contains sketches or photographs and visual annotations, plus appropriate narration or dialogue. It's a storyboard: a series of drawings (however polished or crude) of each proposed scene laid out in continuity developing the progression of a scene or an entire production.

The storyboard details the show's filmic structure. The amount of detail we show in a storyboard is dependent on a host of factors. Complexity is the most important. To develop the storyboard for a complicated show or scene—a complex animation sequence, for instance—the script designer should work with the animator and director to get their opinions regarding the technical complexity and the cost involved to execute the scenes correctly.

The storyboard is not an absolute dictate. Actually, it is a flexible visual-planning guide for the production team, a cooperative effort among the director, cinematographer, art director, and editor. In almost all instances, the final filmic structure, as seen in the projected images on the screen, is somewhat different than detailed in the storyboard. This difference results from adapting to contingencies in cinematography, director's prerogatives, and editorial decisions.

Commentary

It is an immutable fact that the communication effectiveness of an information motion-media show lies primarily in the kinetic visuals and secondarily in the commentary. As we've seen, about 70 percent of the information in motion-media communication ought to be in the visuals and only 30 percent in the commentary. Such a 70/30 ratio bodes well for long-term audience retention of our messages. The 30 percent for the commentary appears to be the effective maximum limit and is applicable only when the commentary directly complements the visuals, that is, show-and-tell. Commentary that's inconsistent with the visuals interferes with communication and reduces a show's effectiveness. Coherence between visuals and commentary is absolutely essential.

One symptom of failure to understand our visual media is commentary that is written as if it were to be read by a reading audience instead of being spoken for a listening audience. These writing styles are very different, and the reading style clearly is inappropriate for motion-media. In the listening style, almost anything goes—and does. What is critical is that the commentary *sounds* right.

Effective Commentary

Effective commentary must be brief, trenchant, and not intrude on or upstage the visuals. Commentary may be a curt phrase, an exclamation, a flashing thought, a complete sentence, or any manner of a well-informed utterance. It may be narrative, meditative thought, rhyming poetry, or blank verse. No matter what its content or form, *commentary's exclusive function is to amplify and explain what the audience cannot perceive from the visuals yet must know for complete understanding.* Commentary is first, foremost, and always an ancillary function to the visuals.

Ideally, scripts are completed and approved before cinematography begins. Oftentimes, however, it is not possible to develop the script, especially the commentary, in detail before cinematography starts. This situation would apply, for instance, in those information motion-media shows that are composed mostly of stock, instrumentation, medical, or scientific footage and of news events or of other events that cannot be preplanned, controlled, or staged. Such lack of pre-scripting would also apply in sequences that show military, technical, or other specialists speaking their own jargon and doing their own jobs in their own particular way.

Even when the commentary is preplanned in detail for tightly controlled situations, flexibility is key. To meet changing circumstances during production, commentary must be adapted to conform to the cinematography.

The Script Designer's Role

The script designer is suited best to translate the script into information motion-media. In any phase of production, he or she is the one who can adapt, change, rearrange, redefine, add, or delete filmic elements to meet current circumstances, which in this business have a severe proclivity to change frequently.

As the former manager of an in-house information motion-media group, I established the job of filmmaker as our standard professional position. The filmmaker is the jack of all trades who is accomplished in all phases of scripting and production. On average, it takes a neophyte about six or seven years to become a polished professional. The filmmaker also serves as the script designer. Script designer–produced shows have a high order of communication effectiveness resulting directly from the powerful synergism generated by the combination of talents and responsibilities in one professional. In addition, we realized major economies in total resource expenditures—effort, money, time, equipment, and labor. Another advantage we realized was the script designer's high degree of job satisfaction resulting from fulfillment of creative needs, pride of accomplishment in an end product, and definitive recognition by peers.

Today, most motion-media professionals are free-lancers. In-house groups usually are small, having a permanent staff of three or four professionals on the average. Most of these professionals have multiple production responsibilities. Management uses free-lance personnel and contractors for specialized services, such as sound, art and animation, laboratory, and reproduction to round out the group's total production capability.

Development of professionals into script designers may not be feasible for all in-house groups. Nonetheless, management should consider the advantages of this concept, especially among beginning professionals whose skills are just developing. Use of a script designer as the person totally responsible for the show warrants for full realization of practical solutions of communication problems through information motion-media—solutions that are accomplished economically and professionally.

Information Film/Video Archives

Part of our job as script designers is to know and evaluate the cost and expected results of the scenes we develop. For instance, if we were to go to all the worldwide locations to film the various types of scarves called for in our storyboard in appendix 3, *The Scarf: The Perennial Fashion Statement,* our production budget would skyrocket, and we'd most probably be out of business. The answer: use stock footage and tape. Quite literally, there are millions and millions of feet of scenes of all types and descriptions available for our use in this country and throughout the world. Stock footage is available through:

- stock footage and tape libraries
- television networks (broadcast and cable) and local stations
- film/video production houses
- corporations
- universities
- motion-picture organizations
- museums and libraries
- government offices

Sometimes the footage is free; most of the time it costs. Cost usually is based on the amount of footage used in the final show and on how the show is to be distributed. Unless we're familiar with an organization's stock-footage catalog, we'll have to hire a re-searcher to find the specific scenes we need. On a per-hour basis, the cost of a researcher may seem high, but using an experienced researcher is a worthwhile investment and can result in significant savings, particularly if the researcher knows the library. Additional costs also include paying for duplication and shipping.

Also found in stock libraries are still photographs, music, and sound effects. It's imperative that we always get written permission and a license agreement any time we use stock material. Such is especially the case with music; otherwise, we may well end up as defendants in court.

There's no standard script format. However, there are several formats that work for most of us. Which format to use depends on the show's *mise en scène*. Traditionally, we use the split-page for information motion-media scripts that call for voice-over narra-tion—the anonymous, authoritative, and unseen voice. We prefer the teleplay format for the slice-of-life and real-life dramatization scenarios in which actors speak scripted lines in synchronous sound. The teleplay format has several alternate names: *business teleplay, corporate teleplay,* or *information teleplay.* These types of informa-tion motion-media shows mimic the style of the entertainment industry's narrative motion-picture films and television programs. And there are combinations of these two basic script formats. Nowadays, script designers in the information motion-media pro-fession are using the teleplay format more frequently, because more and more of our scripts are set in the narrative *mise en scène*.

No matter which format you use, what's important is that the script is organized clearly, is graphically lucid, and is vividly un-ambiguous.

As an aside, there are a number of computer programs that'll help get your script into the format of your choice.

To illustrate the primary script formats, I've included four samples in the appendixes:

Appendix 3 has a split-page script and storyboard. The script is for the show *The Scarf: The Perennial Fashion Statement.* Please note that there is no narration or dialogue in this script.

Appendix 4 is in the information teleplay format with a few pages from the script *Gambling Addiction and the Family.*

Appendix 5 is a split-page script with voice-over narration, using a sample of the script *Desert Stewardship*.

Appendix 6 is a teleplay and split-page combination with the opening sequence of the show *Pacific Frontier.*

17

Scripting for Information Motion-Media

Information motion-media is primarily a visual communication medium. Accordingly, narration and dialogue should be kept to a minimum, used only to amplify or explain what the audience cannot perceive from the visuals on the screen. Overwriting is a primary fault—too many words *telling* the audience too many things, not *showing* them.

Accordingly, writing per se is probably the least-important component in scripting an information motion-media show. Motion-media scripting is, in fact, kinetic-visual designing. "Don't write, draw" is an ideal maxim to follow in script designing—that is, don't *write* a script, *draw* a storyboard.

An information motion-media script—no matter how well conceived and detailed—should be no more than a flexible visual planning guide. Our scripts must be mutable to meet varying requirements, new perspectives, and unforeseen production difficulties and to encourage industry and opportunism during production and postproduction. Important points we need to consider are:

- A script includes the storyboard and the preproduction plan
- A script doesn't have to be a minutely detailed prescription for production (don't direct from the script)
- The script is not sacrosanct

In the production of medical and test-and-evaluation shows, for example, the script designer has little or no control over the activities being photographed and can't predict with any certainty the outcome. Success hinges on the script designer's keen perception and ability to adapt to changing events during all phases of the production process (assuming that the script designer has continuing responsibilities from conception to completion of the show).

Scripting Components

Our responsibility as script designers is to identify, analyze, and resolve all the key issues of the scripting components. We can identify six discrete components that constitute the scripting function. The components are mutually related and interdependent, and they combine in an interlocking synergism to form the composite scripting function. The components are:

- communication analysis
- topic research
- client concerns
- medium selection
- filmic approach
- kinetic-visual planning

Each of these components, in turn, is composed of a number of key elements or issues. Regardless of where in the production process our script is completed, we would have considered and resolved all issues relating to these components.

Communication Analysis

The entire scripting function is based on a communication analysis that addresses the following basic issues:

- What is the problem we're going to solve?
- What are the communication goals?
- Who is the target audience? Secondary audience?
- What are the essential elements of information?

Since all these elements of communication analysis are intrinsically connected, we can't isolate one from the other. Rather, in practical terms, we gather data on all elements more or less concurrently. It is nigh impossible, for instance, to define the problem and communication goals without identifying the target audience. (For details, see chapter 14, "Creating a Communication Analysis Plan.")

Topic Research

Using the results of our communication analysis, we ferret out and gather information through on-site visits to locales to see, hear, feel, touch, and smell the living scene. We interview the client and technical consultant, and we discuss the topic with the target audience (not always possible, however). Interviews with ancillary people may give important and perceptive insights—for example, a dissatisfied customer, an injured worker, or a failing student. We review the literature, screen related motion-media shows, and peruse still photographs. All research options should be considered and explored. It's imperative that we keep an open mind so that we recognize unexpected new information or an unforeseen nuance on a preconceived idea. This directed topic-research approach is significantly more productive and cost-effective than the scatter-gun attempts I've seen all too often.

Organization and evaluation of the information in terms of relevance and associations are our follow-through procedures. We distill the gathered information into that which is germane and organize it in a structure. The organizational structure may be spatial, chronological, operational, logical, or by critical area. As a rule, one structure usually evolves as the most propitious. Fact-finding is not complete until we consider the client's concerns.

Client Concerns

Clients zealously strive to project and maintain a positive image. For some, it may be their most important asset. They are particularly sensitive to images projected or perceived in mass communication media, where negative interpretations are easily made and hard to rectify.

Also of concern to clients are such sensitive issues as company policy, legal aspects, political implications, classified information, privileged and proprietary data or processes, and future goals. Though not directly related to image, these issues are often critical elements in the client's communication policy.

Therefore, it's incumbent on us to ascertain the particulars of our client's concerns in order to ensure that our script reflects a fitting image, is inoffensive, and that only releasable information is included. Usually, the client and technical advisor will spot any inappropriate or offensive details during the various script reviews, but don't count on it. In any case, we must make sure we get script approval *in writing*.

Medium Selection

Before we start designing the script, we must select the appropriate medium. Though we discussed medium selection in earlier chapters, here are a few more details. Our final choice of medium depends on the answers to the following questions:

- Which medium engenders optimum communication in the most cost-effective way?
- Is some combination of media required?
- Are the messages so important that cost is only a minor consideration? How soon does the audience need the information?
- When are results expected?
- Lastly, what's the optimum way to package and distribute the information?

Recall that a medium is composed of many parts. For example, the information film is composed of the program (the physical motion-picture film) and requires a projectionist and projection equipment, electrical power, and an appropriate screening environment—all melded into an all-encompassing motion-media presentation. To view a multimedia show, one needs a computer, power, etc.

Close liaison with the client is essential when selecting the medium. We need to negotiate a mutually agreeable choice that considers the client's preferences and what's best for the audience.

I've coined three terms—*medium advantage, communication surround,* and *controlling factors*—to describe the all-encompassing communication environment. These concepts are intimately related and inseparable in theory and practice. Nevertheless, there are some intrinsic and discrete factors in each concept.

Medium advantage describes that unique overall psychological ambiance that engenders optimum communication. Of all the media available, there will be one system that has the greatest potential for maximum communication in any particular show. (For details, see chapter 14.)

Communication surround describes the physical environment in which communication occurs.

Controlling factors are usually client-imposed conditions that are concerned with production and distribution. (For details, see chapter 14.)

The potential of any medium to facilitate communication is dependent on a host of complex factors. The properties of a medium or channel define its overall communication effectiveness. These general properties are: credibility, accessibility, strength, permanency, reinforcement, and feedback. Other channel dimensions we consider are:

- *capacity:* rate at which the channel transmits messages that are error-free or nearly so
- *coding:* the physical and psychological effort required to encode the messages into the channel and the system that decodes them for the audience
- *treatment:* the way the messages are presented in the channel in terms of authority, emphasis, believability, redundancy, and style
- *noise:* the inherent noise factor of the coding and decoding functions and of the channel itself; noise is both physical and psychological

Thus, the medium-selection process is markedly more complicated than it appears to be at first glance. Consider these examples:

- For large, widely separated, heterogeneous audiences who need general information quickly, e-mail may be the appropriate medium. When immediate feedback is required, a teleconference or a speakerphone conference telephone call may be best. If the need is not immediately pressing and feedback can be delayed slightly, perhaps some form of publication is fitting.
- To train an audience in a perceptual motor skill, an interactive multimedia show is in order.
- To motivate a small, homogeneous audience to do the "right thing," a film/video is applicable.
- To teach a cognitive skill with just a few key points, an information film or video may be appropriate. If the skill is complicated—learning a foreign language, for example—then it's multimedia.
- If the audience must learn a large amount of technical data or how to perform a complex series of actions that must be done in sequence—for example, field-stripping an M16 rifle—communication is best accomplished by instruction-proctored, interactive multimedia, and hands-on practice, with follow-through by liberally illustrated backup printed material.

There are no easy or right answers. In many instances, any one of the media will accomplish the communication task. We should weigh all possibilities in selecting the appropriate medium for the problem, message, and the audience.

Filmic Approach

The filmic approach is the *mise en scène*. It's based on the show's tenor, milieu, characteristics, and form. Though I've discussed filmic approach in chapter 14, I'm repeating it here for those who've skipped that chapter.

Tenor refers to the overall personality of the show. Is it frank or subtle, serious or humorous, calm or excited, telling or asking, authoritative or dubitable? Perhaps it is a combination.

Milieu deals with the setting or environment. Where and under what conditions does the scenario occur? Is the atmosphere real, fictional, or surreal? Dramatic, documentary, or cinema verité?

Characteristics are the production characteristics. Will actors or real employees be used? Does cinematography include slow motion, time-lapse, microphotography, digital effects? Will production take place on location or on stage? Is stock footage used? Art and animation? How about sound—synchronous dialogue or voice-over narration, theater of the mind, or stream of consciousness? Or some concoction of all these? What language is spoken? Stock or original music?

Form refers to the form of the media of production and distribution: length, gauge, analog or digital, black-and-white or color, compatible with what screening/viewing devices. Is the show complete unto itself, or does it have supporting material?

Kinetic-Visual Planning

There is no one method of designing the script. Nor is there any one correct structure or style. Each script is designed to meet the unique situation described by the components. Here's my four-step scripting method:

Outline. I organize the data into a skeletal structure that highlights key points and puts them into a perspective that defines their interrelationships.

Treatment. Here I expand the outline into a narrative synopsis that gives an overview of the entire show. It describes in some detail the major visual sequences and significant lines of dialogue or narration, all couched in the elements of the filmic approach. It's in this phase that we fashion the show's *mise en scène*—its structure and style. It's the guiding hand that leads the audience through the communication process, sorting messages into meaningful patterns.

Script. The treatment is enlarged into a detailed production plan in which kinetic visuals are developed scene-for-scene and the complete dialogue or narration is written. Suggestions are made regarding type and location of effects, titles, and other production and postproduction details. In practice, the final decisions about these details are made in the postproduction phase.

Storyboard. This is a series of drawings, sketches, or still photographs depicting proposed scenes in their filmic continuity. Narration/dialogue is shown with each storyboard frame. A storyboard isn't needed for every motion-media show, but it's rare when it isn't. Detailed storyboards are essential for animation scenes.

Outline for Generic Information Motion-Media Scripts

The generic script outline I'm suggesting will fit many of our information motion-media communication tasks. It's a formula, modified in many ways that I've used over the years with some measure of success.

- Open the show with a grabber to get and hold the audience's attention—to whet their appetite. My grabbers usually are a fast-paced, dynamic filmic montage of relevant scenes underscored with upbeat music. Minimal, if any, commentary.
- Set the stage by summarizing what the show is about, and state the communication goals.
- Communicate to your audience why this show is important to them. What advantage will the audience obtain? How will it affect them?
- Communicate the main points rationally, cogently, and empathetically. Such communication is accomplished through trenchant and dynamic visuals and graphic words in a pinpoint communication thrust.
- Tie concepts together in a memory chain linked together with smooth and relevant transitions.[1]
- Answer the primary questions expected from the audience. A pre-script test with a sample of the target audience helps define such questions.
- Use logic and persuasion to lead the audience to a conclusion (your communication goal) that is obvious and inevitable.
- Summarize the main points.
- Communicate the audience's action items and time frame for completion.
- End on a positive note, if appropriate, with a short filmic montage or another upbeat short sequence.

In its simplest form, the basic outline is:

- Show 'em what you're going to show 'em
- Show 'em
- Show 'em what you showed 'em

I'm not suggesting that we should repeat the information three times. What I'm saying is that we must first introduce the topic: set the stage, as it were. Next, expand the information in appropriate detail. Last, summarize key points and state the audience's action items—what, in effect, you want them to do, say, or think as a result of having viewed your show.

Use this generic outline as a guide in your scripting ventures. It's flexible. Add to it, subtract, or revise it to fit the communication goals of your show. It's not the outline that counts. It's your thinking that counts—your ability to devise a filmic solution to the communication problem at hand. Often, the particular circumstances of each show dictate the appropriate structure. (In chapter 19, I discuss guidelines for writing narration and dialogue.)

Remember, *short is sweet*. Motion-media shows with a pinpoint communication thrust, stripped of nearly all the folderol and most of the technical data, are highly effective communication tools. Audiences empathize easily with shows that are clear and concise. I recommend using multimedia accompanied by a liberally illustrated publication to communicate technical data.

Pace

Today's audiences are accustomed to fifteen-second and thirty-second television commercials with their rapid-fire repetitiveness that inundates the viewer in barrages of hard-sell messages—an effective technique if administered in small doses. If used to excess in information motion-media, the audience will escape mentally. It's important to give the audience reflective time to assimilate and integrate newly presented information. We need to vary the pace of our shows to get and maintain audience interest.

A well-scripted information motion-media show portends success. Communication goals are achieved, and resource expenditure is optimal. In such a scenario, clients and film designer benefit, and the audience does not try to escape.

18

My Contrary Principles
of Script Design

The scripts for most information motion-media shows are inept. Mimicking commercial television or the movies, most scripts employ dialogue or narration to carry the bulk of the information. These scripts may read well on paper, but they don't engender much communication when translated to kinetic motion-media sight-and-sound shows.

Designing an effective information motion-media script is not easy. There isn't any shortcut. Hard work, common sense, initiative, perhaps a touch of verve, and extensive understanding of how our media communicate ideas are the essential attributes of the professional information motion-media script designer.

Becoming an accomplished script designer in our profession demands a long and arduous learning process. The foundation of this process is to understand the media's *language, grammar,* and *syntax*. We also need to have a working knowledge of the technical processes available: their advantages, disadvantages, and costs. Sadly, not many script designers spend the time and effort to truly master these fundamentals.

To illustrate, I've codified the most common scriptwriting problems that comprise my "contrary principles." (From this point on, I use *scriptwriter* in a pejorative sense.) The following list is not in any particular order, nor do I pretend that it is complete. I fully realize I'm criticizing concepts, values, and basic plots that many scriptwriters hold in high esteem.

Overwritten. Narration/dialogue tells the audience everything they'd ever want to know about the topic. The audience is be-clouded in irrelevance. They cannot perceive the essential elements of information nor what is expected of them. Rather than inundate the audience with drivel, concentrate on the kinetic visuals, and make the verbiage sharp and concise, lean and mean.

One more comment on overwriting. Some years ago, when I was the manager of the motion-media competition for a major communication society, we received a video whose target audience was deaf people. As incredible as it sounds, the talking head was the video's entire filmic milieu. We can't assume that the viewers were lip readers.

Prolix. Wall-to-wall narration or dialogue pounds the audience into a cacophonous-induced stupor. It's abominable verbosity. The scriptwriter uses the narration or dialogue as the primary communication medium, and an endless stream of machine-gunned words suffocates the audience. In motion-media, silence is golden.

Punctilious. To ensure 100 percent correct grammar, form, and syntax, the scriptwriter writes narration or dialogue to be read rather than heard. When it's heard, it sounds stilted and academic. Scripts are not an extension of literature. It's okay to develop narration/dialogue in non-sentences, to use idioms and slang, and in general to be less formal than when writing for a reading audience. Conversational style is appropriate for a listening audience.

Discordant. Dichotomy between visuals and audio: Two disparate messages are sent simultaneously, each element going its own independent way. The audience is confused by the mixed signals. In effective motion-media, there is *absolute coherence* between visuals and audio. Audio reinforces the visuals to form a synergism that greatly enhances communication—show and tell.

Tautological. Visuals and narration are redundant. Words tell the audience exactly what they can see on the screen. Instead, words must be used only to tell the audience members what they cannot perceive from the visuals yet must know for complete understanding.

Radioish. Vapid and irrelevant visuals are used as a mechanical device to use up screen time while the bulk of the information is transmitted in the narration. The visuals do not pertain to the points being discussed, but they don't directly interfere either. Consciously or subconsciously, the audience tries to interpret the visuals (in what ought to be the primary communication source in the sight-and-sound media) but cannot. They become confused and distracted, and the result is poor communication. Such motion-media shows are, at best, illustrated radio programs.

Question: Why is radio such a powerful communication medium, especially radio drama? It's because we, the listening audience, create our own perfect and powerful visuals. We're not confused with irrelevant visuals that distract our concentration.

Malapropos. Narration is not in a style and tone appropriate to the target audience. Some of the styles under this malady are:

- *passive:* Passive voice dulls the audience's mind. Active voice in present tense stimulates and involves the audience—and stimulation and involvement are essential ingredients in communication.
- *pedantic:* Pompous language and scenarios are used to impress the audience or client about how learned the scriptwriter is.
- *telling:* Telling style tends to alienate many audiences—use carefully.
- *over and under:* Narration is cast in a form that is either orotund or patronizing to the audience; it misses the understanding and needs of the audience.

Desultory. The show rambles and lacks structure, so audiences cannot follow its development. I firmly believe a motion-media show should have a beginning, middle, and end. The sequences ought to be linked in a chain of associated ideas that build to a logical conclusion. Such shows, however, do not necessarily have to have linear development. To use the old standby, "Tell them what you're going to tell them. Tell them. Then tell them what you told them."

Farraginous. A hodgepodge; a confused mixture resulting from too many goals for too many audiences. The show is too ambitious and lacks a critical focus. It's like an ice-cream sundae made from a dash of dozens of flavors. It tastes okay, but what flavor is it? What's the message the target audience is supposed to get from the show?

Vacuous. In an attempt not to offend anyone, the show communicates nothing to anybody. It would be better if these sorts of shows were never produced. However, they are politically correct and engender feel-goodism.

Self-Indulgent. "Creativity" is used for creativity's sake and to massage the scriptwriter's ego. "Here's my chance to write a 'great' movie. I'll be 'creative.' I'll entertain the audience with production value, actors, locations, special and digital effects, and lots of razzle-dazzle, and in stereophonic sound." Wonderful! Hope you had a great time at the client's expense. But did the show accomplish the communication goal set for it? And was it worth the client's money and resources? Probably not! As Charles "Cap" Palmer said, "The only conceptual kinship between a good [informational] film and a 'movie' is the accident of being packaged on long narrow strips of cellulose acetate through which a beam of light shines."

Gimmicky. Overabundance or misapplication of novel ideas, styles, and devices that call attention to themselves and detract from communication. Gimmicks are noise in the communication process.

Monotonous. The show lacks variety in rhythm and accent. It has one speed from beginning to end, no dramatic sense or development. Since motion-media is plastic, the effective script designer manipulates time and space to arouse the audience's emotions in order to engender commitment and empathy.

Rough. No transitions to lead the audience smoothly from one concept to the next—nothing to integrate the scenes. Today, many scriptwriters and producers have the notion that "audiences are TV smart. Hit 'em on the head with raw information as fast as you can." From what I've seen in such shows, I'm convinced these folks are rationalizing. They won't (or can't) put out the initiative, industry, and imagination needed to make an all-around professional show.

Inept. Just plain incompetence in all facets of scripting and production. The scriptwriter doesn't know the syntax of filmic design, is not familiar with techniques or processes, and doesn't comprehend the scope of the resources required to execute these techniques successfully. Thus, the scriptwriter fails to use the medium effectively by either under-utilizing or over-utilizing techniques.

Stilted scenarios. In an attempt to be creative and to make a narrative movie, some scriptwriters couch the essential elements of information in a dramaturgical scenario laced with trite dialogue. Such scenarios are hackneyed and implausible and are best avoided. The fact that the dialogue carries the bulk of the communication burden should give us a clue to the inherent problem in these scenarios—scenarios that I find particularly ineffective and insulting.

Below, I've listed some particularly egregious stilted scenarios. These samples are generic, and there are many variations within each of the basic themes:

- *man on the street:* In "spontaneous" utterance, random characters extol the virtues and evils of whatever point the show is trying to make. Almost no one believes that such dialogue is unrehearsed and undirected, and credibility is seriously eroded by such chicanery.

- *newscast*: Contrived to a crippling fault, scenarios of a "newscaster" in the pressroom or on location, faking a broadcast with a news bulletin, always fail. Sophisticated audiences recognize the flim-flammery instantly and are insulted, guaranteeing communication failure.

- *interview:* Under the guise of a no-holds-barred interview, some "big-time journalist" questions the chief executive officer to get the "real" facts. Sure! The journalist asks the obligatory, scripted, arranged-in-advance, tell-me-what-we-both-already-know question, which is followed by the dittoed answer. It's patent tomfoolery and ineffective.

- *old guy talking to the young guy:* By far, this is the most popular and notorious stilted scenario. It's the scenario that I abhor with the greatest vigor! The basic premise of this scenario is that the sage (old guy) tells the novice (young guy), in ping-pong question-and-answer routine, why to buy it or how to do it. *It* can be anything from coffee ("Madam, here's how to save your marriage with a better cup of coffee"), to automobiles ("Sir, here's how to inveigle that attractive female"), to home mortgages ("Folks, here's your path to upward mobility, even if you're fiscally overextended"), to field-stripping an M16 rifle ("Recruit, your rifle is your best friend"). I wholeheartedly resent that if I'm to get information from this scenario, I must eavesdrop on the actors' conversation to get the information I need. This stilted scenario dominates radio commercials and is even more obnoxious in that context.

- *talking head:* Our information motion-media shows are laced with talking heads that talk, talk, and talk. Ensconced in an appropriate setting decorated with pertinent trappings (CEO's office, perhaps), the talking head tells us why the Acme Toxic Waste Disposal Company is people—and tells and tells and tells! At best, such a scenario is a photographically recorded lecture that almost no one cares a hoot about. Novices should reject all temptation to use this scenario.

- *parody:* Frequently done, seldom successful, and always a self-evident reflection of the scriptwriter's limited imagination is parody. The scriptwriter tries to imitate the style of a well-known artist or the form of a popular television show or motion picture in a feeble attempt at humor or parody. Many audiences feel cheated and patronized at such second-rate imitations of the real thing. "Don't we deserve, at least, an original idea?" they might rightly wonder. This kind of audience perception does not engender much communication, at least not the kind intended by the scriptwriter and client.

- *real-life dramatization:* In an outlandish photoplay, some down-trodden character's problem, either emotional, social, or financial, is solved by the character doing what's "required"—usually dictated by family, friends, or coworkers. For instance, "Your nose warts disappear when you start using Acme Nose Wart Nostrum." Artificial plots, tediously developed in such scenarios, do not achieve communication.
- *slice of life:* A hard-working, good-natured bumpkin is in deep trouble because of lack of insight or knowledge. Someone with a special interest in the bumpkin sets him or her right by dispensing the missing insight or knowledge. The problem is solved, and all live happily ever after. Who's kidding whom? With today's attuned audiences, such a jejune scenario will elicit scorn and giggles.

Admittedly, I've skewed the thrust of my arguments here to fit my own predilections. I'll also reluctantly admit that, in some instances, under certain circumstances, perhaps an exceptionally well-crafted dramatic scenario might work just fine. For instance, when we are dealing with sociological themes such as sexual abuse, child molestation, and gambling addiction, our audience needs to identify and empathize with the show's characters to enhance communication.

However, I recommend that beginners and longtime professionals always avoid stilted scenarios. When a narrative show is required, I suggest that only an experienced script designer skilled in dramaturgy can successfully develop such a script.

My prescription for universal success is to keep your scripts and shows *simple, short,* and *straightforward.* The only proven way to improve your script-designing skills is to visualize, visualize, visualize, then draw, draw, draw your storyboard, no matter how crude. Finally, write a few lines of commentary—if absolutely necessary.

Design Scripts

Use filmic design to develop the kinetic-visual continuity. Then have your scripts critiqued by your peers and those whom you respect. If you're super-serious about this business, pay for such critiques from an honest broker, someone who is recognized by our profession.

19

Guidelines for Writing Narration and Dialogue

Here's the problem: No matter how hard you've tried, you can't get all the information in the kinetic visuals. Your storyboard is brilliant. The visuals you've planned are relevant, dynamic, and cogent, but they just don't complete the communication task. After lots of soul-searching, you're forced to admit that you've got to use commentary to tell the audience what they can't perceive from the visuals, voice-over narration, dialogue, or a talking head. What do you write? How do you write it?

In the following sections, I suggest some guidelines that'll help you develop commentary that contributes to communication. These guidelines are listed in their descending order of importance.

General Guidelines

Ensure that the narration and the kinetic visuals reinforce and complement each other—that they are in coherence. Ensure that the narration does not send one message, the visuals another. When the visuals and narration are in near-perfect coherence, a synergism is created. Such a synergism is a powerful dual sense that significantly enhances the communication potency of motion-media. The show is harmonious.

Write narration and dialogue as if every word you write costs you two hours of pay. Too many words telling the audience too much information pounds the audience into a stupefying catatonic state. The eye is our primary sensor. The eye receives information at a significantly faster rate than does the ear.

All factors being equal, voice-over narration is the voice of authority for most audiences. The anonymous narrator speaks from on high—presuming that the narrator is a first-class professional. Direct the narrator to use the right mix of vocal tone and pace to emphasize the importance or urgency of the messages.

Narration and dialogue are heard, not read. A conversational style is appropriate for the listening audience. Write for the ear, not the eye. A good test is to have someone read the narration and dialogue to you. How does it sound?

Sometimes narration can be blank verse, as in the "Voices of Commerce" sequence in the *Song of Ceylon.* In *Night Mail,* the narration in the concluding scene is rhyming couplets spoken in the tempo of the clickety-clack of the fast-moving train as it approaches Glasgow. Use such techniques with caution.

Don't write narration that tells the audience what they can see for themselves from the visuals or just to keep the narrator talking.

Specific Guidelines

Here's a potpourri of some specifics I recommend to help ensure that your commentary is as excellent as it can be. Obviously, no list such as this can be complete. But do with it as you will: add, modify, or (I pray not) delete from it.

- Include only one thought per well-formed utterance (or sentence).
- Short sentences and well-formed utterances are best.
- Narration doesn't necessarily have to have coherence and continuity in itself. Such factors should come from the kinetic visuals through montage editing and manipulation of the plasticity of the medium—filmic design.
- Narration should not be noticed. It must be natural to the scene and natural in tone and syntax. Narration that calls attention to itself usually becomes noise in the communication process.
- Write the narration in a natural, conversational style. Be careful of tongue twisters.
- Short comments are best. Concise, direct, easy-to-understand words and phrases communicate effectively.
- Narration and dialogue must be written in a tone appropriate to the particular audience. Talking up or down to audiences ensures communication breakdown.
- Use colloquialisms with caution.
- Be personal in your writing. In many instances, it's better to use personal pronouns such as *we* and *you* to establish a warm and

friendly ambiance. Be cautious, however: don't overdo it or you'll become smarmy. It's okay to use contractions from time to time—*we'll, I'm,* and *it's,* for example.

- Use everyday words for your particular audience, and use them simply. Be natural.
- Use precise language. Say exactly what you mean, and mean exactly what you say.
- Use simple, unambiguous words.
- Use concrete nouns and verbs.
- Keep the nouns next to their verbs, and follow with the object. Such a verbal arrangement in oral communication optimizes communication. A natural order and uncomplicated construction are basic to conversation.
- Use dynamic, active-voice verbs in the present tense. Such verbs are stimulating and have an involving effect that maintains the audience's interest.
- Avoid passive voice, which dulls the audience's mind. Sometimes, however, the passive voice is appropriate, such as when the emphasis is on the subject rather than the actor. For example, "Airplanes are made of aluminum," or "I was fired!"
- Develop vocal variety, rhythm, and pattern in the sound of the commentary.
- Repetition reinforces communication.
- Write the narration in a positive tone for maximum impact. Use *remember* instead of *don't forget,* for instance.
- Introduce new information in context with old information. In some instances, it's best to start a comment with a bit of old information and use a connector to end with new, important information.
- In some show-and-tell sequences, presenting information via the laundry-list narration technique is appropriate. For instance, "The veterinarian inoculated poodles, terriers, setters, and hounds."
- Keep construction parallel for maximum impact.
- Use acronyms only after you're positive the audience will understand their full meaning. Tread prudently.
- If you must use technical terms, use them—but use them sparingly. Consider using a superimposed title of the technical term over the visual to reinforce communication.
- Abstract ideas are communicated effectively through trenchant visuals (animation, perhaps) and graphic words.
- If you must use foreign-sounding names and words, give the narrator a break and spell them out phonetically in parentheses in your script.

- Use alliteration, simile, and metaphor with caution. Often these rhetorical devices are best used in writing to be read.
- Use idioms, slang, clichés, etc., with extreme caution. I've found over the years that such sayings contribute little to the communication.
- Round off numbers, if appropriate. Reinforce the communication with a superimposed title of that number.
- When dealing with the size of things, make comparisons with objects familiar to the audience. For example, "about the size of a dime." (Better yet, show a dime next to the object, and skip the narration.)
- Be scrupulously honest. Any false comment or perceived attempt to mislead the audience ensures communication failure. The entire show is discredited.
- Avoid imperatives. Telling tends to alienate many audiences.
- Avoid adjectives and adverbs that reflect your personal interpretation—for example, *beautiful, quickly, azure blue.* Audiences make their own judgments and may resent your imposition.
- Avoid superlatives, such as *greatest, bluest, most.*
- Avoid pronouns whenever possible. In aural communication, antecedents get lost quickly and frequently.
- Avoid, if possible, comments that date the production.
- Avoid starting too many comments with *th* words. Such writing sounds stilted and lacks variety and rhythm.
- Avoid overusing *you* and *yours.* A few *you*s go a long way.
- "Gobbledygook obfuscates ratiocination."

Such a list is endless. What I have noted here, however, are some of the primary guidelines you'll need to consider in writing narration or dialogue. Application of these guidelines with professional élan is the key to enhanced communication in motion-media. Admittedly, there are exceptions. In that rare instance when you believe that you've got an exception, proceed with caution.

To illustrate some of the points I've made, I've included a superior example of voice-over narration. The following quotation is part of the narration of the award-winning seven-minute film *Vision Lab,* a sales film for a (then) new computer graphics system. Through use of a highly stylized format, we see the system in operation to demonstrate its capabilities. William "Bill" Mauger, president of Sunbreak Productions, was the executive producer of *Vision Lab.*

Vision Lab
The means to an end.
The end. Limitless transformation.
Imagination.
The means.
Vision Lab.
Nondedicated distributed workstation image processing.
Software. A high-resolution monitor . . .
Vision Lab. Every function you imagined.
Archive. The storage and retrieval of images on disk.
Digitize. To capture an image thirty times a second or to freeze a
   single frame.
Analyze. Zoom. Pan. Region of interest.
Pixel coordinates and values. Plot pixel values.
Filter. Sharpening. Smoothing. Convolute an entire image.
Erode and dilate gray scale.
Image edit. Paint. Airbrush. Erase.
Cut. Paste. Insert text. . . .[1]

Notice that the narration lacks continuity, detail, coherence, and formal grammatical structure. Also, please note that the narration is sparse. Mauger optimizes communication in this film by couching most of the information in relevant and dynamic visuals. He uses the narration only to tell the audience the information they must know for a complete understanding of the film's message. This film is a classic show-and-tell, having the visuals and narration in near-perfect coherence.

Unfortunately, on this printed page, you can't see the film. You must see it to fully comprehend how Mauger uses the syntax of the medium to communicate commanding messages, to understand how he uses kinetic visuals and graphic words in harmonious coherence to form a powerful synergistic communication tool.

I'll conclude this chapter on writing narration with a comment from a student who attended my script-design seminar a few years ago. She is a senior technical writer/editor working for a large organization that has no in-house motion-media capability. She was tasked to write a video script on a technical subject. Here are her comments: "Script design *works!* I find that the thing that works for me in writing narration is to 'hear' it in my head as I go—then I go back and pronounce the words. This inevitably leads to reducing syllables and eliminating words. Then I'm visualizing how the words and the images will be, as an audience member. The customer was very pleased."[2]

20

The Talking Head

We're inundated with talking heads in our kinetic sight-and-sound media. We *hear* everybody from the chief executive officer to the local politico, the television news-talker on the evening news, actors bantering in television commercials, to the man or woman on the street *telling* us all about it (whatever *it* may be). The talking-head scenario is popular, quick, and cheap. Admittedly, the talking head does affect some communication, in varying degrees, to some audiences. But it's tedious, unfilmic, and woefully inefficient in communicating ideas. More often than not, the talking-head scenario reflects the script designer's lack of cinematic skill and filmic imagination or just plain laziness.

Partial Communication Power

As a communication tool, the talking head functions only minimally because the visual of the head does not contain much information. Instead, the communication thrust in shows using a talking head is concentrated in the spoken word. We're not utilizing motion-media's full communication potential. We know that optimum communication is achieved in those motion-media shows in which 70 to 80 percent of the information is contained in the visuals. It takes me a long time to *tell* you what I want to communicate. But I can *show* it to you more quickly and much more effectively.

Here's another way to illustrate why the talking-head scenario is so inefficient. Let's suppose our task is to drive from Los Angeles to Las Vegas as effectively and efficiently as possible. We have several options. We can drive our finely tuned, eight-cylinder roadster at 70 mph on the interstate highway all the way. Or we can drive Honest Harold's used jalopy that runs on only three cylinders and take unpaved desert back roads. We'll get to Las Vegas either way. But when will we arrive? How much effort did we expend? More important, what's our frame of mind after we arrive? Our eight-cylinder roadster is a finely tuned filmic-design show. The jalopy is the talking-head show.

I'll admit that there is some visual information in the talking-head scenario but not enough to justify its use as often as it is. As we *see* the persons talking, their affect projects through the screen; we may discern their authority, intellect, demeanor, and sincerity (or we can be fooled). The setting and background help set the ambiance. In addition, other visual clues contribute to the communication process—a person's dynamics, delivery, dress, accessories, grooming, etc. But on the whole, such shows dodder along to communication oblivion.

Filmic the Talking Head Is Not

Far more times than I care to recall, I've seen talking heads in shows that reflect the worst in filmic communication. One classic example is the CEO sitting (hiding) behind the desk, looking off-camera, and droning on and on, *telling* the audience what they generally don't care about and don't need to know. Rapid-fire babble couched in gobbledygook pounds the audience into stupefying catatonia.

Particularly vexing is that nowadays it's common practice to have the talking head look off-camera. That is, look at someone we can't see—a person who is out of the camera's view (perhaps an imaginary interviewer). Television news is the progenitor of this perversion. It's dishonest! If someone is going to talk to me, I want that person to look me directly in the eye and tell me forthrightly what's on his or her mind. I resent having to eavesdrop on a conversation to find out what's going on.

Here's about the only directorial advice you'll get in this entire book. If you *must* have a talking head, always have the talking head look directly into the camera's lens. And have the lens positioned at that person's eye level.

The talking head can be, and all too often is, the death knell to effective communication. Some in the audience may receive the message, or at least part of it. For those remaining (those who are nodding a bit and wondering when the lights will come on), the motion-media script designer has missed the mark by not understanding the target audience profile—who they are, their motivations, and what information they need.

The Talking Head Communicates

I reluctantly admit that in certain cases, the talking head scenario may be appropriate when critical information must be transmitted urgently and economically to concerned audiences who may be in different locations and when prompt audience reaction is required. The validity of this kind of show increases with the speaker's importance, credentials, and authority and with his or her ability to deliver messages with verve and conviction. It's better to have some communication now rather than to have delayed communication with a high-efficient filmic show when the value of the information has expired or the required audience action is delayed and of no, or minimal, value. Use of relevant props, graphics, still photography, and stock footage/tape will enhance significantly the communication effectiveness of the talking-head scenario, making the show more filmic.

The degree of communication achieved is related directly to the intensity of the audience's need or desire for the information, which is dependent on importance (how critical), urgency (how soon needed), and currency (how soon the value perishes). (See Shelton's Theory of Communication in chapter 4.) No matter how dull or inept a motion-media presentation may be, communication will occur if the audience has a critical need for the information. Of course, there are probably better ways to design a show to effect the intended communication, perhaps even to increase communication. But the fundamental question is: For the message's relevance to the target audience, what production technique can, at a minimum acceptable level in terms of turnaround time and cost, best bring about the show's communication objectives? Such a presentation must satisfy audience needs so that they'll understand and accept the messages.

Here are some instances when the talking head may be appropriate and effective:

- CEO announcing that tomorrow the plant will close permanently and all employees are dismissed; printed details to follow shortly
- renowned scientist lecturing on the latest unified-field theory to a group of graduate students majoring in physics; formal paper to be published in the *Acme Scientific Journal* next month
- evangelist preaching the evils of sin to the sinners; the book of divine inspiration is your guide
- television newscaster describing little green men emerging from their flying saucer, which has landed on the White House lawn; video footage to follow

Though these shows aren't cinematic masterpieces, they'll get the minimally acceptable communication job done.

If we are to communicate with disinterested or hostile audiences, we must produce motion-media shows that engender intense empathy—those that mentally seduce the audience. Empathy can be engendered by use of refined filmic design coupled with keen psychological manipulation. An enhanced version of the talking-head presentation, produced with such refined techniques, might accomplish communication objectives. However, I urge caution. In some instances, no matter how well produced, the talking-head scenario will fail. Audience resistance to the information transmitted is just too strong, or the talking-head scenario is inappropriate for the communication problem at hand.

What can we do to enhance the communication power of the talking-head show? How can we get our show to operate at a level of communication efficiency significantly more than the 30 percent theoretical limit? How do we ease the audience's eye exhaustion caused by staring constantly at the head? We need to enrich the visual ambiance through filmic design.

Visual Ambiance

In the enhanced version of the talking-head motion-media show, many visual elements contribute to communication, some directly, others at a secondary level. It's the visual ambiance of the milieu— the setting in which the talking head speaks—that strengthens communication by establishing the mood, providing visual clues, lending credence, and piquing audience interest. Included are such visual elements as the location and the background. Importantly, the setting needs to be an integral part of the story. The *mise en scène* is the natural environment—the place where the talking head works, lives, or does whatever the show is about.

Also, by using relevant visual aids, the efficiency of the show is increased substantially. Such visual aids may be props, models, uncomplicated charts or graphs, titles, artwork, still photographs, stock footage, or tape. Perhaps original film or tape can be shot/recorded quickly and cleanly to cover key points. Scenes of these visual aids can be used as cutaways from the talking head to show what's being said. It's the classic show-and-tell. This is the combination that makes effective communication. It's imperative that the visuals be absolutely relevant—that is, that there is absolute coherence between the visuals and the spoken word. If there's minimal or no coherence, we've introduced visual noise that seriously impairs communication.

Imaginative cinematography/videography is yet another way to enhance the visual efficiency of the talking head. Some techniques to consider are strong composition, appropriate lighting (either high or low key), variety of camera angles (including lots of close-ups), zooms, dollies, or trucks. We use the full gamut of cinematic techniques to heighten the visual design. Make the presentation as filmic as possible. And do it with *understanding* and *restraint*.

It's easy to get carried away and overdo the cinematography. When overdone, the techniques call attention to themselves. They get too cutesy and become noise by interfering with the information that is supposedly being transmitted.

One excellent example of a talking-head presentation that capitalizes on a host of visual elements in the natural environment is the Public Broadcasting Service's series *Ancient Lives,* produced by station WTTW in Chicago. The series is hosted by John Romer, archaeologist, historian, and storyteller extraordinaire. In one episode entitled "A Village of Craftsmen," Romer escorts us on a tour of ancient Egypt. The point is to impart some history and to give us a sociological perspective on the times. Romer is on-camera only about 40 percent of the time, weaving his story around a host of strong visual scenes. He interprets the hieroglyphs, shown in dramatic close-up shots, and takes us to locations in the story such as Thebes, the Valley of the Kings, Tutankhamen's tomb, and to the Cairo Museum where we see artifacts, works of art, mummies, and other antiquities, each exactly fitting to the points being made.

Aside from its technical excellence and inherent subject interest, several factors combine to make this talking-head presentation a highly effective communication tool. For instance:

- The background is natural, dramatic, and heightens our interest
- Romer gives scale to the environment and to the props
- Relevant cutaway visuals are used extensively
- Romer convinces us that he is the expert Egyptologist; we tend to believe him; he's established his credentials
- Romer looks directly into the camera's lens—that is, he looks us in the eye
- Romer is a consummate storyteller; his personality projects through to give the series a personal flavor

Personal Approach

When the talking head looks directly at us, with strong eye contact, the communication is personal. It's one-on-one. We get a perceptive insight into the personality and character of the person talking to us. We can evaluate this person and make conclusions. Is this someone I can trust? Is the message true? Relevant? Do I care?

The personal approach often is preferred for the dissemination of "bad news." For example, if the CEO has to announce the closing of a plant to the effected employees, the talking-head *mise en scène* is appropriate. By couching the message in a personal, compassionate way, the CEO may be able to soften the bad news. The personal approach cuts through the layers of interpretation that are inevitable. Jobs are being eliminated. Our audience becomes deeply involved and strongly identifies with what's happening.

Identification

Fundamentally, the talking head is a storyteller with varying degrees of communication power. Contributing to this communication power are the persona and charisma of our host and the ambiance of the location. Also contributing are filmic-design elements, such as use of relevant and powerful kinetic visuals and effective use of the plasticity of the medium. It's these characteristics that are the critical elements that enchant our audience, generating identification or empathy. The stronger these factors are, the stronger will be the empathy and the more the audience will participate in the communication process by projection into the scenario. Our audience is on location with the storyteller, and they'll fill in many of the on-camera scenes of the talking head with their own perfect images of what's being talked about.

Charisma, or stage presence, is hard to define, and all of us tend to perceive it somewhat differently. To one person, a talking head may exude charisma. To another, the same talking head is a dullard. It's a matter of how we relate—how we feel about the talking head, topic, and surround. Some of the factors that contribute to charisma are projection of authority, sincerity, understanding, and trustworthiness; others are demeanor, mannerisms, élan, looks, and dress.

The charisma of the talking head is so critical in the communication process that, depending on circumstances, a highly charismatic talking head may well communicate even if speaking a language that is foreign to the audience. For instance, the Reverend Billy Graham, speaking English, mesmerizes his television and live audiences in Germany, Scandinavia, and Africa. The words his interpreters speak are almost anticlimactic.

Clearly, Graham communicates to a host of different audiences. How does this happen? In communication theory, it is axiomatic that we tend to view, read, and talk about subjects that we already believe in or want to believe in. So, additional communication on these subjects is reinforcement of what we already believe. Graham is a charismatic and inspirational speaker, and his messages are critically important to many in his audience. How about an atheist or agnostic? Would Graham communicate to them? Perhaps. To answer the question, we need to know why such persons would want to watch and hear him. Some reasons might be curiosity, mental challenge, or peer pressure, or perhaps there is a need for the information or for inspiration. We'd need to know their preconceived notions about Graham and his message—hostile, neutral, or sympathetic. All these factors of the audience's mind-set can and will influence the level of communication achieved.

In another example, some years ago the actor James Whitmore portrayed President Harry S. Truman in a monologue performance in a limbo setting. Audiences raved about the performance. They identified closely and learned more about Truman than most would ever want to know. But we might ask, "Would an ardent fan of General Douglas MacArthur identify and sympathize with Whitmore's interpretation of the Truman-MacArthur conflict?" I wonder.

Exceptions

There are a few exceptions to consider. If the talking head is omnipotent or is the ultimate knowledge authority and if the message transmitted is critically important to the audience, no matter how churlish or inept the talking head or how technically incompetent the show, a high level of communication most likely will occur because the audience will force themselves to pay close attention. They need the information for their advantage, and action items are required.

Here is one classic example of such an exception. The U.S. Navy produced a ten-minute show to implement a tough new no-tolerance crackdown on drug abuse in the navy. A series of fatal aircraft accidents caused by personnel high on drugs precipitated this policy. The target audience was all naval personnel. The show featured Admiral Thomas Hayward, Chief of Naval Operations, in a talking-head solo performance. The setting was his office. Production techniques were basic—one continuous, ten-minute take from a fixed-camera position. No cutaways or visual aids of any kind were used. Occasionally, a zoom-in or zoom-out was used. All the audience saw was the admiral talking directly to them—sailor to sailor—for the entire ten minutes. And the admiral was not a polished speaker; he stumbled several times. Ordinarily, such a film would communicate nothing to anybody. But this film was the exception. It was eminently successful. Why?

Admiral Hayward cut an impressive figure in his service dress-blue uniform with its array of gold stripes and row upon row of decorations. He was the authority—the father figure, the boss. His message was cogent, timely, and critically important. His sincerity, commitment, and concern projected right through the screen. He cared about each member of the audience, his shipmates, and the navy. Empathy was intense. He made the severe consequences of any future drug abuse crystal clear. The audience got the message, and drug abuse in the navy was reduced significantly.

Could this show have been made better with enhanced filmic design? Sure. Would such a better show have been more effective? Maybe. Would it be as timely? No! (There was an immediate need to distribute the message to the fleet.)

For the communication problem at hand, Admiral Hayward talking directly to the camera—to each audience member—was the solution. Here's a classic example of the message transcending all filmic-design inadequacies and the "unprofessional" delivery of the talking head. Perhaps the admiral's amateurism in front of the camera enhanced his sincerity and commitment to the audience. Though a professional actor could have made a much more polished delivery, the actor probably could not have convinced the audience.

Professional Actor

The professional actor does have an important place in the talking-head scenario. It's the actor who is probably the better all-around storyteller, effective frequently with even neutral or hostile audiences. Seeing the makeup, costume, setting, and props, it's easy for us to project—we see the "real" character instead of an actor playing the part. It's the willing suspension of disbelief. We want to believe in the reality of the scenario—and we do. Reality is further enhanced by our prior knowledge about the character or subject. We provide imagery from our memory, triggered by visual and aural cues.

For example, in a memorable solo performance, the actor Hal Holbrook played Mark Twain on stage, and the performance was also broadcast on television. The show was an outstanding success. It's uncanny how deeply audiences projected into the scenario. Holbrook *was* Twain! We saw and heard Mark Twain talking to us, in a scenario aided by nothing more than makeup, several cigars, a white suit, and a simple set.

Generally, I've found that it's best not to use actors as authority or power figures in information motion-media shows—unless, of course, they already are. Most actors in such roles are unconvincing, and audiences tend to resent the deception. In such instances, communication almost always fails.

One way to ameliorate communication failure when using a professional actor as the voice of authority is to have the actor look directly into the camera lens and say, for example, "Mr. Caspar Gutman-Cario has asked me to speak to you about . . ." In special situations, a professional actor is required. For example, when I produced the film *The Man from* LOX, I needed to use an actor. The purpose of the film was to motivate liquid-oxygen (LOX) handlers to work safely. The selected *mise en scène* was a fantasyland, nearly avant-garde in conception, in which an exceptionally gifted character actor portrayed the "Man" in a series of short, parodistic vignettes. Only a skilled actor could have played this out-of-the-ordinary part with conviction, and, in large measure, he made the film the success it was.

I almost always recommend that professional actors/narrators be used for off-camera narration—the anonymous voice of authority. No matter what the pressures are, don't compromise on this point. Audiences just won't accept an unprofessional narration, no matter who is doing it, and communication failure is guaranteed.

The talking head has become very popular in information motion-media. While fully realizing that for some communication problems, there is a case for the talking head, the talking head is being overused to a crippling fault. It's become a crutch. When we use the talking head, we lose the power of our dynamic visual medium. I understand the reasons. Today's designers got most of their filmic-design education from watching dramatic scenarios on commercial television. Unfortunately, commercial television—either by technical limitations or default—stresses the spoken word rather than visual dynamics. Increasingly, television is the producing medium for information motion-media shows. All too often, our shows mimic commercial television.

Misapplication of the talking head and its overuse are deadly. Such presentations are lectures, illustrated only somewhat—radio with a portrait. Nonetheless, in some instances, the talking head is a valid use of the medium. It's personal, quick, and economical, and it is an appropriate way to transmit some messages to certain audiences. The talking head is a special case, to be used with judicious skill and discretion.

21

The Sound Track

Sound is a key communication and dramaturgical element in motion-media. It helps set the tone and pace of our shows. Though secondary to the kinetic visuals, sound in some scenes can be an important communication tool.

Elements in the sound track of motion-media are voice, music, and sound effects—although with computer-controlled sound generators, it's difficult to distinguish between music and sound effects and even sometimes between sound effects and voice.

Sound's power lies in its invisibility, its unobtrusiveness. Our audience should not "hear" (i.e., be cognizant of) the sound. Sound should be a natural, inconspicuous element of our shows. Sound has to sound right. If our audience focuses on the sound, it will infringe on their absorption of the messages being transmitted by the kinetic visuals; accordingly, sound's power is lost. For instance, wall-to-wall narration and wall-to-wall elevator music soon become noise in the communication process, no matter how expertly done. Ditto with overly done sound effects. An inept narrator or amateur players will generate lots of noise. It's to our advantage, therefore, to eschew amateur talent, off- and on-screen, and to choose professionals to narrate and act in our shows. We must resist to the depths of our professional being pressure from client to put the CEO or whomever on camera to tell us all about *it*. There are exceptions, as I've noted in the previous chapter.

Effective Sound Track

What's critical is that the sound and visuals work in harmony. If the audience notices that a sound doesn't sound right, then the illusion of reality is broken, and empathy is lost. It's critically important that music and sound effects not intrude on the commentary. If they do, they become noise that interferes with what's being said. Of course, if the sound elements are clear of commentary for a while, then "pot" them up to normal volume. In many of the shows I see and hear, the intrusion of music and sound effects into the commentary destroys the show's effectiveness.

To be unobtrusive, sound must mimic the perspective of the scene. For instance, if our scene is a long shot of an automobile driving on a lonely desert road, the volume, pitch, and tone of the automobile sound effect must seem as if it's emanating from the automobile and heard from the camera's (i.e., our) perspective. That is, the sound effect our audience hears ought to sound as if it comes from a microphone near the camera, not from a microphone on the automobile or on the side of the road as the automobile whizzes by. Maintaining proper sound perspective is challenging when we select sound effects from a library. However, most sound houses have the wherewithal to modify sound effects to meet the scene's requirements. Naturally, all of this effort costs money. But I've found over the years that I kept postproduction expenses within budget by working with a professional sound house. It's truly amazing what wizardry these engineers and artists accomplish.

Silence can also be a telling dramatic effect. Such is particularly the case when a period of silence is broken by a startling and unexpected musical sting or an unforeseen sound effect—or the reverse, when music or effect quickly cuts to silence. The old adage "Silence is golden" has much merit for our shows. Bela Balazs, filmmaker par excellence and author, notes, "No other art can reproduce silence."[1]

Types of Sound

Various sounds have an important role in setting the ambiance and pace of our shows. Here are some examples of the many factors involved:

- Voice talent is male, female, or obviously computer talk
- Commentary intonation is hard or soft, fast or slow
- Music is fortissimo or pianissimo or something in-between, presto or adagio, euphonious or cacophonous, staccato or legato
- Sound effects that are appropriate add realism and presence to a scene. Note: If you use one sound effect in a scene, all elements in the scene must have appropriate sound effects. Otherwise, the scene calls attention to itself

A scene in which we edited shots in rhythm to a musical beat (or sound effects) is particularly effective in setting the ambience and pace of the scene or sequence (a series of related scenes). This is especially true in a montage sequence. Or we can do it the other way around: have music composed (or find canned music) that matches the tempo of our edited visuals.

Music

We can use a musical theme to bind disparate or widely separated scenes with continuity. Notice that we introduce music into a scene gradually. In the business, we dub this technique *fade-in*. Ditto the reverse with a *fade-out*. When we introduce a different music selection between scenes, we segue the tunes seamlessly: Outgoing tune fades-out while simultaneously the incoming tune fades-in.

How do we obtain music to support our shows? The first thing to remember is that we must pay, one way or another, for the right to use any piece of music. So it's best to follow the rules religiously.

Basically, there are three ways to obtain music. But first, please understand that I'm not an attorney. The laws on these matters are complex and vary from country to country. Always seek competent legal advice.

Original music. Commission a composer to write the tunes, contract with an arranger to orchestrate the music, hire a band or an orchestra to record the music, and book a sound studio for the recording session. The expenses involved with this task are considerable. If you choose this route, it's imperative that you get a work-for-hire release from everyone involved in the process. Such a release must relinquish all copyrighted material to you or your client to use in any way you choose in any medium. Make no exceptions, or else you or your client may well be paying royalties every time your show is screened. Of course, owning the copyright of original music ensures that your music will never be used by anyone else, unless you license it.

Copyrighted music. Buy the music that's on a commercial CD from the copyright owner, performers, publishers, etc.—a tough road that I don't recommend. There are, however, copyright houses that specialize in making these kinds of deals for us. They're super-expensive, but they usually get the job done. The process can be long and laborious. The payments to get the right to use this music may well be astronomical. Some of this copyrighted music is virtually unobtainable because of artist and publisher concerns or perhaps union restrictions.

It won't do to simply visit the local CD store and incorporate music from a favorite recording into our motion-media show. That would violate federal copyright and piracy laws and invite expensive lawsuits and fines that would cost lots and lots more money and headaches than obtaining music the legal way. Copyright-infringement laws apply to *any* use of someone else's creative property. It matters not whether we use the music in a company-produced video to encourage employees to work safely or in a TV commercial to publicize the Acme Company's new XYZ widget or for any government or nonprofit institution, no matter who and no matter for what purpose. *No exceptions!*

It's true that after time, copyright protection expires, and the musical work enters the public domain. In such a case, we're free to use the work *as originally published*. Congress sets this public-domain time limit and changes it from time to time. The copyright laws of other countries vary widely from those of the United States. Consult competent legal advice to ensure that the music you want is, in fact, in the public domain. Then it's back to the arranger, band, sound house, etc.

Music library. Purchasing music from a music library offers a number of advantages. It's easy, quick, and much cheaper than the other options. Getting licenses is routine. The amount and kind of music available in these libraries are enormous, and the performances are high quality—just about anything we'd ever want. Okay, it's not original music composed especially for your show, but it's relatively inexpensive, appropriate, and maybe even artistic! The type of music offered by these libraries is sometimes called "production music," since it is used for motion-media shows.

Another valuable advantage of music libraries is that the music is designed for motion-media use. The music is easier to edit than popular songs because the music has been scored with editing in mind—an important factor when we're trying to match an exact scene length timed to the tenth of a second. I well remember, back in the analog days, working with music editors who could edit a tune to fit a scene: take an element from one tune and blend it into another, extend the time of a tune or contract it, and make the tune sound as if it was recorded that way. Today, with digital sound, such sorcery is routine.

Evaluate carefully several music libraries for the value they offer. Merely providing numerous themes is not enough for the discerning motion-media designer. The key is to find a library that offers the type of production music we want—including, perhaps, several edited or remixed alternate versions of a tune or theme, acoustic and electronic sounds, and sound effects. The size and depth of a library are critical; it should offer a wide variety of settings, periods, and moods.

Licenses

Depending on the music library, we may have a choice of several types of licenses. What we pay for is the license to use the music we select. We've got several options:

Annual or long-term license. Buy the license for the entire library, or a part of it, for a year or some other specific time (perhaps indefinitely) and at an agreed-upon exhibition use. In such an instance, we take possession of the library in whatever medium it's recorded on. This option gives us a quantity of music with rights to use any of it in our shows. We log what tunes we've used and report our use to the library. Sometimes we may negotiate a deal in which there are no reporting requirements.

Individual license. Buy a license to use the music in a specific show and for a specific exhibition or distribution: internal use only, commercial television, worldwide sales meeting(s), rental or sales to users, etc. Sometimes there's a time limitation: no use beyond a set number of years without additional payments. We buy this kind of music license by the cut, the minute, the show, or the use, depending on the arrangement we make. In the ol' days, this type of agreement was known as a *needle drop.* This term comes from the time when we placed a mechanical stylus on a vinyl long-playing record.

No matter which method we choose to get our music, we must make sure that we have a 100 percent right to use the music for our show and in the exhibition manner we've agreed upon. To this end, we must have:

- ownership; or
- synchronization rights (to synchronize the music with visuals or spoken words and to reproduce copies); and
- performance rights, to publicly perform the music in our show

Audio considerations should be part of the overall motion-media production plan. We need to start thinking about music and all other sound elements early in our scripting and to budget for it. Such early planning and budgeting for sound ensures balance and cohesion in our shows: an unobtrusive and supportive sound track.

Sound Editor

Finally, a proficient sound editor who specializes in music and sound effects is worth his or her weight in platinum. With comprehensive knowledge of various music and sound-effects libraries, a sound editor is instrumental in selecting the music and effects that are best for our shows. We need to work closely with the sound editor to communicate our vision of what's to be accomplished. The professional sound editor can make judgments and suggestions that will benefit the final show, unifying the elements of the sound track to focus the impact of our shows. These music-selecting and editing talents are a combination of the skill, taste, and artistry that helps bind our shows into coherent productions.

22

Distribution

Now that we've produced the great American information motion-media show, what are we going to do with it? How do we get our show in front of the target audience? Of all the elements in our sight-and-sound profession, distribution is least understood, least planned for, and least successful.

No matter how compelling and empathetic our show is, it's worthless unless the target audience views it. Distribution is complicated by the fact that motion-media shows require that the audience has access to sophisticated playback equipment. Such stuff is not always available, especially in Third World countries. In this respect, publications have the clear advantage over motion-media.

How the show is distributed depends mostly on the client's goal and to some extent on input from the producer. At the start of the project, the distribution scheme details the number of copies to be duplicated for release in the appropriate medium or media. Such media may be motion-picture prints, digital tapes, or disks, or it may be by direct digital transmission without the show ever being in a physical form.

Clients sponsor most shows. Sometimes we produce shows on speculation for profit or for the pure artistic pleasure of it. Consequently, there are three basic modes for the distribution of our shows

- within an organization (to employees, clients, visitors)
- through a professional motion-media distribution house (to the general public, specialized audiences, a professional organization, or high-school students, for example)
- self-marketing (direct marketing to the target audience)

There are many ways in which we distribute our shows to the target audiences: via the World Wide Web, over digital networks, direct mailing, cable television, broadcast television, teleconferencing, direct broadcast satellite, or any other way we can think of.

If the client chooses a professional distribution house for a film/video show, the house charges the client for direct costs such as reproduction, distribution, and other expenses. Also charged is an agreed-upon fee per screening/viewing based on the number of people in the audience. Usually, the distribution house collects audience comments, collates, and evaluates them, and sends them to the client. There are lots of permutations on this basic scheme. Such is especially the case when distribution is done electronically. The actual cost of a film/video should not be calculated in dollars per screen-minute but rather in dollars per idea remembered by our audiences and results garnered—admittedly, a tough task.

If the show is multimedia, we've got a new set of factors to deal with. Instead of being intended for mass audiences, multimedia shows are designed almost exclusively for individual viewing. Most of these kinds of shows are distributed internally or sold directly to the consumer. The final consideration is the cost per result per audience member (and profit isn't a bad idea).

If we use a distribution house for our own shows, there are several options. We can sell the show outright, copyright and all. Or we can negotiate a deal where we get a percentage of sales and rental receipts. Such fees usually are meager because of the house's high expenses incurred in reproduction, distribution, advertising, overhead, and profit.

In this chapter, I've highlighted just a few of the many permutations of the distribution scheme. I hope there's enough information to give you an idea of the fundamentals. Distribution is far too complicated and customized to delve into it any further here. It's beyond the scope of this book and of my experience.

23

Your Career Growth in Our Profession

Career Choice

Fundamentally, there are only two choices in the way you pursue your career: work for yourself or work for someone else. Of course, you can alternate between these options over the years—seizing opportunities as found. Occasionally, I've known folks who've combined these options in some sort of hybrid concoction.

First, however, make sure that you're committed to the information motion-media profession and plan to give it your very best. Nothing else will do. Second best is unacceptable. For example, sometimes I've worked with folks, especially beginners, who don't have total commitment. All too often, these folks attempt to use our profession as a stepping stone or entrée into the movie or television industry—the narrative film/TV industry. They manipulate our profession to learn the fundamentals, pad their résumés, and enhance their careers at our profession's expense. From long experience, I can state categorically that the vast majority of these people fail in both careers. Most of the shows they design and produce in our profession are communication failures—rife with unneeded dramatic scenarios and out-of-control technological effects. The shows may be creative, but they're not memorable.

We must understand and accept the basic fact that these two professions are vastly different. They have divergent goals: communication as opposed to entertaining and making a profit. Production styles are dissimilar. Budgets are vastly different. Distribution schemes and media formats are different. In other words, there's not much in common between these two professions. The best advice I can offer is to make your decision on which profession is your career choice. Then stick with it and excel.

As I mentioned in the preface, I've enjoyed great job satisfaction and wonderful personal rewards working in our information motion-media profession. In large measure, I contribute this fulfillment to the fact that I wasn't infected with the Hollywood virus. I concentrated wholeheartedly on the communication task at hand, thereby achieving some measure of success.

Attitude

Your attitude is critical. Over the years, as the manager of a highly professional and award-winning in-house, motion-media group, I've hired lots of people—mostly novices. I concentrated my recruiting efforts largely on folks who had recently graduated with advanced degrees in our profession. What I looked for was attitude, not skill level. I'd prefer to work with and train a novice. Without fail, those that I hired had the "can do" attitude and were willing to work—to get their hands dirty and body sweaty—and to learn. My philosophy was that one had to learn the profession from the bottom up to become well rounded in all facets of design and production and to constantly produce top-notch shows.

In an attempt to discern an interviewee's attitude, my opening comments were totally candid. They went something like, "Your task, if hired, is to be the 'gofer.' You'll haul boxes, hold reflectors, pull cables, make the coffee, drive the truck, run errands, and do whatever it takes to support the professionals in our group." Some of the interviewees' responses were amazing. The classic of all time was, "You mean I'm not going to produce movies for you?" (as the starting assignment). I got this attitude in many variations from many of the candidates. Naturally, these candidates didn't get hired.

Perspectives on Choices

Working for someone else has a measure of security (emotional, pay, and benefits) and offers on-the-job training and an opportunity for professional growth into more responsible and demanding tasks. On the other hand, there's no guaranteed job security because of management decisions and business fluctuations. One can be stuck in a no-growth position, or the general work environment may be distasteful. Lots of other factors are involved, far too many for me to discuss here. But you get the idea.

The heyday of large in-house motion-media groups is over. Corporations and governments have either eliminated or significantly reduced in-house groups. Only a few key people are left in the few remaining groups. Most motion-media production is accomplished with contract help or totally on contract. This is especially the case with the federal government. I know of only a few remaining federal government in-house groups, and they are reduced to just a few professionals. On the other hand, there are opportunities with the contractors.

Working for yourself (freelance or on short-term contract) is tough, especially if you're a beginner. You'll spend most of your time looking for work instead of working for pay. Establishing a network with colleagues and professional associations is essential. Also of critical import is maintaining currency in emerging technology and business trends. Using employment agencies and employment leasing outfits ("body shops") are ways to get short-term jobs and contracts. Sometimes, such jobs and contracts can result in long-term commitments with your clients.

No matter if you decide to work for someone else or to freelance, networking is critically important. Few jobs or opportunities are advertised in the help-wanted section of the classified pages of the newspaper. Most openings are found through word-of-mouth in networking sessions and through job postings with professional associations and on the Internet.

Résumé

You need a current and professional résumé. Unless you're super-skilled in résumé development, hire a professional. Your résumé is you. It's your introduction to prospective employers and clients. There are several different styles and formats, depending on the experience of the individual and the type of job sought. Again, I'll not get into too much detail here since there're lots of books and professionals around to help you. I've read/scanned/tossed dozens of résumés over the years. My advice is to make your résumé concise, factual, and visually appealing. No exaggeration, half-truths, lies, or twists. Such chicanery is always discovered and is guaranteed to quash any prospects of getting hired. Or, if hired, it's a sure ticket to the pink slip. Integrity counts. In fact it's the only thing. Prospective employers and clients almost always check the details on the résumé of someone in whom they have serious interest.

Demonstration Reel/Tape

Another essential element you ought to have in seeking employment or finding a client is the demonstration reel/tape or "demo" reel. It's on this reel (film, video, disk, or electronic media) that you display your designing and producing skills—segments of your completed shows. If you're just beginning, use your student projects. Obviously, you'll want to highlight only your outstanding success, and that's as it ought to be.

However, I view demo reels with a jaundiced eye. The first question in my mind is "Is it the work of the applicant?" There's no way to tell for sure, but skillful interviewing with in-depth questions regarding the shows on the reel can usually uncover the facts. For example: Who was the client? What were the budget and production schedule? Who was the audience? What were the goals? What measure of success was there?

A second set of questions is: If these are the successes, where are the failures? How many are there? What's the ratio of success to failure? Please understand, failure is not always bad. Ideally, it's a learning experience. What I really want to see is the raw footage right out of the camera—the unedited dailies. It's through this process that I can see the filmic-design skills of the applicant. It's in the dailies that I can see the applicant's gems and warts, skill and style, and understanding of our media as a communication tool. Unfortunately, it was rare that dailies were available.

Sample Scripts

Sometimes applicants submitted sample scripts they had written. Only a few had storyboards. Most of these scripts reveal the applicant's writing skills rather than their script-designing skills. Also, the questions arise: Is this script the work of the applicant? What influence did other folks have on the development of these scripts? Does the script reflect client-imposed direction? On the whole, I'd rather screen completed shows where I can see and evaluate the applicant's filmic-design skills in action.

Growth in Our Profession

As professionals, each of us is obligated to adhere to the highest performance standards. To continually hone our skills, broaden our perspectives, advance our profession, never settle for the status quo, behave honorably by responding to ethical dilemmas in an honest and forthright manner, develop and maintain an inquisitive mind, and adopt new technology to enhance communication—not create more whizzbang tomfoolery. Lastly, we have a compelling responsibility to leave a legacy to our profession.

No matter if you're a long-time professional or a budding novice, it's difficult to know and understand the rapidly developing technology of our profession. To know your peers and see their work. To discern industry trends and styles. To get feedback on your ideas and work. To continually upgrade your education. In essence, you and I and all the rest of us must fulfill our professional obligations today to ensure our professional stature tomorrow. Such obligations can be realized, in large measure by professional growth.

Here are some suggestions that can help you develop professional skills and grow in our profession:

Attend classes. Go to classes at community colleges, universities, trade schools, or museums. Most post–high school institutions offer courses in film, television, communications, and graphics. Some of these courses are short courses, and many are offered in evening classes. Take all the courses you can, even those that may not be directly related to but are oriented toward visual communication.

Corporations involved with producing motion-media shows and services and products for our profession also offer short courses. Many are free; some have a registration fee. Special interest and professional organizations offer short courses, seminars, and workshops. So do any number of private (for-profit) organizations.

Practice. Hone your scripting skills by using your filmic-design to develop scenarios that communicate effectively. Try designing scripts for some of the communication problems I've listed in appendix 8. Draw storyboards. Write narration and dialogue sparingly as I've suggested in chapter 19. If you're super-serious about this profession, pay for critiques from those who are recognized and respected by our profession.

Read voraciously. Study every book that is marked with an asterisk in this book's bibliography. Take notes, and heed. Read as many of the remainder as you can. Public and college libraries are excellent sources for these books.

Subscribe. Subscribe to some of the professional journals and trade magazines dealing with our profession. I'll not cite specific examples because the various publications appear and disappear routinely. Search the Internet and library to learn about these publications and to assess which have interest for you.

Look. Screen/view as many information motion-media shows as you can. Evaluate these shows using the Motion-Media Evaluation sheet in appendix 1. Based on what you've learned in this book, decide what's terrific, what's awful, and how you could improve these shows. Be cautious; don't become hypercritical or jaded.

Talk. Network with motion-media professionals, pick their brains, share ideas, and take notes. Meet these professionals at conferences, workshops, chapter meetings, film/video festivals, and classes.

Visit. Go to workplaces where information motion-media shows are designed and produced. See how it's done. Ask questions.

Work. Work on assignments with an organization that produces information motion-media shows. Start as an apprentice if necessary. Work for minimum wage or classroom credit as a co-op or mentor student.

Affiliate. If you are going to be a first-class professional in our profession, you need to join one or more professional organizations that focus on motion-media. However, joining is not enough; you must be active in the association—participate in all manner of activities. Be motivated to make long-term and heartfelt commitments to the association. Association dues and other expenses are minor when compared to the benefits you'll accrue. Such costs are an investment in your future.

Recommended Activities

Here are some of the activities I recommend for involvement as a member of professional associations. Importantly, if you volunteer for these activities, perform them to the best of your ability. Do them with commitment, skill, verve, and industry. Anything less is unsatisfactory.

- Serve on committees to gain in-depth knowledge of a specific activity and to contribute to the growth of the profession.
- Become an officer in your local chapter or at the national level. Learn and practice leadership and interpersonal skills. Be a manager.
- Network with other professionals. Meet and parlay. Develop contacts. Share experiences, ideas, and mutual concerns. Get inspired. Broaden perspective. Seize opportunities. Learn about job openings and contracts being let. Develop mentors and protégés, advisors and audiences, and maybe even some long-term friends.
- Present a program, give a seminar, host a workshop. Build your reputation and credentials.

- Become a mentor. Share your experience with those less experienced. Such activity sharpens your understanding and contributes to the long-term enhancement of our profession.
- Write and publish a formal paper in the association's journal or magazine. Write an article for your chapter's newsletter. Preserve our heritage by sharing knowledge and experiences and by editorializing. Writing is the best way to teach yourself about a specific topic, clarify your thinking, and earn peer recognition.
- Attend conferences, seminars, workshops, and local chapter meetings. Make contact with others in our profession. Learn about the latest technology. Note trends and attitudes. Discuss philosophies. Develop a broader understanding of our profession than is possible in your day-to-day localized activities.
- Host a chapter meeting, and plan the program. Expand your professional capabilities and people skills.
- Serve as a juror in the associations' competitions—an ideal way to see and evaluate the best work of your peers and to keep abreast of contemporary standards.
- Enter your work in competitions and exhibitions. Heed comments on critique sheets. Look critically at the winners. Why did some entries earn awards and your entry did not? Be brutally honest with yourself.
- Plan a conference program. This is a challenging task not to be undertaken unless you have the resources, well-being, time, energy, and wherewithal to accomplish the task properly and in a timely manner. In dealing with your conference committee, you'll hone your cooperation and negotiating skills, develop win-win solutions, and learn fiscal responsibility.

You get the message. Passivity is passé. Activity is the key. Involvement is essential if you're going to maintain currency. Without such involvement, you'll rarely discover the challenge, experience, opportunity, recognition, and education that are essential for professional growth. All of us need to learn something every day. Else, we become professional dinosaurs as our motion-media profession passes us by.

Benefits

So far we've been discussing what we can contribute to the association to enhance our professional status. Let's see what associations can do for us. As I've discussed, the most important function of an association is to provide the opportunity to participate and grow professionally. Here are some of the activities and benefits (listed in no particular order) that I've not mentioned so far that associations may provide to its members:

- maintenance of currency through formal and informal training
- membership directories, which are valuable in networking and program planning and as a resource for crew members, potential employers, and clients
- special interest groups (SIGs), networking groups with a focused, narrow interest in one facet of the profession
- screening of the winning entries in the competitions—often found in the associations' libraries; the best way to see what your competition and peers are doing and to get new ideas
- review of résumés by experts
- salary surveys, which tell what the current pay is for the jobs in the industry in the various areas of the country; an excellent method to know how you're doing and what to expect
- demographics of the association, which tell the member's skills, where they work, and where they live
- job hot lines and job fairs, which provide employer and employee clearinghouses and get-togethers; learn about new career opportunities; get a job or a contract
- chapter newsletters, which keep us informed at the local level
- society journals and publications, in-depth studies of the various aspects of our profession: technical, philosophical, and tutorial; also included are national association information, columns, book and article reviews
- library, the source for the associations' publications and other material
- reduced fees for competitions, publications, conferences, seminars, etc.
- continuing education, conducted or sponsored at universities and colleges and in regional and chapter areas
- sponsorship via grants or loans for research in fields that are relevant to the profession
- certification of professional competence, which attests that those certified have completed certain professional education and training and have requisite experience
- code of conduct is the association's formalized set of ethical standards governing members' professional conduct

- dissemination of specialized information to members, such as tax information, legal considerations, government regulations, contracting, copyright laws, etc.
- group health, medical, life, and accident insurance
- liability and equipment damage-and-loss insurance
- completion bonds
- discounts on travel, automobile rental, lodging, theme parks, etc.
- membership certificates, lapel pins, and various thingamabobs that promote the association (coffee cups, T-shirts, paperweights, etc.)

It's an absolute truism that what we get out of a professional association is a direct function of the efforts we put into the association. The realization of such efforts results in mental satisfaction, confidence, competence, peer recognition, and fiscal reward—a potent combination of attributes that define professionalism.

Changing Profession

Let's pause and get a personal perspective of what's happening. You're a professional, right? Look around: Note how different your job is today from what it was just a few years ago. Developing styles, trends and technologies are changing dramatically every facet.

Think about it. Note how many jobs there are today that require new skills and attitudes. Note how many of the old jobs just don't exist anymore. Take a few minutes to speculate on how much different your job and the entire field of motion-media communications will be in a few more years. You might not be far off!

The questions are, however, Are you keeping pace? Are you developing your skills and refining your attitudes to be an effective communicator using communication-age media in the years ahead? Or will you be an anachronism? A professional dinosaur? Is your vision exciting? Challenging? It had better be. Else, you'll be just so much flotsam in the waves of the onrushing communication age. It's up to you.

Leave a Legacy

Lastly, I want to expand on my earlier comment that we have a compelling responsibility to leave a legacy to our profession. I'm convinced that the true professionals are those who give more to the profession than they gain from it. A true professional is one who eagerly shares knowledge with protégés and peers through written and oral communication-books, papers, lectures, and seminars. One who inspires. Teaches. Contributes. Leads. Those who fulfill their obligations by being active in professional associations secure their status as professionals and enhance the profession as a whole.

With these few insights I've offered here, perhaps you'll have a head start. The point is you've got to help yourself. You're the only one who can. Make your own breaks. See opportunities and seize them. Be self-confident, not arrogant. Be mentally honest. Be your own toughest critic. Keep the mind open, inquisitive, and unfulfilled. Be totally committed. And be a great success in this wonderful profession of ours.

Part Five

*Some Thoughts on
the Business of Our
Profession*

24

Our Client Isn't the Enemy

The information motion-media industry is big business and growing apace. Unfortunately, all too often, an adversarial relationship develops between the client and the script designer or producer. As a result, the show suffers. Sticking our egos in our pockets and following a few simple professional guidelines enhance understanding and make our tasks of designing and producing information motion-media shows easier, lots more fun, profitable, and effective.

Essentially, our industry is not that much different from any other enterprise. A customer buys a product from a merchant at an agreed-upon price and delivery date. The customer is our client, the product is equipment, services, or a complete show. The show can be tailor-made or delivered off-the-shelf. The merchant or retailer is the script designer or producer—you and me.

Selecting a Designer/Producer

Most motion-media shows are unique, custom-tailored to meet the client's needs. As a one-time event, motion-media shows are relatively expensive, have high visibility, are important, and are not returnable—there are no guarantees. How then do our clients select someone to design and produce their shows? It's not easy. Selecting a designer/producer is much like selecting an architect to design an expensive home: It has to be right the first time.

Unlike architects who are licensed, have peer review, and are relatively scarce, motion-media designers/producers have no licensing requirements, no professional or peer review, and there are hordes of us vying for the business. We come in all stripes: entrepreneurs and salaried in-house personnel, skilled and inept, chevalier and blackguard, generalist and specialist. Some of the specialty fields in which we work are training, public relations, information, and marketing. It's a mélange of possibilities with no easy way to identify the market.

Unfortunately, there are too many hustlers in our profession more interested in making a fast buck than in producing quality shows. Such hustlers spew technical mumbo-jumbo, make wild and empty promises, and couldn't care less about repeat business. Fortunately, prudent clients have a caveat emptor attitude and are much aware of the witch-doctoring flummery in such sales pitches.

Usually the first item a potential client checks is our reputation: professional and fiscal. What recommendations do our previous clients make? How do we get along with clients? How do our peers regard us? Vendors? What is our work ethic? What experience do we have in relation to the proposed project? What sort of organization do we have—full-fledged or shoestring? How's our credit? Are we members of professional organizations? If so, which ones, and how involved are we? What have we contributed to our profession?

Next, the potential client is likely to ask to view and critique the shows we've produced. Checking with previous clients, they're likely to ask such questions as: Were communication objectives met to full measure? Did we design/produce the shows with a judicious use of resources? Were the shows delivered on time and within budget? How readily were changes accomplished? Did they enjoy working with us?

Also, we can expect an inquiry about who we are—our persona. Traits that are likely to be probed are our integrity, communication skills, reasoning abilities, flexibility, sensitivity, responsiveness, consistency, and commitment.

Lastly, the prospective client must have an intuitive feeling that we're right for the assignment. The "chemistry" between the client and the designer/producer has to feel right for success before we reach an agreement.

Clarity Is Paramount

No matter how simple or complex the agreement—oral or written—we've established a contract. If we and our client conduct ourselves professionally, the goals of each are fulfilled. The completed motion-media show solves the client's needs, and we've made a reasonable profit, learned something, had some fun, and enhanced our client base for repeat business.

Such a scenario seldom develops so favorably, however. Problems arise from a dearth of clear communication or commonsense business practices or from unrealistic promises and expectations. Sometimes, problems occur from unethical behavior, the client's or ours. All too often, in the natural sequence of events, we can count on such problems to develop into disputes over:

- budget and cost control
- unplanned changes
- missed or late delivery
- creativity versus message
- who said what to whom, when?

The ethics committee of the Producers' Guild notes that "usually the blame [for cost overruns, missed schedules, and poor results] is two-way. We as clients are not totally sure of what we want; [and] vendors will sell us whatever they think we will buy."[1]

It's imperative, therefore, that we make our contract correct before beginning the project. When problems do arise, we've got to resolve them amicably and quickly according to the terms of the contract. Otherwise, we've begun an adversarial relationship with our client, now perceived as the enemy. We're now in a no-win predicament.

Unfortunately, in such hostile scenarios, the motion-media show's communication effectiveness is significantly reduced. And it's the communication business we're supposed to be in! Sometimes our egos cloud our understanding of just what we're supposed to be doing. We lose perspective of our common goal.

Divergent Goals

In this "creative" profession of ours, it's easy for the client's and producer's goals to diverge. I've frequently found that much of the divergence stems from the interpretation of *creativity* and *communication*. The designer/producer may feel that the client is stifling his/her artistic abilities, resulting in yet another nuts-and-bolts show. Conversely, the client may feel that the producer is gouging the budget and jeopardizing the schedule by creating another *Heaven's Gate* (one of the all-time super-expensive movie-extravaganza flops), massaging his/her creative ego, and aiming at winning another award rather than focusing on communication.

It is important to remember that these two concepts, creativity and communication, are not at odds. Creativity may well enhance the communication of the client's message and make our motion-media show soar with unbounded energy and compelling interest. Sadly, all too often, creativity becomes its own end: It is misunderstood and misused.

We may produce a great motion-media show, but if it doesn't do its communication job and the client isn't pleased, it may well be our last, no matter how creative it is or how many awards it wins. As John Grierson said, "People are good enough at making films but not at using them to shape ideas, to dig out the heart of the matter. And in fact, the client may well be fearful and mistrustful of anything to do with art and aesthetics." Grierson often tried to avoid the words *art* and *documentary* in favor of *information* and *public service*.[2]

A first step we can take to prevent an adversarial relationship from developing is to keep to the fore what we're up to—why our clients hired us. Essentially, clients have communication problems. They've decided that a motion-media show can best solve these problems. Just about the only reason a client invests in such a show is to persuade the target audience to do something, think something, feel or decide something—to motivate the audience toward realization of the communication objective. As Charles "Cap" Palmer noted, "The aim is the residual impression we want the film to leave—what our viewers will think or feel, perhaps subconsciously, as they leave our screening and hopefully for some time afterward."[3] Essential to accomplishing such communication goals are razor-sharp communication analysis and preproduction planning, topics covered elsewhere in this book. Here we want to focus on communications between ourselves and our clients.

Interpersonal Communication

Our success in the motion-media communication business is a primary function of our interpersonal communication skills—the ability to deal successfully with clients, crew, financiers, and others. Though our designing/producing skills are also critical, we'll not have the opportunity to use them unless we've communicated with prospective clients and convinced them that we can best solve their communication problem with our talent, expertise, integrity, and business acumen.

Communication with our clients must be clear and open. It must engender mutual trust and an explicit understanding of what's to be accomplished and how it's to be accomplished. Prospective clients want to work with friendly and sincere professionals. Technical competence may open the door, but interpersonal skills will close the deal.[4]

Essential to successful interpersonal communication skills is *listening*. We must listen carefully to our clients to understand their concerns so that we can articulate an appropriate solution for their communication problems. Up front, listening is a difficult task that requires significantly more concentration than does talking. Since we understand spoken concepts much more quickly than it takes to say them, our minds tend to wander, to develop a private plan, to debate, to hear less and less of what our client is saying.[5]

Also, we tend to hear with our own bias, which skews our understanding of what's being said. Oftentimes, we hear what we want to hear. Difficult as it is, we need to keep our bias in our pocket and not let it become noise in the conversation. Listening is actually a form of persuasion. People like to be listened to and understood; it demonstrates that you are interested in them and their problems.

As skillful listeners, we give feedback, verbally and through body language. An utterance such as "I understand" or "I hear you" and a head nod from time to time let the client know we're still tuned in. Ask questions, restate key points, make ancillary comments—convince the client that you're sincerely interested in his/her problem and know how to solve it in a way that optimizes communication, costs, and schedule.

Team Activity

Listening is only part of our communication responsibility. Communication is a two-way interactive function—a team activity. Our clients must articulate their needs if we are to listen and understand. Regrettably, for many of our clients, the only experience they have with motion-media communication is viewing narrative television and motion pictures. As we know, both of these media impart a distorted concept of information motion-media. Many clients are honestly ignorant. They don't know what's best or how to tell us what they want or need or to suggest how they'll want it accomplished. Here's where our listening and professional skills come to the fore.

Working with our client, we'll use our professionalism and communication skills to develop a viable communication analysis and preproduction plan, detailing concept, budget, schedule, and producer and client responsibilities. We'll pool our expertise synergistically to ensure that the motion-media show is technically accurate and its goals are met within the client's approved framework.

Client Responsibilities

We need lots of help from our client. Our client has serious obligations and responsibilities to fulfill, just as we do. We'll highlight a
few key points here; it's in the contract that we detail full particulars regarding client and designer/producer responsibilities.

A well-drafted contract bodes well for a successful relationship.
The contract is a legal promise between client and designer/pro-
ducer, detailing each party's obligations and rights—who does what,
when, and for how much. Our client's responsibilities lie in four
primary areas:

- *consistency:* The client stays locked into the agreed plan. Except
  for an extreme emergency, nothing changes (schedule, scope, etc.).
  Our client has the authority to get the job done the way it was
  planned. No vacillating.
- *support:* The client performs tasks in a timely manner. Clears the
  way for us in his/her organization. Ensures cooperation. Has
  people, equipment, locations, etc. available on schedule. Is efficient.
- *deadlines:* Client has a clear approval process within the spon-
  soring organization. Ensures that approvals—script, first cut, payments, etc.—are executed promptly. Knows that delays add to
  cost.
- *hands off:* Client lets us do our job without interference. Is not a
  frustrated designer/producer whose mantra sounds like "Let's
  make a movie!" or "My niece is an aspiring actress." Knows that
  meddling is expensive.[6]

Unfortunately, seldom do we have an ideal client. And perhaps
we're not all that ideal either. Do we understand and appreciate our
client's problems and struggles—the politics in the office? Are we
totally responsible? Under less than ideal conditions, what sort of
relationship can be fashioned that will get the job done with a minimum of disruption and misunderstanding?

Client-Producer Relations

Designing and producing a motion-media show is a lot easier, more
profitable, and more fun if we've established a harmonious relationship with our clients. In large measure, it's up to us to kindle a
positive ambiance. Our clients are in our game, with our rules—a
game and rules with which they, most likely, are unfamiliar. I'm not
recommending that we kowtow to our clients or that they don't

have to be professional. What I am suggesting is that the impetus should come from us to set the positive tone for our relationship, a tone of understanding.

In an atmosphere of understanding and coherence of purpose, our shows have a reasonable chance for success, communicating our client's message to the target audience. In such instances, our product can emerge with aesthetic qualities and with audience and critical appeal beyond the expectations of the client. In essence, our clients expect fresh ideas from us in a constructive partnership with effective communication.[7]

Should the client override our recommendations—which is the client's prerogative—and propose a solution that we're convinced will be undesirable or foolhardy, we're obligated to express our negative opinion. We express our opinion politely, cogently, and constructively, of course. However, if our client insists on proceeding with such a solution, notwithstanding our protest, we are ethically obligated to seek a compromise (seldom attainable in such situations), to comply wholeheartedly, or to withdraw from the project.

If our client proposes something unethical, illegal, or immoral, we ought to retire from the project. It's a matter of integrity. Just how much is our reputation worth? That's the question. In the long term, no amount of largess can redeem a tarnished reputation. And we must always strive for the long-term gain. Sometimes, from the beginning of our negotiations, we know that a particular client relationship is untenable. This is the exact time to drop out of the negotiations.

I don't have a magic formula (for it would have to be magic) that would guarantee a positive and harmonious relationship with all clients. It takes a lot of maturity on our part to set the positive tone and to maintain our professionalism, no matter how excellent or inferior our client may be, and to ensure that our client doesn't become our enemy. Perhaps the most irksome of all client/producer activities, the one that taxes our professionalism the most, is the approval process and the inevitable changes it involves.

Approvals and Changes

As much as we dislike the approval process, it is essential. Approvals are the primary means by which we ensure that client and designer/producer are communicating, that the terms of the contract are being fulfilled, and that the final show meets expectations. Without approvals, we'll not have feedback, and we'll be well on the way to professional ruin. No matter how competent we think we are, we need feedback.[8] It's all too easy to detour from our primary goal. Sure enough, someone just might have a relevant idea or see something we've missed.

It's tough to see our aesthetic work critiqued by the bureaucracy: the killer committees where all members feel obligated to say something to impress the boss; legal departments that are constantly in the defensive mode; and nascent executives who fear and avoid decisions. We're in a strange profession when a novice can tell an expert what to do.[9] But that is the nature of our business. The novice is our client.

In the designing/producing process, there are several key stages where our client should approve our work and approve it in writing. Though all shows are different, the primary approval stages in film and video are at the completion of:

- communication analysis and preproduction plan (includes budget and schedule details)
- script treatment
- first-draft script and storyboard
- additional script drafts
- final script and storyboard
- production plan and schedule (with contingencies)
- interlock with edited work-print picture and narration/dialogue tracks only
- interlock with final edited picture and master-dub soundtrack (with all sound elements)
- first-answer print/video
- first-release print/videocassette/disk

With multimedia, the approval process is much the same, though the terms and process may differ somewhat—for example, instructional design strategy, flowchart, and beta testing. It's important to remember that the more approvals there are, the longer the schedule and the more opportunities there are for the client to recommend (impose) changes, whether justified or not.

In my script-approval sessions, I usually don't hand the script to the client. Instead, I provide a copy of the storyboard. As I review the kinetic-visuals detailed on the storyboard, I read the appropriate narration or dialogue, if any. My reason for this gambit is that clients almost always read the commentary and forgo reviewing the scene descriptions. Consequently, they expect all the information to be in the commentary. They read the script as if it were a publication for the audience to peruse. It's difficult to convince them otherwise.

Critical hazards to brace for in the approval process are the almost-assured presence of *the* review committees. They're "killers," mostly composed of inefficient, time-consuming ne'er-do-wells. Do all you can to avoid them. Try, with all your persuasive skill, to get the client to designate just one person as the approving authority. (Good luck!)

Usually, however, we'll be stuck to suffer the whims of review committees. Significantly, the composition of these committees fluctuates with a continual flow of new members ad infinitum and ad nauseam. Most haven't a clue about what's happening or why. Be assured, nonetheless, that they do know they're supposed to make suggestions for "improvements"—and they do! These approval committee members have an unfailing tendency to demonstrate their alertness and keen acumen by spotting faults, errors, or misinterpretations—real or imagined—all with much hullabaloo. They'll nitpick to distraction with requests for frivolous changes. Some of these pundits may well recommend changes that vector the show away from the original plan.

Another major problem with review committees is that they try to satisfy everyone, which satisfies no one. It's "Let's have everybody's input so there won't be any complaints." This does nothing for anybody. Also, review committees almost always focus on what's wrong rather than on what's right. Parry the review-committee comments with keen wit, consummate skill, resolute purpose, and the contract. Such is the genius of the approval process.

One strategy I use to mitigate negative mind-sets in approval sessions is to encourage the client to look only for the positive points on the first review—those points that have particular appeal and engender communication. On subsequent reviews, we look for and discuss the negatives. It's then that we decide which negative points are important enough to justify change. Some changes are supercostly, especially those surprises seen at interlock or first-answer print. Clear and open communication throughout designing and producing is mandatory to avoid such surprises.

Resolution of requests for changes is a critical and challenging task. We can usually resolve requested changes readily if none of us has developed a private plan, and we're still working toward our common goal. Needed are lots of understanding, compromise, and diplomacy.

Normally, we, the designer/producer, are financially responsible for changes or redos caused by technical problems, inept execution, or delays we've caused. Those changes dealing with content, design, scope, concept, technical accuracy, and the like are the client's responsibility.[10] I'm assuming that these basics were agreed upon in an earlier approval session. Such basics are initially decided on in the communication analysis and preproduction phase and confirmed on approval of the second-draft script/storyboard.

Financial responsibility for client-requested changes over aesthetics is usually not clear-cut. Ideally, we'll work with our client to make the determination on a case-by-case basis. In such instances, common sense and professionalism must prevail—there's no ready answer.

Naturally, we have to protect ourselves. For instance, after delivery of the second-draft script and storyboard that incorporates all agreed-upon changes and additions, some script designers charge an hourly rate to make additional changes in scope, direction, etc. Such charges cover costs of conferences, research, travel, and designing time. In other words, charge extra for any script or storyboard drafts beyond the second.

Here's the ultimate gambit that will keep the number of changes low and improve the show's ultimate effectiveness: tell the client how much the suggested changes will raise the cost above the contract budget.

The Budget Belongs on the Screen/Monitor

Spend the client's money judiciously. Spend it on brains and craftsmanship. Put the budget on the screen where it counts. Avoid costly frills and high-tech stuff that don't enhance communication. It's simple enough to produce a self-important, supercolossal extravaganza: All it takes is money and chutzpah. In these cases, we've put the production cart before the content horse.[11]

But it takes brains, craftsmanship, and commitment to design and produce a motion-media show that excels, one that is markedly superior in communicating our client's message to the target audience with an economy of resources. Such a show has an inherent dignity. Content is relevant and expressed with an honest simplicity and an underlying sense of purpose. Regardless of budget, craftsmanship is masterful. There are no excuses for awkward direction, inept cinematography/videography, unintelligible narration or dialogue, incoherent editing, unbalanced dubbing, or sloppy laboratory or transfer work.[12]

Notwithstanding that there are no excuses, all too many of our motion-media shows are inadequately crafted. They reek of amateurism—apathetically conceived, shoddily executed, and hastily completed. Significantly, inadequate craftsmanship is not unique to our generation. In 1949, Grierson lamented, "The camera work is less fresh and moving today, the cutting less dynamic, the sound less exploratory and inventive than they were ten years ago, nor is it by accident that the writing, in general, is terrible and the habit of work less satisfactory to all concerned."[13]

Is such inadequate craftsmanship the symptom of an inherited disease, passed on to generations of designers and producers? Have we fooled ourselves into believing that we're more skilled than we really are? Has the idiot tube anesthetized our senses into wholesale mediocrity and passivity? Or is it that we just don't care?

Make your motion-media shows sing with professionalism. Build a reputation on quality. Integrity. Reliability. Commitment. Sensitivity. Communication skills. Ensure that you and your clients work together harmoniously—professional associates pursuing a common goal.

25

Contracting for Information Motion-Media

In this chapter, I'll just give a brief layman's overview on some broad aspects of motion-media contracting. Always consult an attorney on all contracting matters to minimize risk and avoid legal problems. In other words, don't consider what I say here as the final word.

Trends

To meet the need for timely and effective motion-media services and products, organizations contract for complete shows or series and for support services. Some organizations fulfill their needs from vendors, either through open purchases or contracts. Others have an in-house motion-media capability. With the trend to downsize in-house groups, certain organizations augment their own limited design and production capability with specialty-service contracts. One aspect of these contracts is to provide, on a quick-response basis, professional talent and equipment to augment the in-house group. Such contracts furnish the flexible manpower necessary to respond to widely varying demands for particular projects—for example, a videographer and crew with camera, lighting, and grip equipment.

Another attribute of these contracts is to provide access to specialty houses for motion-media functions that are outside the capabilities of the in-house group. Such functions might include computer and optical effects, complex digital animation design and production, sound, laboratory, and transfer services. Accordingly, the use of specialty-service contracts results in increased production capability and professionalism and usually decreased costs. Such specialty-service contracts are long-term, usually for a year or so with options for renewal.

With the increased emphasis on contracting, it's imperative that the client and the contractor have a mutual understanding of the general aspects of contracting. The process of purchasing via contract can be as simple as buying a roll of film or as complex as contracting for a complete show. A successful contract is profitable to both the client and the contractor. The client gets a fair product at a fair price. The contractor gets monetary reward and enjoys professional accomplishment, satisfaction, and growth.

Aspects of Contracting

The following is a brief overview of the aspects of contracts, a subject that is intensely complex. Obviously, specific contract situations require expert legal advice. *Legally defined, a contract is a promise, or group of promises, between parties to perform, or refrain from, some specific act(s) that are legally enforceable.*[1] The word *parties* as used here can be people, corporations, partnerships, governments, or any entity that has the legal power to contract. All contracts are:

- *bilateral:* Both parties make promises.
- *express:* Promises are declared in direct terms, either orally or in writing (in writing preferred).[2]

Requirements. For an agreement to be legally enforceable (a valid contract), six fundamental requirements must be met. These are:

- The promises are voluntary.
- The parties have the legal capacity to contract.
- An offer is tendered.
- An acceptance is made.
- The offer and acceptance are supported by consideration.
- The contract is for a legal purpose.

Voluntary promises. The parties making the promises must do so completely voluntarily. The promises must be based on the best available information. If one or both parties believes in an erroneous assumption relating to a material fact in the promises because of misrepresentation, fraud, duress, or undue influence, the contract is voidable—that is, the person induced may elect not to be bound by the promises.

Legal capacity. The parties entering into a contract must have the legal and mental capability to incur liability and to acquire rights. All persons under the law are presumed to have legal capacity. Excepted are infants, insane persons, and persons with temporarily impaired mental faculties due to alcohol, drugs, etc. The law presumes that these persons do not have the mental capacity to protect their interests in the give-and-take of a free marketplace. Therefore, they cannot make a legal contract. (However, legal guardians may make contracts for such persons.)

Offer. With the intent to contract, an offer is a promise of what the offeror shall do, or shall not do, and what is demanded in return. An offer must be communicated to be effective—that is, the other party must receive it. An offer may be made orally or in writing (again, writing is much preferred).

Terms of the offer need not be stated with absolute certainty. However, the terms must be explicit enough for intentions, legal rights, and duties to be determined. If a material term is omitted or left to a future agreement, the contract is invalid because of "uncertainty of terms."

The law presumes that "usage of the trade" terms are intended to be part of a contract unless specifically excluded. This concept is critical in motion-media contracts because of the specialized parlance we use. It's imperative that all parties have agreement on all terms, especially those tossed about so freely in our business. "Complex animation" is but one example that I've seen for which there were widely diverse interpretations of what the client expected and what the contractor delivered.

Sometimes in *negotiated* procurements, the parties may dicker. Each party declares the values of its promises or property in a manner that is not a clear-cut legal offer. Dickering is often to the advantage of both parties, because eventually the best of each proposal is highlighted and properly evaluated.

As a matter of practicality in law, a communicated offer does not remain in effect indefinitely. If no time limit is specified for acceptance, the offer terminates with the passage of a "reasonable time," determined by the circumstances of each offer. Reasonable time in floor trading on a stock exchange would be almost instantly; in a major construction project, it might be several months.

Offers may be terminated by:

- *provision:* A clause in the contract states that the offer must be accepted within a specified time.

- *revocation:* Generally, an offer may be revoked any time before it is accepted. Revocation must be communicated.
- *rejection:* Any of three acts constitutes rejection: refusal of the offer, a counteroffer, or acceptance of the offer with conditions.
- *death or insanity:* The concept that a "meeting of the minds" of the parties is the test of a valid contract evolved from common law. Obviously, no mind exists after death or, by law, in an insane person.
- *destruction:* Clearly, the promises cannot be carried out if the essential subject matter of a contract is destroyed through no fault of either party.
- *illegality:* This proscription describes the circumstances when the performance required in a proposed contract becomes illegal in the intervening time between the offer being made and its acceptance.

In the motion-media contracting business (and in most other businesses), a client who seeks bids for a show or services is soliciting offers. This is a critical point. It is the contractor who makes the offer and the client who accepts or rejects it.

Acceptance. All other conditions being met, a binding contract results when the party to whom an offer has been made communicates the desire to be legally bound by (accepts) all the terms in the offer. Any attempt to alter terms of the offer terminates the offer.

Consideration. To make a binding legal contract, each party must voluntarily relinquish something. It may be money, labor, goods, or a promise to do, or not to do, something (to drop a lawsuit against the other party, for example).[3]

Legal purpose. The performance of the promises in an offer:

- must be legal
- must not cause the commission of a tort (an injury or wrong to another or his or her property)
- must conform to "accepted standards of morality"

If these three conditions are not met fully, the bargain is illegal and automatically void. I use the term *bargain* because by law there cannot be an illegal contract.

Procurement Process

It's axiomatic that a successful contract results only from good planning. Effective procurement planning must begin far in advance of the need for the show or specialty services. Clients need to evaluate critically their technical requirements and the financial aspects of the proposed procurement. These functions are vital to a successful contract: agreement between client and contractor on the work to be accomplished; results expected in terms of quantity, quality, and schedule; responsibilities; contract monitoring; contingencies; and payment schedule. A successful contract is profitable to the client and the contractor and is administered easily.

With few exceptions, the procurement process of contracting comprises these basic functions:

- *definition of requirements:* what's wanted, when, where
- *procurement planning:* what's involved
- *preparation of the solicitation document:* request for proposal or bid
- *selection of contract type:* There are many kinds of contracts.
- *announcement of procurement:* advertisements, conferences, and personal contact
- *evaluation of proposals or bids:* Who has the best technical proposal at the "best" price? Who is the lowest bidder who can do the job to the requirements?
- *contract award:* sign here, please
- *contract administration and performance monitoring*[4]

Don't consider these functions definitive and having finite limits. Rather, they overlap along the contracting continuum.

Definition of Requirements

One of the most difficult and yet essential tasks that clients have in the contracting process is to define the motion-media requirements exactly and then to develop the procurement specifications. Clients accomplish this task by answering precisely such fundamental questions as:

- What exactly is needed? (services, film, video, multimedia, or something else?)
- Why? (What's the problem? target audience? goal?)
- When is it needed?
- How and where are the services or show to be produced?

Obviously, not all the pertinent questions are stated here, but the ones posed are the most critical. Others would need to be developed and answered to meet specific contract requirements. Inherent in this analysis is a precise identification of the services or products (or combination) needed, the goals to be achieved, and an indication of how they are to be accomplished—the requirements statement. If we look at a motion-media show as an example, the requirements statement might involve:

Definitions. With the requirement for an information motion-media show, we need to define the communication goal in terms of the target audience, including the minimum rate of achievement or level of performance required of the audience in the near term and in the long term. After defining the communication goals and the target audience, we must make decisions about medium selection, the distribution plan, and the contracting scheme.

Medium selection. What medium or combination of media will best achieve the goals: film, video, multimedia, filmstrips, sound/tape slide shows, or a liberally illustrated publication?

Distribution plan. How will we distribute the show? Some factors to consider are audience composition, size, and location; viewing environment; equipment needs; projectionist; and discussion leader (if required).

Contracting scheme. How is the contracting scheme structured? Which of the major phases (scripting, production, or distribution) should be contracted for, singly or in combination, and which, if any, should be done in-house? Or is a combination of in-house and contractor support appropriate?

Combination contracts. In my experience, I prefer not to combine the scripting and production phases of a show in a single contract. Rather, I try to contract for each phase separately and at different times. Overall, I've seen superior results produced more quickly and at lower cost by keeping script and production separate. Actually, I'm uneasy with contracts that combine script and production. They smack of the fox-guarding-the-hen-house syndrome. Significantly, I've found that only a vague requirement statement can be developed for these combination contracts, because the requirements for the production phase must be based totally on the completed and approved script. The precision requirement statement, essential for a good production contract, cannot be developed without a script and storyboard. A major pitfall is almost guaranteed when a combination contract is used.

Speculative script treatments. The widespread and abhorrent practice of soliciting speculative script treatments for a proposed motion-media show is simply conniving balderdash. Most often, these are induced by vague assurances of having an edge in getting the scripting or production contract. These schemes are immoral, unethical, unreasonable, and not in anyone's best interests.[5]

Specialty-service contracts. If the client has in-house motion-media producing skills, we should consider the concept of using specialty-service contracts to augment the in-house group or to develop a total motion-media package (including distribution). I've found the use of specialty-service contracts to be very productive and cost-effective.

Contract specialist. Translating the communication analysis, production and distribution plan, and contracting scheme into procurement specifications requires the skills of a contract specialist. Ideally, working together, the client, the in-house motion-media manager (if any), and the contract specialist develop a statement of the requirements that is contractible. Namely, the specifics are definitive and well written in plain English and are legally viable. The attendant contract is easy to understand, easy to administer, and easy to comply with.

These ideal goals, unfortunately, are rarely achieved. Most motion-media contracts in the government and private sector reflect the bureaucracies from which they come. They are tedious, ambiguous, voluminous, and encumbered with inconsequential and politically correct boilerplate. Usually, however, they are legal. (See appendix 9 for Jack Williamson's comments regarding a government request-for-bid.)

Procurement Planning

With the requirements clearly defined, the client and the contract specialist decide on the procurement method, type of contract, schedule, assignment of responsibilities, and a host of other details to ensure that a viable contract is let. A milestone chart is often used to monitor progress and forestall delays. A sound procurement plan is a requisite for a timely and viable contract award, professional business conduct, and responsible contract administration.[6]

Procurement Methods

Procurements (read *contracts*) are classified in two broad categories: noncompetitive and competitive. Each category has numerous subsets.

Noncompetitive. Of primary importance in this category are:

- *single source:* In a competitive market, purchasing from only one source may be advantageous because of that source's experience, ongoing contract work, or other features.

- *sole source:* Only one contractor has the unique capability that meets the requirements—patent ownership, for example.
- *small purchase:* Basic purchase agreements placed with local vendors may be the best source for low-cost, off-the-shelf items.

Competitive. Of the many variations in this category, two are most appropriate to motion-media contracting:

- *formal advertising:* When the requirements have been defined with pinpoint precision to encourage maximum competition, formal advertising is used to *solicit bids.* Contract award is based on the lowest bid from the responsible and responsive bidder. Inherent in this process is sufficient time for the formalities of preparing the invitation to bid, evaluating the bids, and determining the responsibility and responsiveness of the lowest bidder.
- *negotiated procurement:* Quality competition, flexibility, selectivity, and speed in dealing with contractors are the salient points of a negotiated procurement. The client uses a *request for proposal,* which details the requirements and establishes the criteria for evaluation, to solicit offers. The client attempts to get the best possible terms by negotiating with the contractors in the competitive range (client-established estimated-cost range). Contract award is made to the contractor whose price, technical proposal, and other factors appear to offer the most advantages.[7]

Preparation of the Solicitation Document

Information gathered and codified during the definition of requirements and procurement-planning stage is used to prepare the solicitation document (invitation to bid or request for proposal). The solicitation document must include enough data—terms, conditions, responsibilities, schedules, and other pertinent information—to constitute a definitive contract when it is signed and dated by the client and contractor. The *statement of work* in the solicitation document tells the offeror what must be accomplished as an end product. It may be as simple as a one-line statement for an off-the-shelf item or as complex as a complete plan for a motion-media show.

Specifications in the plan detail all the physical aspects needed to describe the show—for example, film, video, or multimedia; color or black-and-white; sound elements, synchronous or voice-over, original or stock music; and approximate length. The solicitation document must also detail all the information a contractor should provide. This is essential so that the client's contract specialist and technical personnel can properly evaluate the offer or bid in terms of costs, technical approach, and contractor qualifications.

Finally, the solicitation document includes (as appropriate) the general provisions, inspection criteria, acceptance procedures, payment schedule, and other contract administration details.

Contract Types

There are as many types of contracts as contract specialists can devise to meet specific situations of risk, responsibility, legal liability, and products and services to be delivered. The two contracts most frequently used to procure motion-media products and services lie at opposite ends of the responsibility spectrum. At one end is cost reimbursement, where profit rather than price is fixed—the client pays actual costs. At the other end is firm fixed price, where the contract price is locked at the bid figure and not subject to adjustments—profit is a function of contractor efficiency and cost control. Between these extremes are contracts with varying degrees of contractor cost responsibility, depending on the amount of uncertainty in the work statement and specifications.

Cost reimbursement. In these contracts, an estimated cost is set during the negotiation process as a ceiling to attain a specified end product or some level of effort. The contractor may exceed this ceiling only with risk. Particulars of the contractor's fee also are agreed on during negotiations. Importantly, statutes forbid contracts in which the fee is a direct function of cost; that is, the fee increases as costs are incurred. In general, the client is obligated to reimburse the contractor for all the allocable, allowable, and reasonable costs incurred, including *approved* cost overruns.

Cost-reimbursement contracts are useful, particularly when flexibility is needed to redirect the contractor's effort to meet changes in requirements that fall within the scope of the contract and when specifications cannot be detailed with pinpoint accuracy in advance. An example would be the production of a documentary show that follows a pharmaceutical company's efforts to develop a drug to cure lung cancer.

Cost plus fixed fee. During negotiations, the contractor's fee is set at a specific dollar amount. The fee does not vary with actual costs, including cost overruns. This contract has minimum incentive for the contractor to manage effectively and tends to increase client costs. We should use such a contract only with caution. If the scope of work is broadened significantly, the fee may be increased proportionally. Conversely, if actual costs for an end product or level of effort are significantly less than estimated or if the schedule is not met, the fee should be decreased to reflect the reduced scope of the contract. Appropriate for this type of contract would be production of a technical motion-media show that reports on an ongoing research and development program for which unknown factors and technical delays cannot be predicted.

Cost plus award fee. The fee paid to the contractor is composed of two parts:

- a fixed amount, or basic fee, that does not vary regardless of performance
- an award fee determined by the client's unilateral and subjective evaluation of the contractor's performance in meeting requirements, schedule, and cost

Because the motivation for contractor excellence is strong in award-fee contracts, clients use them to procure technical, administrative, and housekeeping services—the motion-media distribution phase, for instance.

Cost plus incentive fee. When the uncertainties in the work statement and specifications are moderate (firmer than in award-fee and fixed-fee contracts), the incentive-fee contract is appropriate. The risks are shared about equally between client and contractor. Target costs and target fee are set in the negotiations. If the contractor reduces costs below the estimate, a bonus fee, based on a percentage of cost saved, is awarded. By its nature, the incentive-fee contract exerts exceptional pressure on the contractor to reduce cost, improve performance, and meet schedules. It is appropriate for the operation of a company-owned, contractor-operated motion-media facility—a film laboratory or video-transfer operation, for example.

Time and materials. Time-and-materials contracts are appropriate when the extent, duration, or overall cost of the work cannot be estimated with any degree of certainty. With a ceiling price established, contractor-furnished labor and materials accomplish the task. A fixed hourly (or daily) rate, including profit and overhead, is established for each labor category used on the task. Materials are purchased at contractor cost, and the contractor is usually reimbursed on a cost-plus percentage (15 percent is about average). Time-and-materials contracts are suited to buying engineering or design services (computer or digital effects, for example), and for maintenance, repair, and overhaul functions. A variation of this type of contract is the labor-hour contract, which requires no materials. It is used to buy scripts and storyboards, for instance.

Fixed price. A fixed-price contract is an agreement to pay a specific price (sometimes with adjustments) upon delivery and acceptance of the goods or services contracted for. The contractor's risk ranges from moderate to very high. The fixed-price contract, by its nature, encourages maximum competition and is generally the most cost-effective contract. It is therefore much preferred in industrial practices.

Fixed price redeterminable. Clients use this type of contract to buy quantity production items when adequate estimates of labor and material cannot be made because the specifications are somewhat vague, the initial buy is very small or very large and not reflective of realistic production costs, or the delivery schedule is short. Financial risk, because of uncertainties, is shared about equally between client and contractor. The contract price is adjusted up or down during the life of the contract as specifications are firmed or other variables are controlled. This contract could be used to buy, for example, special laboratory processing of large quantities of film to be exposed under unusual conditions and delivered to the laboratory in varying quantities over an extended period.

Fixed-price incentive. When the contingencies relating to cost, performance, and schedule are less than those associated with a redeterminable contract, an incentive contract is appropriate. Financial risk is shifted toward the contractor because of more certainty in the contingencies. Cost reduction, performance-improvement goals, and the formula for determining profit are agreed on during negotiations. The incentive is strong for the contractor to meet target goals because profit is a direct function of overall performance. This contract might have application in the procurement of a complete multimedia-training package where student performance can be measured objectively.

Fixed price with economic price adjustment. Special contingency clauses in this type of fixed-price contract allow for price adjustment up or down to protect the contractor and client from major fluctuations in labor or material costs. Price adjustments are limited to contingencies that the contractor does not control. Because of the wide variance in the price of silver, this contract would be useful for purchasing raw film stock and for routine laboratory processing and printing.

Fixed price, indefinite quantity. Several factors make this contract especially attractive to client and contractor. A fixed price is set for goods and services as line items in a contract, much like a catalog. Goods and services may be purchased piecemeal to meet varying client requirements over the life of the contract. The client guarantees to buy a stated minimum of each line item. (Sometimes a maximum purchase limitation is established to protect the contractor.) Frequently, the services are categories of highly skilled labor plus the attendant specialized equipment. This type of contract is suited very well to the purchase of specialized motion-media functions, such as art and digital animation, sound, and laboratory and transfer services.

Firm fixed price. In this type of contract, the contractor is obligated legally to deliver an end product that meets specifications on time and at the agreed price regardless of the actual cost or be liable for breach of contract. Profit is the difference between contract price and the contractor's costs. Accordingly, this type of contract places a maximum incentive on the contractor for cost control. Sometimes, however, quality can suffer. A firm-fixed-price contract should be used only for procurements that have few or no uncertainties in cost, end-product description, or schedule. It is the simplest contract to structure and administer and is ideal for buying a complete motion-media show whose script and storyboard are completely detailed and approved and when the contingencies are inconsequential.

Announcement of Procurement

To get maximum competition from responsible contractors, the proposed procurement should be publicized extensively through informal advertising for proposals and by formal advertising for bids. Advertisements may be posted in trade journals and newspapers, word-of-mouth, conferences, etc. The procurement or supply department usually handles the distribution of the announcement to ensure that legal requirements are met.

As a first step, the in-house motion-media manager (or a knowledgeable person) prepares a list of prospective contractors known to have the capability to accomplish the work. Also, the client's records are screened to uncover other prospects. For large procurements, a presolicitation conference may be held with prospective contractors to discuss the work and to pique interest.

In negotiated procurements, the *letter of interest* is useful to solicit interest. Be careful that the letter does not become an informal request for proposal.[8]

Evaluation of Proposals

Clients use the evaluation process in negotiated procurements to discern which offeror has the best prospect of satisfactorily completing the work on schedule and within cost. As part of the procurement package, the solicitation document must state all criteria used to evaluate and rate a prospective contractor's proposal. The criteria should be comprehensive and detailed enough for a critical assessment of all relevant technical and managerial capabilities needed to accomplish the tasks as delineated in the statement of work.[9]

The key criteria used to evaluate contractor capabilities are past performance, client continuity, integrity, credit rating, financial resources, management, organization, quality-control procedures, access to classified information (if appropriate), plant or office location (space and equipment), personnel (staff and free-lance associates), and subcontractor access.

In formally advertised procurements, evaluation criteria may also be used. However, the criteria must be highly specific and essential for contract performance. Since no communication may be had with bidders, after evaluation, their bids may be rated only as acceptable or unacceptable.

My favorite evaluation process is the pre-award survey. It's particularly valuable in determining and evaluating all aspects of an organization's operation. We ferret out the true capabilities of a prospective contractor with a visit to the contractor's place of business to inspect facilities, equipment, and organizational operations and to interview personnel. Oftentimes, I've found that bidders or contractors find it easier to spin fiction in a proposal or bid than it is to produce the facts during a pre-award survey. Over the years, I've seen lots of fiction, some bordering on chicanery. Rigorous pre-award surveys ought be conducted on any proposed contractor with whom the client has no experience and whenever any doubt exists about the contractor's managerial, financial, or professional capabilities.

I'll relate one story about how we exposed monkeyshines during a pre-award survey. A few years ago, we received a proposal from an outfit in the Los Angeles area that was responding to my request for proposal for a production-service contract (directors, cinematographers, editors, grips, etc). The outfit's name had the word *Electronic* in it. Nonetheless, its proposal was fabulous. The proposal listed dozens of motion-media shows the firm had produced for a host of government agencies and Fortune 500 companies. They claimed to employ a dozen or so motion-media specialists and technicians with widespread experience and graduate degrees in film/video from the top universities. Its equipment was state-of-the-art. And its low-bid price was too good to be true. Having extensive knowledge of the production facilities in the area, my suspicions were piqued because I'd never heard of this outfit.

The contract specialist and I visited this organization. The managing director seated us in the conference room. Also in the room were his staff of six managers (no motion-media folks, however). Evasive answers to our questions soon intensified my suspicions. I asked to see some of the shows they'd produced. None were handy. The equipment was in another location. None of the motion-media people were available for us to talk to. It soon became obvious that these folks were in a sweat. They'd not expected such intense scrutiny. Finally, I asked to see the time cards of the motion-media people. The managing director told me they were not available. I responded that the pre-award survey was over and that I was recommending they not be awarded this contract and they be barred from future contract considerations.

Clearly, this outfit had no motion-media production capability whatsoever. I suspect that their goal was to get the contract and then hire the people, buy the equipment, and build the facilities. Even so, they could not have fulfilled this contract in a timely and professional manner, especially considering the unrealistically low prices they'd quoted. This example may be an extreme case, but it reveals the importance of the pre-award survey. I have numerous other examples of fiction in proposals and bids, but my point is made.

Contract Award

In negotiated procurements, the client dickers with the offerors to get the best possible terms. All factors of the proposals may be explored. The contractor's technical approach, resource allocation, and costs are of particular importance. For instance, exactly how is the contractor going to produce the information motion-media show, and what equipment and personnel are to be used? The award is made to that *responsible* and *responsive* offeror whose proposal has the most advantages and least risk for the client.

In formally advertised procurement, prospective contractors submit sealed bids. Bids are opened publicly, and after evaluation, the award is made to the lowest responsible and responsive bidder. Because the award is based on price, the contract, by definition, must be either firm-fixed price or fixed price with escalation clauses.

Contract Administration and Performance Monitoring

Efficient administration and performance monitoring of the contract are critical to satisfactory progress and completion. These functions are accomplished through active cooperation among technical, purchasing, and legal personnel. The gamut of contract administration and performance-monitoring specifics is almost endless. Most elements involve common sense, some are legally complex, and others involve business ethics.

Changes. Frequently, contracts must be modified to meet changing circumstances. If the modification affects a material provision of the contract, a bilateral agreement needs to be completed (a minicontract, in effect). Changes in the work statement or specifications constitute a material change and require some agreement between client and contractor. Examples are cancellation of extensive location photography or doubling the DVD release order. In most organizations, only the contract specialist may negotiate bilateral contract modifications.

Unilateral actions provided for in the original contract, such as administrative changes or exercising of options, require only written notification from the client to be effective.

A word of caution: In government and in most other contracts, clients and their representatives must avoid a *constructive change*. Simply put, a constructive change (order) is an unofficial request (implied or manifest) by an unauthorized person for extra or different work from that agreed upon in the contract. Such constructive changes are not legal and/or not enforceable. Accordingly, they cause serious difficulties and disputes, and contracting and legal experts view them with disdain. Usually, constructive changes are perpetrated inadvertently by the client's representatives while coordinating with the contractor. Or, as sometimes happens, the contractor unwittingly or purposefully misconstrues comments or suggestions as valid change orders. Contractor claims for additional work done because of a constructive change are onerous to resolve because of the difficulty in deciding between client directed and contractor volunteered work.

Other aspects. Problems relating to technical performance, cost, and schedule are expected. However, close monitoring and expeditious reporting will identify potential problems and will permit timely corrective action to be taken. If a problem persists, the contractor may become delinquent by reason of nonperformance. Several remedies are available to the client (and to the contractor if the client becomes delinquent). The easier solution, though not necessarily the

most practical, is to terminate the contract via a default action—
an ugly business in which both parties almost always lose. To pre-
clude these undesirable events, a viable contract between a responsible client and contractor is imperative.

Lastly, delivery and acceptance constitute contract completion.
Usually, a certification of some sort is submitted to conclude formally the business. Practically, however, cashing the final payment
check is "The End."

Though no one contract will fit all situations, or even most of them,
the Standard Motion Picture Production Contract developed by the
International Quorum of Motion Picture Producers is an excellent
example of a firm-fixed-price contract for a film or video show.[10]
If clauses are unsatisfactory, they can be struck.

We've only managed a broad-based treatment of the intricate topic
of motion-media contracting. Although my discussion has a govern-
mental ring to it, the general points should be applicable to all facets of motion-media contracting and for motion-media managers to
gain a keener appreciation of the complexities and pitfalls involved.

One last thought: *Expert counsel is a must.*

26

Managing an Information Motion-Media Group

The day I retired as the manager of an in-house motion-media group was a wondrous day, and it was a horrific day. I was delighted to become a free man—finally, after twenty years, escaping from the day-to-day grind and free of the suffocating bureaucracy. And I was saddened deeply to realize that I no longer would be working with one of the best designing and producing teams in the business, a group of outstanding professionals. I would miss deeply my associates. My apprehension zoomed, knowing that I'd no longer be active in the profession I love. So it goes.

In this chapter, my goal is to share some ideas regarding management of a motion-media group (in-house and outside). There are lots and lots of books, seminars, and formal classes that deal with management. I'm not going to get into those details here. Rather, I want to share a few specifics that I found useful that relate directly to motion-media groups.

Let's set the fundamental truth: In today's austere business climate (and I suspect as far into the future as we can see), the measure of a motion-media group's success and reason for continued existence is based on the group's contribution and responsiveness to clients in solving their communication problems.

Resource Provider

As managers of an information motion-media group, our primary task is to make sure that our clients get the most effective motion-media shows possible, delivered on time and within budget. I define *effective* in terms of communication results garnered with the target audience as a direct function of resources expended. To this end, we need to provide the resources our group needs to do its job of solving communication problems with motion-media.

Because of the unique circumstances of individual motion-media groups, my listing of resources necessarily is incomplete and will contain some resources that are not germane. However, those I've found to have special importance are people (talent), time, contractor support, space, equipment, group administration, and senior management's support. Such resources are the wherewithal the group needs to accomplish its goals. Implicit in the list is the funding to acquire and maintain these resources.

Resources are assets to be acquired, nurtured, and used with judicious care. Such is the manager's major contribution to achievement of group goals. If our group is part of a larger group, we must ensure that we conform to that group's policies and long-term goals while keeping senior managers informed.

On a show-by-show basis, we provide and allocate the resources needed to accomplish the specific task at hand. We monitor their expenditure in the design and production of shows. In our monitoring process, we keep track of resources spent. If we see that too much resource is being used for too little gain, we need to tweak the team back on track. Conversely, if not enough resource is being spent and the show's progress is hampered, we need to determine why.

All too frequently, the problems of the day-to-day routine sidetrack us, and we have less and less time and effort to focus on quality control and our long-term goals. We become reactive rather than proactive. We're forced to concentrate on duties that, albeit important, are narrower in scope and require quick response—for example, personnel problems (morale, discipline, feuds, etc.), group image, administrative details, and senior management's interference and micromanagement.

Understandably, in some groups, it's senior management that sets a narrow direction and tone for the first-line manager to follow in day-to-day operations. Sometimes, to meet these requirements, we may concentrate on boss-pleasing areas, much to the detriment of the group's welfare. I suggest, however, that even under strict dicta from above, we can broaden our focus and over time develop a more comprehensive perspective of our duties as a resource provider. Let's take a closer look at these resources to see if they're applicable to our motion-media group.

People

People are absolutely, positively the first resource we must consider. We need to look at our professionals and craftsmen in terms of inherent talent, motivation, and industry—the spark and fuel of the group. Our task is to ensure that these attributes are nurtured in each employee.

This responsibility begins with the all-important function of recruiting—a much-neglected and relegated duty that more often than not is accomplished by happenstance. I understand why many managers give only cursory service to this task. It's tough to do properly. If done properly, it consumes a vast amount of time in planning, execution, and follow-through; it frequently requires travel; it needs to be conducted with consummate tact, legal precision, and marked deftness. Recruiting demands incisive insight and ruthless objectivity. This kind of effort, in the long term, realizes an overall return that is almost immeasurably positive. Unfortunately, few motion-media managers devote such effort in their recruiting. I've often heard managers say something like, "With the glut of all types of talent on the market today, I can hire an editor (or whatever) any time, any place." This is true. But I also believe it to be painfully myopic.

As managers, we should analyze our recruiting objectives in relation to long-term goals, not for just the immediate need. What do we want the new employee to be doing in one year, five years, ten years? Does the job have growth potential? If not, can it be made so?

As the manager of a small in-house film group, I looked for a job applicant who, though inexperienced, had the potential to become a versatile motion-media professional—a combination script designer, producer, director, and editor. Perhaps also someone who knew how to operate cameras and the other equipment. Such a person can develop into a consummate motion-media professional who can assume total responsibility and authority for the show's design, production, and completion. Obviously, such a special person is not easy to find and recruit. But they are out there. I've found them. It just takes lots of looking and insight.

I've had the most success in fulfilling my long-term people goals by recruiting recent graduates with advanced degrees in motion-media from the recognized universities. The traits I look for in recruiting are inherent talent, motivation, work ethic, commitment to the information motion-media profession, and how well the prospective employee will fit into the group. By and large, I little consider experience. All too often, I've found that experience is not what it seems to be. For instance, a candidate might tell me that he/she has so many years' experience, say ten years. In checking the candidate's qualifications and references, I'll find that, sure enough, he/she does have ten years' experience—but it was the first year done over ten times!

Admittedly, at best, candidate selection is mostly a subjective, educated guess. But when done with judicious care, it usually results in a propitious selection—maybe not the best candidate but a candidate who is clearly among the top few. Only the years gone by will tell.

Training and Mentoring

Next, we develop, train, mentor, and motivate the new employees to achieve. When stuck, we counsel, help, badger, commiserate, and, if we must, retreat. We need to establish an open work atmosphere wherein new ideas are encouraged and flourish. We continually task the new employee with varied and challenging assignments of constantly increasing responsibility and authority. These assignments are made in consonance with the group's workload, at a pace slightly faster than we believe the employee can reasonably handle.

It's important for developing employees to know that it's okay to fail from time to time and especially so when trying a new task. We support our employees in such instances and make sure that it is a learning experience on which the employee can build. If not, our employees will be shy about attempting anything new. Thus, their initiative may well be stifled, and they won't grow professionally as fast or as adeptly as we would want.

In my experience, it takes six or seven years for an advanced-degree graduate to grow into a fully qualified information motion-media professional. At this point, the employee performs satisfactorily in most all of the motion-media tasks and generally excels in several. He/she can analyze communication problems quickly and effect solutions with the best economy of resources and can act independently or in support of others in whatever task is required. I am convinced that a cadre of this kind of professional talent is essential for the success of any motion-media group.

Here's yet one more aside. Some years ago, my management cajoled me into taking a fellow into my group who was billed as a writer. Big mistake! He couldn't write (as if I wanted a writer!). Compounding the problem, he refused to admit that he couldn't write, and he refused to learn anything new—even to the point of refusing to learn how to thread our motion-picture projector. His comments were to the effect, "That's not in my job description!" Within a few months, I purged this fellow from our group. I've relayed this story because I hope it has a message for you, the reader, regarding the work ethic. Do whatever is required to learn and help your group move forward. No task is too menial.

My paternal grandfather, an ol'-line Texan, had a wonderful philosophy on the work ethic. He'd say, "Marty, if you're going to learn to be a farmer, you've got to learn how to slop the hogs." I learned to slop the hogs, but I didn't become a farmer.

Time

Time is the next most important resource—time to get the job done satisfactorily with reasonable economy. Our task as managers is to ensure, as much as possible, that enough time is allocated for the task. Unfortunately, this is the one resource over which we have the least control. Make sure that short deadlines are realistic. Ferret out those that are set falsely by overanxious clients. Working with the client, establish a realistic due date.

In the scheme of our management duties, we should establish and direct a time-management program, ensuring that the time available is used efficiently. Since time is such a deceptively complex resource, there is no easy definition of efficiency. I would like, however, to share a few observations from my experience.

The laws of physics and human nature being as they are, the time available to accomplish the job determines the pace of the work and of the workers; that is, the work will get done in the time allotted, be it short, normal (routine), or long.

The routine job. All factors considered, the routine motion-media show is the most economical in terms of rate of return for resources expended and in overall job satisfaction. The motion-media professional has enough time to plan and create and enough time to execute all the elements carefully. Yet, there is not enough time for any element to atrophy. The elapsed time, from statement of the communication problem to distribution, is short enough for the professional to have a fresh and comprehensive view of the entire process.

One caution: We must prevent the routine show from becoming the job that is worked on just when there is nothing else to do. The routine job has an inherent priority that must be honored, so develop a schedule with a fixed deadline and hold to it.

Long lead-time. I've found that a long lead-time, especially when excessive to the total time needed to complete the job, results in a major increase in resource expenditure with little additional return. In fact, of all the time allocations, the excessively long lead-time usually is the most expensive. It dulls the sharp edge in incisive thinking and efficient work ethic. Things are postponed or re-planned or done over repeatedly. Lack of decisiveness reigns in an attempt to achieve the ultimate perfection. Productivity wanes. It's axiomatic that the more time available, the more complex and important the job becomes.[1]

Crash schedules. Shows that have short or inadequate lead-times present some special problems. Generally, these shows are much more expensive and less effective than those that are routine. Large blocks of inefficient but expensive overtime are used. Normal eco-nomics are skipped in the interest of time; for example, personal messenger service or overnight delivery is used instead of ordinary mail. Falsely, more talent in terms of quantity and quality is em-ployed in all facets of production with far less efficiency. Contin-gency options of all kinds are covered in anticipation of need or trouble. And what should be polished or done over is accepted in the interest of getting the job done.

Sometimes the side effects of this kind of crash effort can be dev-astating: Group moral and team spirit suffer as normal office ameni-ties are short-circuited, tempers rise, egos are bruised, and better judgment fails. Equally important, other work in the group is put aside, and either its deadline is missed, or it, in turn, becomes a crash project in an attempt to recoup lost time—a self-defeating process.

On the other hand, the group can derive some advantages in effecting a rapid response to communication needs. Operating un-der the pressure of the crash or short deadline offers unique oppor-tunities for professional growth. This can be the catalyst needed to build team spirit among the group members. It demands creative and physical discipline from all that participate but especially from the motion-media professional who has responsibility for the show. Communication analysis is done thoroughly yet quickly. Produc-tion shortcuts are devised and executed. In this sharp decision pro-cess, all else is excluded as unnecessary or too expensive in terms of the time resource.

Contract Support

I've found that more and more motion-media groups are concentrat-ing their limited resources in the communication-solving functions—scripting, producing, directing, and editing—and in contract man-agement. Increasingly, contract support is used for the technical and craftsman functions—camera, sound, art/animation, special/computer effects, original conforming—and for laboratory and transfer services.

The manager's task is to develop, let, and administer a series of viable contracts with expert specialty houses that are professionally responsive to the group's needs at reasonable cost. This is no easy or quick task. Sometimes, it took me over seven months to get such a contract in effect. But once let and working, these contracts were worth the effort in every sense of the word. They yield significant advantages in terms of increased professionalism and decreased operating costs.

From the contractor's viewpoint, these contracts must be profitable, monetarily and professionally. They must also be simple: simple to understand, simple to administer, and simple to comply with. That is, the work statement must pinpoint the exact services and materials required and no more, within a specific and reasonable time frame. (See chapter 25 for details on contracting.)

Space

The space resource encompasses much more than the minimum square footage needed to house the group's talent and its equipment. It defines space in terms of human and environmental factors and in its efficient use.

Every employee needs to have a personal space, furniture, and attendant office paraphernalia. This not only offers a security symbol, it *is* security—perhaps more so than the paycheck or managerial plaudits. To demonstrate this principle someday, without any heads-up, announce a radical change in office assignments. After you recover, let me know how it went!

We need first to concentrate on the human factors of the space resource. The space needs to be large enough to prevent crowding, physical or mental. It needs to be designed, decorated, and furnished for reasonable comfort and provided with good communication tools. It must afford enough privacy to encourage creative thinking.

The environmental factors of heat, air conditioning, light, humidity, power, security, and safety must be provided and controlled to the degree that their presence or absence is not noticed. The space must be maintained with efficient janitorial service, repair, and upkeep. All of these are overhead budget items.

We must also decide on the kind and amount of equipment space that the group needs in order to produce its motion-media tasks effectively. Again, the question must be put: What is the most efficient in terms of resource expenditure? My experience has been to provide just the space resource that is used actively in support of the group's work. Space needed on an occasional basis can be rented; for example, sound stages, recording studios, editing rooms, and projection rooms. Inefficiently or seldom-used space is a serious drain on any group's overhead, reducing all resources proportionately.

Equipment

The equipment resource is defined as the hardware and software needed by the group to get its job done. Hardware may be owned or rented. The equipment resource includes equipment maintenance and repair, done in-house or on contract. Office equipment and furniture are included in the equipment resource.

Generally, an equipment-resource purchase must be considered as a capital investment, and as such it must be considered carefully. Again, nonprofitable expenditure taps the lifeblood from all other resources. To get a good return on the investment, personnel must be able to use the equipment to get the job done professionally, and it must be used frequently, must be reliable, must be easily maintainable, and must be the optimum buy. If these conditions are met, the purchase is valid. If not, the best return is realized by leasing or renting from a reliable firm that will provide maintenance and repair.

Lastly, the equipment must work when it is needed. This can be ensured by rigorously following a scheduled preventive maintenance program and by developing quick and reliable access to expert, fully equipped repair personnel who are responsive to needs on short notice.

Administration

Within my frame of reference, the administration resource encompasses all the services and senior-management support the group needs to keep running smoothly. This includes clerical, payroll, transportation, mail, library support, and a myriad of other services—most of which we don't think about very much, all of which contribute to overhead.

Some managers take the administration resource for granted, not recognizing it as a resource that supports the group in getting its job done. Others pay only scant attention to it until some facet bogs down. Then the crash fix is on. This low-profile yet critically important resource must be nurtured and developed as keenly as any other resource, or the group's efficiency will fall off quickly. I've found that poor administration can quickly kill a group's initiative and industry, and only good administration will set it right.

The manager, as resource provider, must ensure that the group has those resources needed to get its job done efficiently—a job with constantly changing requirements. Little if any resource should be expended on nice-to-have and none on anything that gathers dust. Some backup resource should be available to cover those extra crash tasks and as a substitute for primary equipment when it is down for maintenance or repair.

Resource Monitoring

As managers, we should consider taking, from time to time, an inventory of the resources our group uses as to type, quantity, and quality. We should determine those resources the group needs to get its job done and those resources the group does not have or use.

Frittering Away Resources

Information motion-media shows are produced in many styles: narrative, cinema verité, kinestasis, theater of the mind, testimony, and inner thought, for example. While these are valid, fun, and exhilarating, they are expensive. Without careful planning and judicious implementation, these styles can cloud the essential elements of information. Complex structure involving, for example, elaborate subplots, retrograde development, and symbolism tends to confuse the inherent message. On the whole, standard, straightforward exposition and simple linear development will ensure maximum communication.

The list of over-embellished production values is long. Some deserve special mention because they often reflect flagrant squandering of resources and typify overall lack of management oversight. Some are:

- expensive name talent in front of and behind the camera (with the attendant folderol) when equally competent or superior talent is available at much less cost
- exotic locales when inexpensive sets or backdrops or even stock footage would suffice
- expensive sets and stage shooting when a nearby, easily accessible location is more apt
- costly special effects when simple models or other techniques would suffice
- complex effects when straight cuts would suffice

- elaborate staging and execution of a sequence requiring a large crew when a simple documentary approach would be more realistic
- complex digital animation when much simpler techniques would have near-equal communication value
- original score instead of stock music
- esoteric images that have meaning only to the designer/producer when conventional close-up photography has the real communication value

Spend Enough

Production and postproduction should be accomplished with minimum expense to make the show look natural yet not sterile. Spend enough resources to get maximum return on the investment. As managers, we should recognize the delicate balance between extravagance and miserliness. Sometimes in trying to achieve the optimum level, we'll not expend enough to accomplish the goals set for the show. With too many economies made in planning, production, and postproduction, the show may fail in its communication task. A successful show can have professional production values yet be produced under austere conditions. It depends on how the resources are expended. Austerity is achieved by concentrating on essentials.

Insufficient Funding

Sometimes, after the script and storyboard are completed and approved, the budget is cut. The manager must then make the fundamental decision to proceed or not. If the decision is to proceed, the show's scope must be reduced to accommodate the decreased budget. Again, we should strive for optimum communication within the new framework, maintaining a high level of quality and professionalism. If the scope cannot be reduced, it's best not to start. As an alternative, explore those communication media that require fewer resources and yet are communication-effective in their own fashion.

The Challenge

Managing a motion-media group is not for everyone. It's a weighty challenge, not to be taken with a cavalier attitude. Full commitment is required. Nothing else will do. The responsibilities will tax your skills to the maximum. The job is full-time: morning, afternoon, evening, and night. Yet for those who succeed, it's great. Personal reward and satisfaction abound. We know that we were instrumental in solving our client's problems. We were the catalysts in the professional growth of our people. We built a group who grew and flourished. Perhaps we just might get some recognition from senior management and our peers. How much better can professional life get?

Appendixes

Notes

Bibliography

Index

Appendix 1: Evaluating Information Motion-Media

One of the best ways to understand the fundamental essence of our information motion-media profession and to increase our script designing and producing skills is to view and evaluate the shows of others, especially the shows of those who've earned critical acclaim. Screening is not enough, however. We must analyze and critique (evaluate) such shows with the critical eye. Tackle this evaluation task with industry, objectivity, and verve. You'll find the experience most rewarding as you garner keen insight into the fundamentals of our profession.

Evaluating the work of others is serious business! Their work deserves our wholehearted professional commitment. As you might suspect, I've developed some rules and guidelines that you need to follow. Rules, tedious as they may be, are necessary to:

- establish professional standards
- maintain consistency in evaluation and scoring
- protect the integrity of the evaluations

This document (form) is prepared primarily for competition judges. Nonetheless, they will work for anyone with minor modification and innovation.

Evaluation Rules/Guidelines

1. Attached is a copy of the Motion-Media Evaluation sheet. Please be familiar with it before you begin viewing and evaluating. It's okay to duplicate this form for your personal use. If you want to use it in a professional manner, please contact me through the publisher, and let's negotiate a license use fee.

2. Before and after a show is screened, you'll be told the show's primary audience and purpose (communication objectives). If you need more information, just ask. If this information is not available, make an educated guess from the data you have and from what you can discern after you've screened the show.

3. Rely on the total scope of your experience as the basis for your evaluation.

4. Evaluate the show from the perspective, experience, values, and attitudes of the *intended audience*—not your own. Admittedly, this projection is very difficult, yet it's the most critically important criterion in the evaluation process.

5. Evaluate only what you see on the screen/monitor and hear from the speakers. All else is irrelevant! Don't be concerned with the budget or what the show could have been or should be or with the good intentions or effort expended. Only the end results as seen and heard are pertinent.

6. Be concerned with communication values rather than with gratuitous gimmicks and flashy folderol.

7. Immediately after you've screened a show, read each of the ten evaluation criteria on the Motion-Media Evaluation sheet, and mark each criterion with a score from 0 to 10. Decimals are okay. A mark of 5.0 is average. Don't be timid about using any number within the total range. (It's ordinary to have wide fluctuations in scoring marks among the ten criteria of any one show.)

8. It's critically important that you mark a score in each of the ten evaluation criteria. Not to do so results in an unfairly low evaluation. For instance, from time to time some shows have no or minimal artwork/animation, and therefore you can't make an objective evaluation of the art/animation criteria. In such instances, use the average score of the other nine evaluation criteria for the score for the art/animation criterion.

9. Fifty is the average score. That is, 50 is the score a competent, professionally produced show should get. It's rare for a show to score above 90 or below 10—perhaps one or two a session. Infrequently do shows score in the 80s or in the teens.

10. The average score of all the shows you evaluate ought to be about 50. The 50 average can vary somewhat when the shows are extraordinarily proficient or extremely inept.

11. If the average of all your scores is much above or below 50, reevaluate your standards and seriously consider rescoring the shows. Feel completely free to change your marks on a show that you believe you've scored too high or too low.

12. I recommend that you use pencil. It's easier to change.

13. I encourage you to make written comments on the Motion-Media Evaluation sheet. Then compare your scores with the narrative. Are they consistent? Inconsistent?

14. Evaluating a show is a learning experience for all of us. To this end, discussion is encouraged after a screening and during the scoring. Try to keep comments short and to a minimum during the screening.

Motion-Media Evaluation

Title _____ Evaluation Total _____

Target Audience _____

Purpose. To _____

_____

Producer _____

Client/Sponsor _____

_____

Evaluation Criteria

0.0 is total imperfection. 5.0 is average. 10.0 is perfection. Evaluate the ten criteria with a number from 0 to 10. Decimals are OK.

_____

Subjective Evaluation

How did you like this show? Use a number from 0 to 10. Vent your personal prejudices, pro or con here. Then use the remainder of this evaluation sheet to score the show in a detached professional manner.

Score _____

Communication Value

Consider the target audience for this show.

OBJECTIVES. How well does this show accomplish its stated objectives? Consider the appropriateness of this show as a communication tool to achieve the stated goals: goals that must be *fitting*, *realistic*, *worthwhile*, and *well articulated*.

Score _____

THEME. Does this show have a clear vision and tone that communicate a sharply focused central theme to the target audience? Are resources (capital, energy, and screen time) used optimally? Are the essential elements of information developed logically, clearly, succinctly, and in the proper tone? Is communication engendered to maximum effectiveness with *minimum* expenditure of resources?

Score _____

INFORMATION. Is the bulk of the information in the visuals? Do the visuals enhance communication to full measure? Is the show's message communicated effectively through relevant *filmic design* and *visual continuity*? Are visuals and narration in coherence?

Score _____

APPROACH/EMPATHY. Does this show have a fresh and imaginative approach that facilitates information flow? Is the approach *pertinent*? Is creativity basic and *deliberately concealed*? Will the target audience accept this show? Does the approach generate empathy to gain and hold the audience's attention and involvement? Does the approach reinforce audience interest and commitment?

Score _____

AUDIO. Do audio elements reinforce the visuals? Is narration or dialog used only to tell the audience what they cannot perceive from the visuals yet must know for a complete understanding? Do music and sound effects contribute to communication?

Score _____

Technical Quality

CINEMATOGRAPHY. Is the cinematography/videography technically excellent? Is the composition aesthetically pleasing? Does the photography facilitate communication by highlighting important information? Does the lighting set an appropriate mood? Does the lighting have continuity throughout individual scenes?

Score _____

SOUND. Is the sound crisp and clear? Are words pronounced for proper emphasis and spoken at the appropriate pace and style? Are sound elements blended to achieve a harmonious show?

Score _____

EDITING. Are visuals sequenced to achieve optimum communication? Is plasticity of the medium (manipulation of time and space) used optimally to maintain orientation and to facilitate an appropriate information flow? Is the pace appropriately varied, and does it reinforce communication objectives? Is screen direction used effectively to create harmony and dissonance?

Score _____

ART. Is the art style appropriate with the tenor of the show? Are art elements and spatial relationships used to accentuate key points? Is perspective true? Are shading and highlighting used to create depth and for emphasis? Are form, mass, and color arranged in compositions that heighten communication?

Score _____

Add your individual scores and put the total on the top, right side of the front page.

* * *

Please make narrative comments to support your numerical evaluation.

Evaluator _____ Date _____

Appendix 2: 101 Classic Documentary Films

Film data are presented in the following sequence:
- film title
- filmmaker(s)
- length
- release date
- producing organization/sponsor (as applicable)
- country of origin
- significant award(s)

Aero Engine. Arthur Elton; 55 min., 1933, Empire Marketing Board, England.

American Time Capsule. Chuck Braverman; 4 min., 1968, Braverman Productions, U.S.A.

Ballet Adagio. Norman McLaren; 10 min., 1971, National Film Board of Canada, Canada. Bronze Plaque, Columbus Film Festival.

Ballet Robotique. Bob Rogers; 8 min., 1982, Bob Rogers and Company, U.S.A. Academy Award nomination, 1983.

Ballon Rouge, Le (The Red Balloon). Albert Lamorisse; 34 min., 1956, Films Montouris-Col/Col, France. Academy Award, 1957; Palme d'Or, Cannes Film Festival, 1957; Gold Medal, Grand Prix of the French Cinema, 1957.

Battle of San Pietro. Maj. John Huston, U.S. Army; 37 min., 1945, Signal Corps of U.S. Army, U.S.A.

Battleship Potemkin. Sergei Eisenstein; 75 min., 1925, First Studio of Gosinko, Union of Soviet Socialist Republics.

BBC: The Voice of Britain. Stuart Legg and Alberto Cavalcanti; 56 min., 1935, General Post Office Film Unit for the British Broadcasting Corporation, England. Médaille d'Honneur, Brussels International Film Festival, 1935.

Bead Game. Ishu Patel; 6 min., 1977, National Film Board of Canada, Canada.

Belle Époque, La (Paris 1900). Nicole Védres; 91 min., 1947, Pantheon-Productions Pierre Braumberger, France.

Berlin: Die Sinfonie der Grosstadt (Berlin: Symphony of a Great City). Walter Ruttman; 70 min., 1927, Fox-Europa, Germany.

Bolero, The. Allan Miller and William Fertik; 26 min., 1972, Allan Miller Productions, U.S.A. Academy Award, 1973.

Bridge, The. Joris Ivens; 12 min., 1928, Capi-Amsterdam, Holland.

Chelovek S Kinoapparatom (Man with the Movie-Camera, The). Dziga Vertov; 69 min., 1929, Vufku, Ukraine, Union of Soviet Socialist Republics.

Civil War, The. Ken Burns; 7 hours, 1989, Florentine Films and WETA (Public Television), Washington, D.C., U.S.A. Emmy Award, Academy of Television Arts and Sciences, 1991.

City, The. Willard Van Dyke and Ralph Steiner; 44 min., 1939, *American Documentary Films for the American Institute of Planners, U.S.A.*

Claymation. Will Vinton and Susan Shadburne; 18 min., 1978, Will Vinton Productions, U.S.A. First Place, San Francisco International Film Festival.

Coal Face. Stuart Legg and Alberto Cavalcanti; 10 min., 1935, Empo (General Post Office Film Unit), England. Médaille d'Honneur, Brussels International Film Festival, 1935.

Contact. Paul Rotha; 42 min., 1933, British Instructional Films for Imperial Airways, Ltd., Shell-Mex, and British Petroleum, Ltd., England.

Crac! Frédéric Back; 15 min., 1981, Société Radio-Canada, Canada. Academy Award, 1982.

Cummington Story, The. Irving Lerner and Helen Grayson; 20 min., 1945, U.S. Office of War Information, U.S.A.

December 7th. Lt. Comdr. John Ford, U.S. Navy; 34 min., 1942, Coordinator of Information (Office of Strategic Services) for U.S. Navy, U.S.A. Academy Award, 1943.

Desert Victory. Ray Boulting and Major David MacDonald; 60 min., 1943, British Army Film and Photographic Unit and the Royal Air Force Film Production Unit for Ministry of Information, England. Academy Award, 1943.

Diary for Timothy. Humphrey Jennings and Basil Wright; 39 min., 1945, Crown Film Unit, Ministry of Information, England.

Drifters. John Grierson; 50 min., 1929, Empire Marketing Board Film Unit, England.

Eagle Has Landed: The Flight of Apollo 11. 29 min., 1969, National Aeronautics and Space Administration. U.S.A. Ionosphere Award, Atlanta International Film Festival.

Easter Island (original title, *L'Ile de Pâques*). Henri Strock and John Ferno; 25 min., 1935, France/Belgium coproduction.

Enough to Eat. Edgar Anstey; 22 min., 1936, Associated Realist Film Producers for Gas, Light, and Coke Company, England.

Entr'acte (Between the Acts). René Clair; 14 min., 1924, independent production, France.

Face of Britain. Paul Rotha; 19 min., 1935, Gaumont-British Instructional, Ltd., England. Médaille d'Honneur, Brussels International Film Festival, 1936.

Face of Lincoln. Wilber T. Blume and Dick Harber; 22 min., 1954, Cinema Department, University of Southern California, U.S.A. Academy Award, 1955.

Farrebique. Georges Rouquier and Étienne Lallier; 85 min., 1947, L'Ecran Français and Les Films Étienne Lallier, France.

Fiddlededee. Norman McLaren; 3 min., 1947, National Film Board of Canada, Canada. First Prize, Salerno Film Festival.

Fighting Lady, The. Louis de Rochemont; 61 min., 1944, Twentieth-Century Fox for U.S. Navy, U.S.A. Academy Award, 1945.

Fires Were Started. Humphrey Jennings; 74 min., 1943, Crown Film Unit of the Central Office of Information, England.

Flight of the Gossamer Condor. Ben Shedd; 27 min., 1977, Shedd Productions, U.S.A. Academy Award, 1978.

General Line, The (The Old and New). Sergei Eisenstein and Grigori Alexandrov; 90 min., 1929, Sovkino-Moscow, Union of Soviet Socialist Republics.

Granton Trawler. John Grierson; 11 min., 1934, Empire Marketing Board, England.

Harlan County, USA. Barbara Koppel; 103 min., 1975, Cabin Creek Films, U.S.A. Academy Award, 1976.

Housing Problems. Arthur Elton and Edgar Anstey; 17 min., 1935, Associated Realist Film Producers for the British Commercial Gas Association, England.

If You Love This Planet. Terri Nash; 26 min., 1981, National Film Board of Canada, Canada. Academy Award, 1982.

Industrial Britain. John Grierson, Robert Flaherty, and Edgar Anstey; 21 min., 1933, Empire Marketing Board, released by Gaumont British Picture Corporation, England.

John F. Kennedy: Years of Lightning, Days of Drums. Produced by George Stevens Jr., written and directed by Bruce Herschensohn; 88 min., 1964, United States Information Agency for the John F. Kennedy Center for the Performing Arts, U.S.A. Golden Eagle, Council of International Nontheatrical Events, 1965.

Kon Tiki. Thor Heyerdahl; 70 min., 1947, RKO Radio/Janus, Sweden.

Kornet er i Fare (The Corn Is in Danger). Hagen Hasselbalch; 9 min., 1944, Nordisk Films Kompagni, Denmark.

L'Amitié Noire (Black Friendship). Jean Cocteau; 20 min., 1944, independent production, France.

Land, The. Robert Flaherty; 44 min., 1941, U.S. Film Service for the Department of Agriculture, U.S.A.

Las Hurdes (Tierra sin Pan, Land Without Bread). Luis Buñuel and Pierre Unik; 27 min., 1933, Spain.

Lefty. James Thompson; 55 min., 1980, DBA Entertainment, U.S.A. Gold Cindy, Information Film Producers of America, 1982.

Les Mystères du Chateau de Dé (The Mysteries of the Chateau de Dé). Man Ray; 26 min., 1929, independent production, France.

Listen to Britain. Humphrey Jennings and Ian Dalrymple; 18 min., 1942, Crown Film Unit of the Central Office of Information, England. Academy Award nomination, 1943.

Louisiana Story. Robert Flaherty; 45 min., 1948, sponsored by Standard Oil Company of New Jersey, U.S.A.

Magic Rolling Board. Greg MacGillivray and Jim Freeman; 14 min., 1980, MacGillivray-Freeman Productions, U.S.A. Gold Cindy, Information Film Producers of America, 1981.

Man of Aran. Robert Flaherty; 62 min., 1934, Gaumont-British, England.

Memphis Belle. Lt. Col. William Wyler, U.S. Army Air Force; 43 min., 1944, Eighth Air Force of the U.S. Army Air Force, U.S.A.

Moana: A Romance of the Golden Age. Robert Flaherty; 85 min., 1926, Famous-Players-Lasky (Paramount), U.S.A.

Motion Painting I. Oskar Fischinger; 11 min., 1947, U.S.A.

My Father's Son. Gerald T. Rogers; 33 min., 1984, Gerald T. Rogers Productions, U.S.A. Best of Show, Cindy Competition, Information Film Producers of America, 1985.

Nanook of the North. Robert Flaherty; 54 min., 1922, Revillon Frères, U.S.A.

Native Land. Leo Hurwitz and Paul Strand; 88 min., 1942, Frontier Films, U.S.A.

Neighbours. Norman McLaren; 9 min., 1952, National Film Board of Canada, Canada. Academy Award, 1953.

Nieuwe Gronden (New Earth). Joris Ivens; 23 min., 1934, Capi-Amsterdam, Holland.

Night Mail. John Grierson, Harry Watt, and Basil Wright; 23 min., 1936, General Post Office Film Unit, England.

North Sea. Alberto Cavalcanti and Harry Watt; 26 min., 1938, General Post Office Film Unit, England.

Nuit et Brouillard (Night and Fog). Alain Resnais; 31 min., 1955, Cocinor Films, France.

NY, NY. Francis Thompson; 16 min., 1957, Francis Thompson Agency, U.S.A.

Olympia: Fest der Völker (Olympiad) (in two parts). Leni Riefenstahl; 3½ hours, 1936, Olympia Film, Berlin, sponsored by National-sozialistische Deutsche Arbeiterpartei for Reich Ministry of Public Enlightenment and Propaganda, Germany.

Pas de Deux. Norman McLaren; 13 min., 1967, National Film Board of Canada, Canada. Academy Award nomination, 1968.

Plow That Broke the Plains, The. Pare Lorentz; 29 min., 1936, U.S. Resettlement Administration, U.S.A.

Power and the Land. Joris Ivens; 39 min., 1940, U.S. Film Service for the Rural Electrification Administration, U.S.A.

Powers of Ten: A Film Dealing with the Relative Size of Things in the Universe and the Effects of Adding Another Zero. Charles Eames and Ray Eames; 9 min., 1978, Ray and Charles Eames Productions for IBM, U.S.A. Gold Medal, Miami International Film Festival, 1979.

Prelude to War (first of seven films in the *Why We Fight* series). Maj. Frank Capra, U.S. Army; 54 min., 1942, Special Services of the Orientation Branch of the War Department, U.S.A. Academy Award, 1943.

Quiet One, The. Sidney Meyers, Janice Loeb, and James Agee; 67 min., 1949, Film Documents, U.S.A.

Redes (The Wave). Paul Strand and Fred Zinnemann; 60 min., 1936, Secretariat of Education, Mexico.

Regen (Rain). Joris Ivens; 15 min., 1929 (sound added 1932), Capi-Amsterdam, Holland.

Retour, Le (The Return). Henri Cartier-Bresson and André Bac; 34 min., 1946, independent production, photography by U.S. Army Signal Corps and U.S. Army Air Corps cinematographers, France.

Rien que les Heures (Nothing but the Hours). Alberto Cavalcanti; 45 min., 1926, independent production, France.

River, The. Pare Lorentz; 32 min., 1937, U.S.D.A. Farm Security Administration for the U.S. Resettlement Administration, U.S.A. World Prize for Best Documentary, Venice International Film Festival, 1938.

Roma, Città Aperta (Open City). Roberto Rossellini; 103 min., 1945, Excelsia Film, Italy. Grand Prize, Venice International Film Festival, 1946.

School in the Mail Box. Stanley Hawes; 18 min., 1946, Australian News and Information Bureau, Australia. Academy Award nomination, 1947.

Shipyard. Paul Rotha; 24 min., 1935, Gaumont-British Instructional for Orient Shipping Line, England.

Silent Witness, The. David W. Rolfe; 55 min., 1978, U.S.A. Flaherty Award, Best Documentary, British Film Academy, 1979.

Skuggor Over Snon (Shadows on the Snow). Arne Sucksdorff; 10 min., 1945, Svensk Filmindustri, Sweden.

Song of Ceylon. Basil Wright; 40 min., 1935, General Post Office Film Unit for the Ceylon Tea Propaganda Board, England. Prix du Gouvernement, Brussels International Film Festival, 1935.

Spanish Earth. Joris Ivens and Ernest Hemingway; 55 min., 1937, Contemporary Historians, Inc., U.S.A.

Survival Run. Robert Charlton and Joaquin Padro; 12 min., 1981, independent production, U.S.A. Grand Prix, Informfilm European Business and Industry Film Festival, 1982.

Swinging the Lambeth Walk. Lyn Lye; 4 min., 1940, Associated Realist Film Producers for Travel and Industrial Development Association, England.

Target for Tonight. Harry Watt and Ian Dalrymple; 50 min., 1941, Crown Film Unit, Ministry of Information, England.

Ten Days That Shook the World. Sergei Eisenstein; 105 min., 1928, Sovkino-Moscow, Union of Soviet Socialist Republics.

Transfer of Power: The History of the Toothed Wheel. Arthur Elton and Geoffrey Bell; 21 min., 1939, Shell Film Unit, England.

Triumph des Willens (Triumph of the Will). Leni Riefenstahl and Albert Speer; 110 min., 1936, Universum-Film, A.G., Berlin, sponsored by Nationalsozialistische Deutsche Arbeiterpartei for Reich Ministry for Public Enlightenment and Propaganda, Germany.

True Glory, The. Garson Kanin and Carol Reed; 85 min., 1945, Film and Photographic Section of SHAEF (Supreme Headquarters Allied Expeditionary Force) for U.S. Office of War Information and Ministry of Information of Great Britain, U.S.A./England. Academy Award, 1946.

299 Foxtrot. S. Martin Shelton; 10 min., 1977, Naval Weapons Center for U.S. Navy, U.S.A. Gold Camera Award, U.S. Industrial Film Festival, 1978.

Universe. Lester Novros; 26 min., 1976, Graphic Film Corporation for National Aeronautics and Space Administration, U.S.A. Academy Award nomination, 1977.

Un Chien Andalou (An Andalusian Dog). Luis Buñuel and Salvador Dali; 16 min., 1929, independent production, Spain.

Urban Spaces. Paul Winkler; 27 min., 1980, independent production, Australia.

Victory at Sea. Henry Solomon, music by Richard Rogers; 26 half-hour programs, 1952, National Broadcasting System, U.S.A. Emmy Award, Academy of Television Arts and Sciences, 1953.

Walk in the Forest. Randall Hood; 28 min., 1978, independent production, Canada. Best of Show, Cindy Competition, Information Film Producers of America, 1980.

Waverly Steps. John Eldridge; 25 min., 1948, Crown Film Unit of the Central Office of Information, England.

Western Approaches. Pat Jackson; 80 min., 1944, Crown Film Unit of the Central Office of Information, England.

Why Man Creates. Saul Bass; 25 min., 1968, Saul Bass & Associates for Kaiser Aluminum and Chemical Corporation, U.S.A. Academy Award, 1969.

Zem Spieva (The Earth Sings). Karek Plicka; 67 min., 1932, independent production, Czechoslovakia.

Norman McLaren drawing directly on 35 mm film for a scene from his film *Begone Dull Care* (1949). Courtesy National Film Board of Canada.

Leni Riefenstahl directing a scene for the film *Triumph des Willens (Triumph of the Will)* in Nuremberg, Germany, at the National Socialist German Workers Party rally, 1934. Courtesy Deutsche Presse-Agentur, Frankfurt.

Maj. Frank Capra, U.S. Army, in 1943, producer of the *Why We Fight* series of propaganda films for American audiences during World War II. Copyright © Academy of Motion Picture Arts and Sciences.

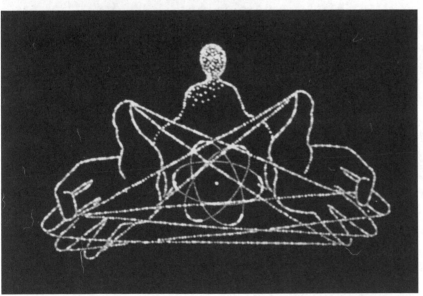

Scene from Ishu Patel's film *Bead Game*, released in 1977 by the National Film Board of Canada. Courtesy National Film Board of Canada.

John Grierson (1898–1972), founder of the documentary film movement and of the National Film Board of Canada *(left)*, working in the studio of the National Film Board of Canada in Montreal, 1945. Courtesy National Film Board of Canada.

Lt. Comdr. John Ford, U.S. Navy, on the sound stage of the Naval Photographic Center, Anacostia, Washington, D.C., directing the Academy Award–winning film *December 7th,* 1943. Ford is the officer with the flat hat in the left center of the photograph. Courtesy National Archives.

Lt. Col. William Wyler at the U.S. Army Air Forces Base in Archbury, England, 1943, directing the Academy Award–winning film *Memphis Belle.* Wyler is the officer in the center of the photograph wearing the flat hat. Courtesy Mrs. William Wyler and the Theater Arts Library, UCLA.

Still frame from *Triumph des Willens (Triumph of the Will)*, directed and produced by Leni Riefenstahl for the National Socialist German Workers Party rally, Nuremberg, Germany, 1934. Courtesy of National Audiovisual Center, Washington, D.C.

After resting for years in the Naval Weapons Center's aircraft boneyard at China Lake, California, the B-29 aircraft *299 Foxtrot* is airborne again after a short takeoff roll from the NWC's Armitage Field on 15 June 1976. The *299 Foxtrot* was restored by a group of aviation historians and air force personnel. The craft is now on display at March Air Force Base in Riverside, California. Courtesy U.S. Navy.

Appendix 3: Communication Analysis Plan, Split-Page Script, and Storyboard

The Scarf: The Perennial Fashion Statement

Split-Page Script by
Louise D. Burnham
and S. Martin Shelton

Storyboard by
Olivia Francis

Copyright © 1996 by
S. Martin Shelton

Communication Analysis Plan

Today's Date: 00 Month 0000

Proposed title: *The Scarf: The Perennial Fashion Statement*
Reason to produce this motion-media show: *To introduce our new scarf line into our nationwide boutique chain*
Target audience: *Upscale female shoppers, keen on fashion*
Purpose: *To motivate the target audience to buy our new line of scarves*

Target audience profile

Identification factors

Demographic: *Youthful (20s to 40s), female, single or married*
Socioeconomic: *Cross-section of female population, leaning toward affluent*
Psychological: *Aggressive, stylish, sophisticated*

Motivation factors

Anticipation: *Piqued through trade-show "pitch"*
Importance of goal achievement: *Fashion conscious, need to be on "cutting edge"*
Urgency of communication: *High. Fashion vogue changes rapidly.*
Information currency/obsolescence: *Six to twelve months*

Predisposition factors

Sponsor: *Sympathetic*
Communicator: *Neutral*
Information: *Interested. The show keeps audience* au courant.
Medium: *Positive. This is the electronic-media generation.*

Secondary audience: Boutique buyers and sales personnel who assist customers by suggesting items to wear and buy

Essential elements of information

1. *Scarves and their derivatives have been used throughout history.*
2. *The scarf is a versatile fashion accessory.*
3. *We offer a potpourri of scarves: sizes, colors, patterns, fabrics.*
4. *The quality of Acme Scarves is preeminent.*

Technical quality needed: *Technically excellent, sophisticated, polished*
Interaction: *Sales associate*

Schedule

Research: *7 days* Production: *14 days*
Treatment: *5 days* Postproduction: *8 days*
Script first draft: *3 days* Duplication: *2 days*
Final script draft: *3 days* Distribution: *1 week*

Filmic approach

Tenor: *Dramatic, upbeat, stylish, fast-paced, exciting*
Milieu: *Various historical and contemporary locations featuring models wearing, as appropriate, our new line of scarves*
Characteristics: *Models/actors, locations, still photographs, original contemporary music*
Form: *Film in Super-16mm color; distribute on* DVD

Communication surround

Audience size at each screening: *In the range of one to four in our boutiques; dozens at our trade shows*
Frequency of screening: *Continuous throughout the day at trade shows; when appropriate for customers in the boutiques*
Physical environment of the viewing site: *Booth at trade shows, and at point-of-sale display near the scarf counter in the boutiques*
Leader or proctor: *Acme sales associates in our boutiques and in our booths at trade shows*
Projection/viewing equipment: *Acme-designed table-top* DVD *player*
Projectionist: *Acme sales associates*
Power requirements: *Standard 110V to 115V, AC*
Backup material and equipment: *Elegant point-of-sale display, models and manikins showing Acme's line of scarves, sample scarves, and color brochure handouts*

Controlling factors

Due date: *Early November: in time for spring fashion-trade shows*
Serialized: *No*
Part of total communication package: *Extensive advertising campaign in appropriate fashion media, sample scarves to boutique buyers, point-of-sale handouts*
Changes or updates: *Yes. Models' attire needs to reflect seasonal offerings.*
Technical and political production considerations: *Need coordination and permission to film on Fifth Avenue in NYC and in the various other locations noted in the script*
Hazards and safety considerations: *Blocking off Fifth Avenue and other concerns we'll determine at each location*

Client concerns

Image projected: *High fashion. Scarves are the answer for variety in all wardrobes.*

Company/organization policy: *Acme Scarves is the vanguard of fashion.*

Legal aspects: *Music and still photographs clearances; model/actor releases; "Work for Hire" document for all crew members; liability insurance and completion bond*

Political impact: *None*

Proprietary information: *All scarf designs are proprietary information. Do not release before the first November trade show.*

Classified information: *Acme Scarves' proprietary*

Budget

Script/storyboard: *$65,000*

Production: *$350,000*

Distribution: *$75,000*

Medium selection

Producing medium: *Super-16mm color-negative film*

Primary distribution medium: *DVD*

Secondary distribution medium: *None*

Distribution scheme: *2,550 DVDs*

Key personnel

Client/sponsor

Organization: *Acme Scarves, Inc.*

Name(s)of contact(s): *Ms. Penelope Worthington-Smythe and Ms. Brigid O'Shaughnessy-Falcon*

Job title: *Marketing Directors*

Telephone number/e-mail/fax: Phone: *(212) xx6-5000*

Address: *One Penn Square, Pennsylvania Station, New York, NY 10011*

Technical advisor/subject matter expert

Name: *Ms. Amelia Ebberhart-Putnam*

Job title: *Coordinator of the Liaison*

Organization: *Public affairs department*

Telephone number/e-mail/fax: *(212) xx6-5001*

Address: *Two Penn Square, Pennsylvania Station, New York, NY 10011*

Client/sponsor approval authority

Name: *Ms. Madeleine de' Sunderman-Wo*
Job title: *Chief Executive Officer*
Organization: *Corporate office*
Telephone number/e-mail/fax: *(212) xx6-5002*
Address: *Three Penn Square, Pennsylvania Station, New York, NY 10011*

Producer

Name: *Ms. Amanda Lupercio-Pirogoff*
Job title: *Executive Producer*
Organization: *Supercolossal Productions, LLC*
Telephone number/e-mail/fax: *(202) xxx-9999*
Address: *1776 Avenue Z, SSW, Washington, DC 20408*

Script designer

Name: *Ms. Miles Archer-Spade*
Job title: *Script designer extraordinaire*
Organization: *Dial-A-Script, Ltd.*
Telephone number/e-mail/fax: *(775) xxx-8888*
Address: *6½ Sagebrush Trail, Tonopah, NV 89050*

Split-Page Script

FADE IN	**FADE IN MUSIC**
Main title. The Scarf: The Perennial Fashion Statement	(Music is soft jazz piano accompanied with bass, snare drums, and xylophone.)
FADE OUT	
FADE IN	**SEGUE**
Scene # 1 A, B, C, and D. Start this scene with a MEDIUM SHOT of old black-and-white photographs of Isadora Duncan dancing. She wears scarves. Build montage of other photographs showing her dancing with scarves wafting about. Vary with CLOSE SHOTS, MEDIUM SHOTS, and LONG SHOTS.	(Music from the Roaring '20s as appropriate to Duncan's dance style.)
DISSOLVE TO	**SEGUE**
Scene # 2 A, B, C, D, E, F, G, and H. Montage of historic "scarves on parade"—people from different cultures wearing scarves: for example, veils and dance paraphernalia on Middle Eastern dancer; sari on Indian woman; babushka on old Russian woman; kerchief on Swiss milkmaid; ascot tucked into overcoat of Dickens-era dandy; turban and scarf on pre–Civil War female slave; Western desperado wearing kerchief over lower face; wraparound scarves on bikini-clad South Pacific islanders. Vary with CLOSE SHOTS, MEDIUM SHOTS, and LONG SHOTS.	(Lively musical vignettes appropriate for the montage.)
DISSOLVE TO	**SEGUE**
Scene # 3A. CLOSE-UP in SLOW MOTION of extremely long chiffon scarf rippling in the breeze against a sunset sky.	(Contemporary romantic mood-music.)

PAN RIGHT TO REVEAL SCENE # 3B

Scene # 3B. MEDIUM SHOT. The scarf is part of an elegant woman's evening attire. She is with a male companion. They are leaning against a cruise ship's rail.

CONTINUE MUSIC

(Music UP slightly.)

DISSOLVE TO

Scene #4. MEDIUM SHOT of upscale shopping district of Fifth Avenue in New York. The scene is busy with shoppers. Most are walking left to right.

SEGUE

(Big-band orchestra plays appropriate "city" music. Add sound effects: beeps, honks, traffic, and other city sounds.)

PAN RIGHT TO REVEAL SCENE # 5

Scene # 5. MEDIUM LONG SHOT. The camera concentrates on a solitary woman walking briskly screen left (opposite most of the foot traffic.) She is outfitted with a yellow wool dress accented with a bright, multihued floral-print-on-black-background scarf worn as a sash and tied at the waist. She is elegant. Carries a briefcase. Obviously, she is a businesswoman.

SEGUE

(Solo saxophone plays a contemporary jazz tune that is counterpoint to the music in scene #4. FADE OUT gradually the sound effects. Music UP as the scene plays.)

FADE OUT MUSIC

CUT TO

Scene # 6. TIGHT CLOSE SHOT of woman looking into a mirror and casually adjusting an earring that is situated below her contemporary and attractive scarf, worn as a headband.

CAMERA DOLLIES BACK slightly to reveal more of the scene. The ambiance of the scene tells us that the woman could be an artist. We see paints and an easel in the mirrored background.

FADE IN MUSIC

(The music is upbeat, soft contemporary-rock played softly.)

CUT TO	SEGUE AND MUSIC UP

Scene # 7 A, B, and C. Build a filmic design MONTAGE of MEDIUM CLOSE and CLOSE SHOTS cut in rhythm to the semi-rapid beat of the music. Several women in different professional environments: bank, hospital, computer laboratory, kindergarten. They sport multi-colored scarves draped variously from front-to-back and side-to-side as shawls, bibs, and cowls.

(Contemporary jazz with a semi-rapid beat.)

CUT TO	CONTINUE MUSIC

Scene # 8. MEDIUM LONG SHOT of woman cinching a long scarf as a belt. She is in front of a free-standing mirror.

(The beat slows.)

CUT TO	SEGUE

Scene # 9 A, B, and C. Build filmic design montage of EXTREME CLOSE SHOTS and CLOSE SHOTS of women roping and knotting scarves on themselves as a necktie, bow tie, rosette, and collar.

(Music is soft jazz piano accompanied with base, snare drums, and xylophone. The same as in the main title scene.)

DISSOLVE TO	CONTINUE MUSIC

Scene # 10. LONG SHOT of a nattily dressed woman in our upscale Fifth Avenue boutique. She is browsing a display of our new line of scarves.

(Beat increases slightly.)

MATCH ACTION CUT	CONTINUE MUSIC

Scene # 11A. EXTREME CLOSE SHOT of scarf display. Our brand, Acme Scarves Inc., is displayed tastefully.

(Volume UP slightly.)

MATCH ACTION CUT	CONTINUE MUSIC

Scene # 11B. MEDIUM SHOT of the woman selecting a multicolored scarf. We see that our brand is sharply focused.

(As we build to the climax, the music is UP gradually.)

MATCH ACTION CUT	CONTINUE MUSIC

Scene # 12A. MEDIUM LONG SHOT of the woman noticing that the colors of the selected scarf complement her outfit.

(The music is UP slightly more.)

MATCH ACTION CUT	CONTINUE MUSIC

Scene # 12B. MEDIUM LONG SHOT of woman. She begins to drape and tie the scarf this way and that. With each variation, she sees harmony.

(Continue building the music to a climatic volume.)

MATCH ACTION CUT	CONTINUE MUSIC

Scene # 12C. MEDIUM CLOSE SHOT (TWO SHOT) of woman and sales associate. Woman smiles, unties the scarf, and hands it over the counter to the sales associate to make a purchase.

(Music is UP.)

ZOOM IN	CONTINUE MUSIC

Scene # 12D. TIGHT CLOSE SHOT of our name and logo, which clearly are visible on the scarf.

(Music is UP FULL and ends with a flourish.)

FADE OUT	FADE OUT MUSIC

Storyboard for *The Scarf: The Perennial Fashion Statement*

1D

CUT TO

Scene continues.

(SOUND)

(Music continues from 1 C.)

2A

DISSOLVE TO CLOSE UPS

A sequence begins of historic "scarves on parade" (live action). Veils and dance accoutrements on Middle Eastern dancer.

(SOUND)

(Lively music appropriate to the scene.)

2B

CUT TO

CLOSE UP. Sari on Indian Woman.

(SOUND)

(Music changes to correspond to scene.)

2C

CUT TO

CLOSE UP. Babushka on old Russian grandmother.

(SOUND)

(Music changes to correspond to scene.)

2D

CUT TO

LONG SHOT of Swiss milkmaid and ZOOM into tight CLOSE UP.

(SOUND)

(Music changes to correspond to scene.)

2E

CUT TO

CLOSE UP. Ascot tucked into overcoat of Dickens-era man in Scotland.

(SOUND)

(Music changes to correspond to scene.)

2F

CUT TO

CLOSE UP. Turbans on pre-civil war female.

(SOUND)

(Music changes to correspond to scene.)

2G

CUT TO

MEDIUM LONG SHOT of western desperado wearing kerchief over lower face, ZOOM into tight CLOSE UP of face.

(SOUND)

(Music changes to correspond to scene.)

CUT TO

Tight CLOSE UP of bikini on South Sea Islander. ZOOM out to full shot to show several dancers. PAN RIGHT and dissolve into scene 3.

(SOUND)

(Music changes to correspond to scene.)

DISSOLVE

To CLOSE UP of long chiffons rippling, SLOW MOTION, in a breeze against a sunset sky. Sunset colors create a smooth transition between 2 H and 3 A. PAN RIGHT to reveal scene 3 B.

(SOUND)

(Contemporary mood music, in sharp contrast to previous music.)

MEDIUM TWO SHOT of woman and man leaning on ship's rail. We see the scarf on the woman — a part of her evening attire.

(SOUND)

(Music continues from 3 A.)

DISSOLVE

MEDIUM SHOT of Fifth Avenue, New York City. It's busy with shoppers. Most are walking left to right. Camera PANS right to scene 5.

(SOUND)

(Orchestra plays appropriate "city" music, mixing occasional beeps, toots and honks for effect.)

Reveals in MEDIUM LONG SHOT a solitary woman walking in opposite direction (left to right) as if to greet the crowd. She is out-fitted with a yellow wool dress, accented with a bright, multihued floral-print-on-black-background scarf worn as a sash and tied at the waist. She is elegant and businesslike carrying a briefcase — obviously a professional woman.

(SOUND)

(Solo saxophone heard, playing a melody that is a counterpoint to a previous music.)

CUT TO

EXTREME CLOSE UP of woman looking into a mirror and casually adjusting an earring that just happens to be situated right below her very contemporary and attractive scarf worn as a headband. She is a painter. There are paints, brushes and an easel seen mirrored in the background.

(SOUND)

(Lively but soft music with a beat.)

CUT TO

Build sequence MEDIUM CLOSE SHOTS of several professional women sporting multicolor scarves in different environments. All sport multicolor scarves drapped variously from front-to-back and side-to-side, as shawl, bib and cowl. Banker with shawl.

(SOUND)

(Music continues.)

CUT TO

Kindergarten teacher with bib.

(SOUND)

(Music continues.)

7C

CUT TO

Systems analyst with cowl.

(SOUND)

(Music continues.)

8

CUT TO

MEDIUM LONG SHOT of woman cinching a long scarf as a belt in front of free-standing mirror.

(SOUND)

(Music continues.)

9A

CUT TO

Extreme CLOSE UPS of women roping and knotting narrow scarves on themselves as neckties, bowties, "rosettes" and collars. CLOSE UP of woman with bowtie.

(SOUND)

(Music continues.)

9B

CUT TO

Extreme CLOSE UP of a woman with a scarf as a "rosette."

(SOUND)

(Music continues.)

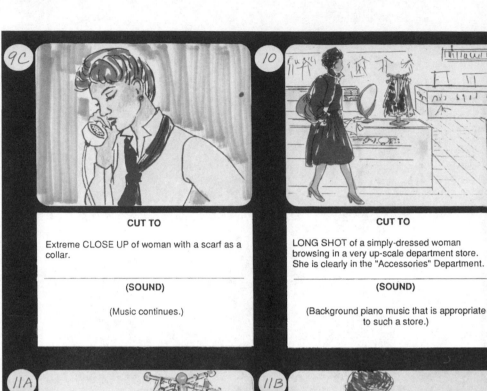

9C

CUT TO

Extreme CLOSE UP of woman with a scarf as a collar.

(SOUND)

(Music continues.)

10

CUT TO

LONG SHOT of a simply-dressed woman browsing in a very up-scale department store. She is clearly in the "Accessories" Department.

(SOUND)

(Background piano music that is appropriate to such a store.)

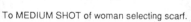

11A

CUT TO

EXTREME CLOSE UP of scarf on display in the Accessories area. Manufacturer's logo is visible. Woman's arm and hand enter frame from screen left to right.

(SOUND)

(Music continues.)

11B

ZOOM OUT

To MEDIUM SHOT of woman selecting scarf.

(SOUND)

(Music continues.)

CUT TO

MEDIUM SHOT of woman with scarf. She checks to ensure that the scarf complements her outfit.

(SOUND)

(Music continues, with a slightly more up tempo beat.)

CUT TO

MEDIUM LONG SHOT of woman as she drapes and ties the scarf this way and that. With each variation she sees harmony.

(SOUND)

(Music continues.)

CUT TO

MEDIUM CLOSE SHOT of woman. She smiles, unties the scarf and hands it to an approaching salesperson. As woman hands scarf to salesperson...

(SOUND)

(Music continues.)

ZOOM IN

To TIGHT CLOSE UP of manufacturers name on the scarf. FADE OUT.

(SOUND)

(Music ends with a flourish.)

(FADE OUT)

Appendix 4: Information Teleplay

Gambling Addiction and the Family

(opening scene)

By Jack Walker

EXT. SUBURBAN NEIGHBORHOOD - DAWN

Gray light and murky shadows. The ghostly, insubstantial hour between night and day. Jane trudges up the sidewalk, a flimsy windbreaker zipped over her pink waitress uniform.

> (NARRATOR)
>> Addicts may spend days and weeks on a binge, gambling away their homes, their savings, even their families.

She walks up the front steps of a shabby tract house and quietly unlocks the front door.

INT. JANE'S HOUSE - DAWN

Cheap, mismatched furniture. Tiptoeing inside, Jane is surprised by a half-deflated toy balloon hovering behind the front door. She sees a sagging "Happy Anniversary" banner overhead.

> JANE
> (under her breath)
>> Damn.

Jane peers into the living room, sees her husband Rick snoring on the threadbare recliner.

Jane moves softly to Rick's side. She reaches for the jacket draped across his midsection, but instead of tucking him in, she rummages through the pockets. Her determined efforts awaken Rick.

> RICK
>> You missed the party.

Startled, Jane makes a half-hearted attempt to hide the twenty-dollar bill she has found.

> RICK
>> Go ahead, take it.

Ashamed, she sets the twenty on the coffee table.

                    JANE

Something came up. I had to cover for
Cherise.

                    RICK

I called. You left work at eight.

                    JANE

I know, but I had things to do.

                    RICK

Alene was here. And Marty and
Bernice. My folks, too. I kept telling
them you were on the way, but they
stopped believing me eventually and let
themselves out.

                    JANE

I was getting you a present.

Rick looks skeptical.

                    JANE

It's the truth. I mean, it *was* the truth.

                    RICK

You were gambling.

                    JANE

I didn't mean to. I borrowed a few
bucks from Cherise. For your present.
That's the only reason she was going to
loan me the money. For that briefcase
you'd been talking about. But even with
her money, I didn't have enough. So I
thought maybe I could turn it into a
little extra.

RICK

At the casino.

JANE

I doubled it right away, I was so hot. I should've come right home, but it would've been nuts to walk away when the cards were saying stay. I mean, I could've bought you the briefcase and fixed the fridge and gotten the TV out of hock.

Appendix 5: Split-Page Script with Voice-Over Narration

Desert Stewardship

(opening scene)

Produced for Naval Weapons Center,
China Lake, California

Script by
Film Projects Branch

CUT TO	SEGUE (NARRATOR)

Scene # 8. EXTERIOR, Mojave Desert at China Lake, California. Long Shot of Joshua Flat. Coso Peak is in the background. In the foreground is Black Spring. It is flowing. We see a forest of Joshua trees and other vegetation.

Most people think of the desert as a barren wasteland where very little can live or grow.

ZOOM IN	(PAUSE)

MEDIUM SHOT of Black Spring. We see the trickle of water coming from the spring. A Mojave ground squirrel sips the water.

Actually, such thoughts are far from the truth.

DISSOLVE	(MUSIC IN)

Scene # 9. EXTERIOR, various locations in the desert at China Lake. Build a filmic montage of CLOSE SHOTS and MEDIUM SHOTS of various desert wildlife in action.

(Softly with a moderate Western theme.)

(NARRATOR)

We cross-cut with scenes having movement in opposite screen directions to emphasize the wide diversity of animal life. For example, sidewinder, partridge, mountain lion, coyote, weasel, deer, etc.

The desert is a delicately balanced ecosystem supporting over two hundred species of wildlife.

CUT TO	(NARRATOR)

Scene # 10. EXTERIOR. Continue the montage. Focus on CLOSE SHOTS of the following animals:

Several of the animals indigenous to this area are legally protected . . .

(show and tell)

bighorn sheep.

. . . bighorn sheep, . . .

golden eagle.

. . . golden eagle, . . .

desert tortoise.

. . . desert tortoise, . . .

Mojave ground squirrel.

. . . Mojave ground squirrel.

CUT TO	(NARRATOR)
	(PAUSE)
Scene 11. EXTERIOR, Black Canyon Area. Build filmic montage of CLOSE SHOTS and MEDIUM CLOSE SHOTS of the flora in the area.	There are more than four hundred species of plants in this desert, ranging from . . .
CUT TO	(NARRATOR)
Scene # 12. EXTERIOR. Black Canyon Area. CUT ON CUE to CLOSE SHOTS of pinyon pine and pickleweed.	. . . pinyon pine . . . . . . pickleweed.

Appendix 6: Teleplay and Split-Page Combination

Pacific Frontier

(opening scene)

Produced for
the Chief of Information,
U.S. Navy

Script by
Erskin Gilbert
(opening narration by
Herman Melville)

FADE IN   (MUSIC IN)

Scene 1. EXTERIOR, THE OCEAN

The gently rolling sea as seen from the hangar deck of an aircraft carrier. As the ship pitches slightly, the scene becomes a CLOSE SHOT. As the sea rises, the scene becomes a LONG SHOT.

FADE IN and SUPERIMPOSE over Scene 1

Title 1. THE UNITED STATES NAVY PRESENTS

FADE OUT Title 1.

Scene 1 continues to play.

SUPERIMPOSE Title 2, PACIFIC FRONTIER. Title 2 ZOOMS IN from infinity to full frame and holds.

FADE OUT Title 2.

Scene 1 continues to play. After a few seconds, the narrator begins.

> (NARRATOR)
>
> There is, one knows not what sweet mystery about this sea, whose gently awful stirrings seems to speak of some hidden soul beneath.

DISSOLVE TO

Scene 2. EXTERIOR, MAKAHA BEACH, HAWAII

Huge rolling breakers as they tumble close to the shore.

> (NARRATOR)
>
> It rolls the midmost waters of the world, the Indian Ocean and Atlantic being but its arms.

DISSOLVE TO

Scene 3. EXTERIOR, LA JOLLA BEACH

CLOSE SHOT of a breaker as it smashes into the rocks on the beach.

> (NARRATOR)
>
> The same waves wash the moles of the new-built California towns, but yesterday . . .

DISSOLVE TO

Scene 4. EXTERIOR, BIG SUR BEACH

HIGH ANGLE SHOT of breakers as they roll onto the beach. Sea gulls are perched on rocks in the foreground.

> (NARRATOR)
>
> . . . planted by the recentest race of men . . .

DISSOLVE TO

Scene 5. EXTERIOR, REPULSE BAY, HONG KONG

MEDIUM LONG SHOT of small Chinese junk with sails rigged putting out to sea. The day is overcast.

> (NARRATOR)
>
> . . . and lave the faded but still gorgeous skirts of Asiatic lands, older than Abraham.

DISSOLVE TO

Scene 6. EXTERIOR, WAIALUA BAY, HAWAII

LOW ANGLE SHOT from the water's surface, a huge breaker smashes over a coral reef. Spray flies.

> (MUSIC UP)

Appendix 7: Shelton's Fundamental Verities of Information Motion-Media

I've listed below the fundamental and factual elements of our motion-media profession. In essence, they are a capsulation of this book, and all have been discussed in the various chapters.

- We're in the communication profession rather than the film, video, or multimedia business.
- Actually, we're in the psychology business. Our task is to manipulate the minds of our audience members.
- The reason to produce a show (the problem to be solved) sometimes is not what it seems to be.
- Be absolutely sure you know precisely what the *real* problem is.
- Select the appropriate medium for the message and audience.
- Motion-media's primary communication advantage is that with filmic design, we manipulate time and space.
- Film and video are linear; multimedia are interactive.
- Film and video are appropriate media for broad-based goals.
- Multimedia are appropriate for "hard-core" training and cognitive learning.
- Only in multimedia can we get real-time feedback.
- Well-done audience analysis augurs well for successful communication.
- Encode motion-media messages in a style, content, and form with which the audience can identify.
- Engendering empathy in the audience is the key to communication.
- Motion-media are kinetic-visual media.
- Aural information must be kept to a minimum.
- Kinetic-visual and aural information in the right mix generate communication synergism—about 70 percent visual, 30 percent aural.
- Script design is kinetic-visual planning.
- Storyboard is the basic script format.
- Filmic design is the key to encoding messages in motion-media communication.

- Simpler and shorter shows are communication- and cost-effective.
- Five is about the maximum number of key points that should be in a linear show.
- Stilted scenarios usually fail.
- Large budgets do not equate to effective shows.
- Information motion-media shows do not have to entertain to communicate.
- Creativity is basic and deliberately concealed.
- Entertainment and creativity all too often are noise, which hinders communication.
- Talking heads are taboo, except in extraordinary cases.
- Clients aren't always right, but they pay the bills.
- You're responsible for your own professional development.
- Know the history and background of our profession—learn from the masters.
- Learn communication theory, psychology, and system analysis.
- Technical skills are developed on the job.
- Develop the critical eye.
- Become a catholic communicator.

Appendix 8: Exercises

Now that you've completed this book and are ready to hone your motion-media script-designing skills, peruse the following real-world communication problems. Try to develop scripts that will solve (or at least alleviate) these communication problems. I've not included all the details for each problem. It's up to you to develop those that are missing as you complete the Communication Analysis Plan (see chapter 14 for the form).

Completion of this plan is a crucial step in your solution of any one problem. Think each question through carefully, and respond with a cogent response. Next, outline your script in narrative form. Then try your hand at a storyboard—stick figures and rough drawings are okay. The goal here is to develop your filmic design for the solution to the problem. Finally, develop the script in one of the formats I've shown in the appendixes. I suspect that you'll need several drafts before you're satisfied. Do your best.

Communication Problems

Problem 1: To motivate. Your client is the manager of a huge warehouse complex. Warehouses are located in several Western states. A new computer system is installed that tracks purchases, inventory, sales, shipping, billing, etc. First-level and mid-level managers are reluctant to use this new computer system. They're comfortable with the ol' way that they know and that always works. Your task is to design a motion-media show that will motivate the managers to use the new computer system.

Problem 2: To sell. The sales of your client's high-end computers are falling. A new computer company is cutting into your client's markets. Your client's computer and the competition's are about equal in cost, capability, and reliability. Design a motion-media show that will boost sales to Fortune 500 companies, governments, and universities.

Problem 3: To persuade. Student drug abuse, alcoholism, and vandalism are rampant in the local junior-high school. The principal has tasked you to design a motion-media show that will assuage this problem. (Clearly, one show will not cure the problem.) What ancillary materials do you suggest be used with the show?

Problem 4: To teach. The folks at the Senior Citizens' Center are trying to learn the basics of personal computing—RAM, ROM, output, etc. They are having a hard time. Design a motion-media show that will teach the senior citizens the basics of personal computing. What medium is best for this type of problem?

Problem 5: To propagandize. The war is going badly. We're suffering defeat after defeat. Casualties are high. Morale on the home front is low and headed lower. Design a motion-media show that will boost morale of the general public on the home front.

Problem 6: To report. Physicists at Acme University have discovered the elusive and long-sought gravity wave—the last of nature's forces to be discovered. Such a discovery revolutionizes science and leads to the development of the unified field theory. Design a motion-media show that will highlight this discovery to the scientific community. The detailed mathematical report will be published later in the *Acme Scientific Journal.*

Problem 7: To canalize (to change or alter an existing belief). Some animal-rights activists are opposed to using animals for any kind of medical research. Design a motion-media show that will cause some of these activists to change their minds or, at the minimum, to reconsider their position.

Problem 8: To inspire. Students in the English Poetry 101 class couldn't care less, and many are failing. This class is a required core class for all entering freshmen at Acme University. Design a motion-media show that will inspire the students to appreciate, become involved with, and thus learn English poetry.

Problem 9: To recruit. Minority representation in professional jobs at the Department of Defense poison gas and biological warfare research and development center is too low. A federal court order tasks the center to increase minorities in the professions by 12.45 percent. This goal must be reached within two years. The center is located in a remote desert region of Nevada, 250 miles from the nearest town. It's hot in the summer and cold in the winter. Design a motion-media show that will recruit minority professionals to long-term employment at the center.

Problem 10: To inform. Traffic in the center of town is a nightmare. To alleviate this situation, the city council is planning to eliminate all street parking and to make all streets one-way in this area. The council anticipates lots of opposition from merchants, the public, and various special-interest groups. Members of the city council are to face the voters in the upcoming November elections. Design a motion-media show that will inform the public about the council's plan and that will ease the opposition.

Appendix 9: Quotable Quotes

Over the years I've jotted down comments regarding our profession that I've heard associates say or I've read in articles or in personal correspondence. Some are insightful, some are funny, and some strip away the veneer and expose the true essence of what's happening in our profession. I didn't fabricate any of these quotes. They're exactly as I heard or read them. On hearing a quotable quote, I'd write it down as soon as I could. I've listed some of these quotes below. They're in no particular order. Enjoy, reflect, and understand the intrinsic meaning in these quotes.

"*First law of inverse correlations.* The sophistication level of a project is inversely proportional to its importance." Gary Glendening, media producer, quoted in *Audio-Visual Communications*, November, 1981, p. 46.

"The standard notion is that for full appreciation, films and plays demand the willing suspension of disbelief on the part of the viewer." Charles Champlin, art critic, *Los Angeles Times*, 3 October 1980.

"This show is straight show-and-tell. Trouble is you can't see anything." The late John Dunker, filmmaker and former associate, commenting on a show submitted for judging in an international film-competition. In this film, the vast majority of the information was in the narration—no filmic design. Visuals were almost irrelevant. 3 February 1976, Ridgecrest, California.

"Anytime there was anything exciting happening (aerial combat), my combat photographers were either out of film or picking their noses." The late General Curtis E. LeMay, USAF, former Commander of the Twentieth Air Force (B-29 bombers in the Pacific Theatre) and later the Commander of the U. S. Air Force's Strategic Air Command. General LeMay made this comment to me in my office at the Naval Weapons Center (NWC), China Lake, California, on 27 July 1977, after screening my film *299 Foxtrot*. His comment expressed his frustration with his film people who produced the mediocre documentary film *The Last Bomb* (the story of the B-29 raids on Japan). General LeMay wanted his film to compete with and overshadow William Wyler's Academy Award–winning documentary *Memphis Belle*—the story of the Eight Air Force's B-17 raids over Germany.

"We're not dealing with the truth here (in this film). What we're dealing with is an illusion (of the truth)." Filmmaker and former associate in a discussion with me on how a certain sequence in the film should be edited to overcome the shortcomings in footage needed to cover the information that had to be communicated. 14 April 1985, Film Projects Branch, NWC.

Charles Kettering, physicist, summed his lifetime experience with evaluation committees, "Their reaction is to seek the wrongness: to ignore 90 percent of the rightness." Quoted by Charles "Cap" Palmer in "Open Mike," *Film World and A-V News,* February, 1965, p. 270.

"Let's have everybody's input so there won't be any complaints." Sam Stalos, editor and columnist, sarcastic comment regarding script-review committees in "Stalos AV Shrink," *Audiovisual Directions,* January, 1984, p. 53.

"Anything can happen in the world of make-believe. The *silence* is the most important part of our show" (emphasis added). Hedda Sharapan, associate producer, Family Communications, Inc., *Mister Rogers's Neighborhood,* on accepting the Distinguished Technical Communication award at the Society for Technical Communication's annual conference, Pittsburgh, Pennsylvania, 21 May 1981.

"This film is a variety of scenes to complement the narration." The late Everett Baker, filmmaker, to me on screening his film in interlock to justify the show's lack of filmic design. 16 July 1981, NWC.

"The resulting proliferation of documents, addenda, declarations, and self-supporting regulations vomit forth in [an] effort [that] is without merit, logic, or adequate word description." Jack Williamson, independent filmmaker, responding to the request-for-bid package of documents for a government film. "No Bid," *Business Screen,* May/June 1974.

"It (television) is adored and vilified. It's feared by some as a mind-altering drug or a subliminal messenger, ridiculed by others as a trivial boob tube, an idiot box; a vast, gray, barren, parched wilderness." Howard Rosenberg, television critic, *Los Angeles Times,* in his column "50 years of TV: A Wasteland and a Wonder," 10 April 1989, Part VI, p. 1.

"Film is a bisensual medium." Tony Gurria, instructor at the London Film School, to me in a private conversation at the Society of Motion Picture and Television Engineers Conference, Los Angeles, California, 8 December 1975.

Does the following metaphoric quote apply to your career? "The best scene is always at the bottom of the trim barrel." Chuck Bodwell, owner of Filmline Productions in Los Angeles, to me at an interlock screening of his film in my office at NWC, November 1979.

"Television is (a melange of) disconnected sights, sounds, images, and pleasing personalities that pretend to offer us coherence. As a result we no longer prefer to confront reality directly. There is, in fact, no reality any more. It's all artifact. We have so thoroughly merged symbols, information, and entertainment that few of us can distinguish between them. That (television), in short, is responsible for the downfall of civilization. We're in the midst of a new 'Dark Age'." Ian I. Mitroff, professor of business policy, University of Southern California, "False Images Lead Us Back to Dark Ages," *Los Angeles Times* 11 October 1989, 2, B7.

"You simply can't cheat on a one-project show and pull it off." Jean O'Neal, CEO of Corporate Image, Des Moines, Iowa, in personal correspondence to me, 4 March 1981. Jean was discussing multi-image shows that had lots of "creativity" but little communications. Such shows ranged from two to thirty or forty, 35mm slide projectors.

"Television has seduced us away from reality, deprives us of self-awareness and growth, given us ersatz excitement and vicarious adventure, fantasized our sex life, brutalized our consciousness with violence, stolen our time, homogenized us, and turned us into zombies, couch potatoes, slobs, and mindless consumers." The late Jack Smith, columnist, *Los Angeles Times,* 20 February 1989, Part V, p. 1.

"No Navy training film never taught nobody nothing." Lt. Comdr. M. R. McClure, USN, production supervisor, Naval Photographic Center, to me in disgust after we'd screened the first-answer print of a contractor-produced film for the navy. The film was totally inept and was reflective of the total scope of the training films being produced. Washington, D.C., April 1965.

An exceptionally talented filmmaker and former associate submitted his script to me for review. The film's subject dealt with a complicated research-and-development project. The meaning of several lines of narration was unclear. I asked my associate to explain this narration. In a burst of unintentional candor, the filmmaker replied with the ultimate faux pas, "I don't know what I'm talking about." NWC, 10 May 1985.

In a stinging rebuke regarding television viewing by African Americans, Derrick Z. Jackson, *Boston Globe,* says, "Television viewing has become a total public health menace. Brain rot from toxic, stereotyped shows." Derrick Z. Jackson, "NAACP fight is a tired rerun," *Boston Globe,* 29 August 2001.

Not all is lost. Even some of Hollywood's giants recognize the pitfalls of technology over story. For example, Robert Zemeckis, a technology-effects aficionado, notes that the true story line comes first and foremost over technique. "I think it's the only way that a movie ultimately works under any circumstance. The technology is only there to *serve the story.* The story can never serve the technology" (emphasis added). Quoted in John Zollinger's article "Giving Back to the Future," in *USC Trojan Family Magazine,* Autumn 2001, p. 3.

Lastly, Steven Spielberg said when discussing the thread that ties all of his films together, "It (the script) has got to be a good story: compelling that will engage the audience." Quoted in "Profile Steven Spielberg Talks about Technology and Storytelling." Frank Barron and Margie Barron, *UPDATE,* January 2004, p. 13.

Notes

2. The Message and Motion-Media

1. Alvin Toffler, *Future Shock* (New York: Bantam Books, 1972), 166.

2. Everett L. Jones, "Subject A: The Class Increases," *Los Angeles Times,* 8 Dec. 1984.

3. Mike Wallace, "Would CBS' Mike Wallace Switch Off His Own Show?" *Los Angeles Times,* 10 Mar. 1976.

4. Charles R. Wright, *Mass Communications* (New York: Random, 1959).

5. Reed H. Blake and Edwin O. Haroldsen, *A Taxonomy of Concepts in Communication* (New York: Hastings, 1975).

6. Paul Lazerfield and Robert Merton, "Mass Communication, Popular Taste, and Organized Social Action," in *The Communication of Ideas: A Series of Addresses,* ed. Lyman Bryson (New York: Institute for Religious and Social Studies, 1948).

7. Rudolf Arnheim, *Visual Thinking* (Berkeley: U of California P, 1969).

8. Marshall McLuhan, *Understanding Media: The Extensions of Man,* 2nd ed. (New York: New American Library, 1964).

9. Arnheim, *Visual Thinking.*

10. Charles F. Hoban Jr. and Edward B. Van Ormer, *Instructional Film Research (Rapid Mass Learning) 1918–1950* (University Park: Pennsylvania State College, 1951).

3. Motion-Media in the Communication Society

1. Nicholas Negroponte, "The Future of TV and the Electronic Communication Media," speech delivered to the International Television Association's 23rd International Conference, Boston, 30 May 1991.

2. Charles S. Steinberg, *Mass Media and Communication,* 2nd ed. (New York: Hastings, 1972).

3. John Fiske, *Introduction to Communication Studies,* 2nd ed. (New York: Routledge, 1990).

4. Louis Reile, "Movies Major Prophet of Our Time," *Gold and Blue* (San Antonio: St. Mary's University, October 1978), 2.

5. Arnheim, *Visual Thinking.*

4. Information, Communication, and Meaning

1. David K. Berlo, *The Process of Communication* (New York: Holt, 1960), 30.

2. Fiske, *Introduction to Communication Studies.*

3. C. L. Shannon and Warren Weaver, "A Mathematical Theory of Communications," *Bell System Technical Journal* (July–Oct. 1948).

4. Jeremy Campbell, *Grammatical Man: Information, Entropy, Language, and Life* (New York: Simon, 1982).

5. James Gleick, *Chaos: Making a New Science* (New York: Penguin, 1987), 257–58.

6. If your interest is piqued by entropy and you'd like more information, I recommend reading Campbell, *Grammatical Man;* Gleick, *Chaos;* and Hans Christian von Baeyer, *Maxwell's Demon: Why Warmth Dispenses and Time Passes* (New York: Random House, 1998).

5. Creativity May Not Equal Communication

1. Lou Clement, *Acquisition of Motion Pictures and Videotape Productions* (Washington, D.C.: Office of the Assistant Secretary of Defense for Public Affairs, 1984), 3.

2. Ed Gray, "Better Business Through Creative Freedom," *Audio-Visual Communications* (June 1981), 50.

3. David MacLeod, "Creativity: The Essence of Communication," *COMMTEX International NAVA/AECT Daily,* 22 Jan. 1984, 1.

4. Charles "Cap" Palmer, "A Personal Philosophy about 'Business Films,'" in *Exit Lines: A Personal Philosophy about Factual Films* (Ames: Iowa State University, 1982), 3.

5. Barbara Saltzman, "Sinatra Credits German 'Stranger,'" *Los Angeles Times,* 11 Sept. 1982, iv–3.

6. Jean O'Neal, personal correspondence with the author, 4 Mar. 1981.

7. John Grierson, "The Documentary Idea, 1942," in *Grierson on Documentary,* ed. Forsyth Hardy (New York: Praeger, 1975), 257.

8. Eleanor Wright, "How Creativity Turns Facts into Usable Information," *Technical Communication* (1985), 29.

9. Charles F. Hoban Jr., "The State of the Art of Film in Instruction: A Second Look," *Audio-Visual Instruction* (Apr. 1975), 30–34.

10. Robert Davis, "The Art of Creation," *Audio-Visual Communications* (Nov. 1981): 26.

6. Information Motion-Media

1. John Grierson, "The E.M.B. Film Unit," in *Grierson on Documentary,* 165.

2. John Grierson, "A Movement Is Founded," in *Grierson on Documentary,* 185.

3. J. Walter Klein, *The Sponsored Film* (New York: Hastings, 1976).

4. Joseph V. Mascelli, *The Five C's of Cinematography: Motion Picture Filming Techniques,* 1965, rprt. (Los Angeles: Silman James, 1998).

5. Hoban and Van Ormer, *Instructional Film Research,* 8–30.

6. Lloyd Engler, "A Commercial Message," *Audio-Visual Communications* (Apr. 1980): 45.

7. Charles "Cap" Palmer, "Single Concept Comes of Age," *Educational Screen and Audiovisual Guide* (Dec. 1963): 17.

8. Lloyd Harvey, "Thoughts on Making Short Films and Other Pleasures," *Business Screen* (Sept.–Oct. 1975): 27.

7. Film and Video

1. Don Dillon, "Hearing, Seeing, Reading," survey by the National Audiovisual Association reported in the thirtieth anniversary issue of *Crowley Commentary Newsletter* (Toronto: Crowley Film Ltd., 1980), quoted in *Industrial Communication Council Newsletter* (July 1980).

2. Wilson Bryan Key. *Subliminal Seduction* (New York: Plume, 1973), 163.

3. Hoban and Van Ormer, *Instructional Film Research.*

4. Karel Reisz, *The Techniques of Film Editing* (New York: Visual Arts, 1953), 265.

5. John Grierson in *Grierson on Documentary.*

6. Sergei Eisenstein, with Jay Leyda, *The Film Sense* (New York: Harcourt, 1942), 4.

8. The False Reality of Motion-Media

1. Brian Henderson, *A Critique of Film Theory* (New York: Dutton, 1980), 19–21.

2. Siegfried Kracauer, *Theory of Film: The Redemption of Physical Reality* (London: Oxford UP, 1978); André Bazin, "The Ontology of the Photographic Image," in *What Is Cinema?: Essays,* ed. and trans. Hugh Grey (Berkeley: U of California P, 1968), 9.

3. Jay Leyda, *Kino* (New York: Collier, 1973), 162.

4. Paul Rotha, *The Film Till Now* (London: Spring, 1967), 122.

5. Rotha, *The Film Till Now,* 83–85; Paul Rotha, *Documentary Diary* (New York: Hilland, 1972), xvi; Grierson, *Grierson on Documentary,* 13.

6. Allardyce Nicoll, "Film Reality: The Cinema and the Theatre," in *Film: An Anthology,* edited by Daniel Talbot (Berkeley: U of California P, 1972), 49.

7. Leon Barsacq, *Caligari's Cabinet and Other Grand Illusions* (New York: New American Library, 1976), 46.

8. Grierson, *Grierson on Documentary*, 13.

9. Rotha, *The Film Till Now*, 113–25; Klein, *The Sponsored Film*, 12.

10. S. Martin Shelton, "What Happens When the Lights Come On?" *Proceedings of the 27th International Technical Communication Conference, May 14–17, 1980, Minneapolis, Minnesota* (Washington, DC: Society for Technical Communication, 1980), G81.

11. Alan Rosenthal, *The New Documentary in Action: A Casebook in Film Making* (Berkeley: U of California P, 1971), 189–90.

12. Richard Dyer MacCann, *The People's Films* (New York: Hastings, 1973), 169–70; Erik Barnouw, *Documentary: A History of the Non-Fiction Film* (New York: Dell, 1974), 181.

13. Barnouw, *Documentary*, 91–94; Ralph Stephenson and J. R. Debrix, *The Cinema as Art* (Baltimore: Penguin, 1969), 199; Rotha, *Documentary Diary*, 125.

14. Barnouw, *Documentary*, 97–99; Richard Corliss, "Robert Flaherty: The Man in the Iron Myth," in *Nonfiction Film Theory and Criticism*, edited by Richard Meran Barsam (New York: Dutton, 1975), 234–35.

9. Documentary Film: A Learning Tool

1. John Grierson, quoted in *Grierson on Documentary*, edited by Forsyth Hardy. New York: Praeger, 1975, 16.

2. Paul Rotha, *Documentary Diary*, New York: Hilland, 1972, xv.

3. John Grierson, quoted in Rachel Low, *Documentary and Educational Films of the 1930s* (London: George Allen, 1979), 176.

4. Roger Manvell, *The Film and the Public* (Harmondsworth, Middlesex, Engl.: Penguin, 1955).

5. Paul Rotha. *Documentary Film* (New York: Communication Arts, Hasting, 3rd ed. 1968), 79.

6. John Grierson, "First Principles of Documentary," in *Grierson on Documentary*, edited by Forsyth Hardy (New York: Praeger, 1975), 146–47.

7. John Grierson. "First Principles of Documentary," 146–47.

8. Paul Rotha, *The Film Till Now* (London: Spring, 1967), 123.

9. Ivor Montagu, *Film World: A Guide to Cinema* (Baltimore: Penguin, 1964), 285.

10. Robert L. Snyder, *Pare Lorentz and the Documentary Film* (Norman: U of Oklahoma P, 1968), 3.

11. John Grierson, "Documentary: A World Perspective," in *Grierson on Documentary*, edited by Forsyth Hardy (New York: Praeger, 1975), 385.

10. Introduction to Multimedia

1. Jeff Berger, *The Desktop Multimedia Bible* (New York: Addison Wesley, 1993).

2. Dawn Stover, "Hypermedia," *Popular Science* 234.5 (May 1989): 122–24, 160.

3. Gillen Interactive Group, "Creating Your First Compact Disc Interactive Project," Press release, Laytonsville, MD, Nov. 1990.

4. Nathan Kolowski, "Development of Effective Interactive Instruction Materials," *Instruction Delivery Systems* 1.2 (Mar.–Apr. 1987), 19.

5. Gregory L. Adams, "Why Interactive," *Multimedia and Videodisc Monitor* 10.3 (1992): 20–24.

6. Peter Crown, "The Power of a New Medium," *Millimeter* 14.7 (July 1986): 121.

7. Clara Lazzareschi, "AT&T Enters Race to Offer Interactive TV," *Los Angeles Times* (6 May 1993) D1–D3.

8. Michael Antonoff, "Living in a Virtual World," *Popular Science* 242.6 (1993): 83-86.

13. Who's Our Audience?

1. Melvin L. DeFleur, *Sociology: Man in Society* (Glenview, IL: Scott, 1974), 419; Hoban and Van Ormer, *Instructional Film Research*; J. Christopher Reid and Donald W. MacLennan, eds., *Research in Instructional Television and Film,* Catalogue 23434041 (Washington, DC: U.S. GPO, 1967).

2. Melvin L. DeFleur, *Theories of Mass Communications* (New York: McKay, 1961), 121.

3. Joseph T. Klapper, *The Effects of Mass Communication* (New York: Free, 1960).

4. Bernard Berelson and Gary A. Steiner, *Human Behavior* (New York: Harcourt, 1964).

5. Klapper, *The Effects of Mass Communication.*

6. Hoban and Van Ormer, *Instructional Film Research,* 8-1 to 8-43.

7. McLuhan, *Understanding Media,* 24.

8. Hoban and Van Ormer, *Instructional Film Research,* 3-11.

17. Scripting for Information Motion-Media

1. Donna Matrazza, *The Corporate Scriptwriting Book* (Boston: Medial Concepts, 1976).

19. Guidelines for Writing Narration and Dialogue

1. Quoted by permission of Sunbreak Inc.

2. Marily Morgan, personal correspondence with the author, 18 Oct. 2000.

21. The Sound Track

1. Bela Balazs, *Theory of Film* (New York: Dover, 1970), 205–6.

24. Our Client Isn't the Enemy

1. Producers' Guild Ethics Committee, "The Work Ethic," *Audio-Visual Communications* (June 1987), 26.

2. John Grierson, "The Malaise of Disillusionment," in *Grierson on Documentary,* 358.

3. Charles "Cap" Palmer, "Open Mike," *Film World and AV News* (Feb. 1965): 10.

4. Susan Sherman and Jay Libby, "Meeting the Client's Needs," *Video Systems* (Feb. 1986): 44.

5. Raul Da Silva and Richard H. Rogers, *The Business of Filmmaking* (Rochester: Eastman Kodak, 1978), 6.

6. Alan Amenda, "A Gallery of Audio-Visual Hang-Ups," *Audio-Visual Communications* (Dec. 1975): 25.

7. Thomas R. Carlisle, "Point of View," *Industrial Cine Video* (Oct. 1984): A34.

8. Murry C. Christensen, "What Every Client Should Know," *Audio-Visual Communications* (Apr. 1982): 38.

9. Mark Pahuta, "Perceptions of the In-House Film Unit by an Audiovisual Apprentice," *Proceedings, 25th International Technical Communication Conference May 10–13, 1978* (Washington, DC: Society for Technical Communication, 1978), 123.

10. Sam Stalos, "Stalos: AV Shrink," *Audio-Visual Directions* (Jan. 1984): 53.

11. Ralph Metzner, "Video Vanities," *Audio-Visual Communications* (Nov. 1986): 15.

12. Palmer, *Exit Lines,* 3.

13. John Grierson, "Progress and Prospect," in *Grierson on Documentary,* 356.

25. Contracting for Information Motion-Media

1. *The New Columbia Encyclopedia* (New York: Columbia UP, 1975), 646.

2. Harold F. Lusk et al., *Business Law Principles and Cases,* 3rd U.C.C. ed. (Homewood, IL: Irwin, 1974), 93–96.

3. Charles Maher, "3 Key Elements in All Contracts," *Los Angeles Times,* 10 Sept. 1980.

4. Lusk et al., *Business Law Principles*.

5. Mollie Gregory, *Making Films Your Business* (New York: Schocken, 1979), 41.

6. J. D. Killoran, *NWC Procurement Guidelines* (China Lake, CA: Naval Weapons Center, 1977), 1–3.

7. Greg MacFarlan and Edward Pulsifer, *Navy Research and Development Contracting* (Washington, DC: Sterling Institute [DAC], 1976), 20.

8. Killoran, *NWC Procurement Guidelines*.

9. Charles Gaisor, *Defense Procurement Management* (Boston: Harbridge, 1976), 1–11.

10. International Quorum of Motion Picture Producers, *Standard Motion Picture Production Contract* (Oakton, VA: IQ, 1984).

26. Managing an Information Motion-Media Group

1. Lawrence J. Peter, *The Peter Principle* (Toronto: Bantam, 1970), 170–71.

Bibliography

Titles marked with an asterisk are especially recommended for further reading.

Adams, Gregory L. "Why Interactive." *Multimedia and Videodisc Monitor* 10.3 (1992): 20–24.

Alber, A. F. *Interactive Computer Systems: Videotext Multimedia.* New York: Plenum, 1989.

Amenda, Alan. "Audiovisual Writing." In *Jobs for Writers.* New York: Writer's Digest, 1984.

———. "A Gallery of Audio-Visual Hang-Ups." *Audio-Visual Communications* (Dec. 1975).

Arijon, Daniel. *Grammar of the Film Language.* London: Focal, 1976.

Arnheim, Rudolf. *Visual Thinking.* Berkeley: U of California P, 1969.

*Atkins, P. W. *The Second Law.* New York: Scientific American, 1984.

Balazs, Bela. *Theory of Film.* New York: Dover, 1970.

Barnouw, Erik. *Documentary: A History of the Non-Fiction Film.* New York: Dell, 1974.

Barsacq, Leon. *Caligari's Cabinet and Other Grand Illusions.* New York: New American, 1976.

Barsam, Richard Meran, ed. *Nonfiction Film Theory and Criticism.* New York: Dutton, 1976.

Bazin, André. "The Ontology of the Photographic Image." In *What Is Cinema?: Essays.* Edited and translated by Hugh Grey. Berkeley: U of California P, 1968.

Beraman, Robert E., and Thomas V. Moore. *Managing Interactive Video and Multimedia Projects.* Boston: Knowledge, 1990.

Berelson, Bernard, and Gary A. Steiner. *Human Behavior.* New York: Harcourt, 1964.

Berger, Jeff. *The Desktop Multimedia Bible.* New York: Addison Wesley, 1993.

Berlo, David K. *The Process of Communication.* New York: Holt, 1960.

Blake, Reed H., and Edwin O. Haroldsen. *A Taxonomy of Concepts in Communication.* New York: Hastings, 1975.

Blakefield, Bill. *Documentary Film Classics.* Washington, DC: National Audiovisual, 1985.

Blum, Richard A. *Television Writing*. New York: Focal, 1984.

*Campbell, Jeremy. *Grammatical Man: Information, Entropy, Language, and Life*. New York: Simon, 1982.

Carlisle, Thomas R. "Point of View." *Industrial Cine Video* (Oct. 1984).

Christensen, Murry C. "What Every Client Should Know." *Audio-Visual Communications* (Apr. 1982).

Clement, Lou, *Acquisition of Motion Pictures and Videotape Productions*. Washington, DC: Office of the Assistant Secretary of Defense for Public Affairs, 1984.

Corliss, Richard. "Robert Flaherty: The Man in the Iron Myth." In *Nonfiction Film Theory and Criticism*. Ed. Richard Meran Barsam. New York: Dutton, 1975.

Cotton, Bob, and Richard Oliver. *Understanding Hypermedia: From Multimedia to Virtual Reality*. London: Phaidon, 1990.

Da Silva, Raul, and Richard H. Rogers. *The Business of Filmmaking*. Rochester: Eastman Kodak, 1978.

Davis, Robert. "The Art of Creation." *Audio-Visual Communications* (Nov. 1981).

DeFleur, Melvin L. *Sociology: Man in Society*. Glenview, IL: Scott, 1974.

———. *Theories of Mass Communications*. New York: McKay, 1961.

Desmarais, Norman. *Multimedia on the PC: A Guide for Information Professionals*. New York: Meckler, 1993.

Dillon, Don. "Hearing, Seeing, Reading." Survey by the National Audiovisual Association reported in the thirtieth anniversary issue of *Crowley Commentary Newsletter* (Toronto: Crowley, 1980). Qtd. in *Industrial Communication Council Newsletter* (July 1980).

*Dillon, Patrick M., and David C. Leonard. *Multimedia and the Web from A to Z*. Phoenix: Oryx, 1999.

Eastman Kodak Company. *How to Be a Knockout with AV!* Kodak Pub. 884. Rochester, NY: Eastman Kodak, 1984.

———. *Movies with a Purpose*. Kodak Pub. V113. Rochester, NY: Eastman Kodak, 1976.

Eisenstein, Sergei. *The Film Sense*. New York: Harcourt, 1942.

Eisenstein, Sergei, and Jay Leyda. *Film Form*. New York: Harcourt, 1949.

Emonds, Robert. *Scriptwriting for the Audio-Visual Media*. 2nd ed. New York: Columbia U Teachers College P, 1984.

Engler, Lloyd. "A Commercial Message." *Audio-Visual Communications* (Apr. 1980).

Feldman, Tony. *An Introduction to Digital Media*. New York: Routledge, 1997.

Fiske, John. *Introduction to Communication Studies*. 2nd ed. New York: Routledge, 1990.

Gaisor, Charles. *Defense Procurement Management*. Boston: Harbridge, 1976.

Gange, Robert M. *Selecting Media for Instruction*. Englewood Cliffs, NJ: Education Technology, 1983.

Gayeski, Diane M. *Interactive Toolkit*. Stoneham, MA: Focal, 1989.

Gayeski, Diane M., and David Williams. *Interactive Media*. Englewood Cliffs, NJ: Prentice, 1985.

Gillen Interactive Group. "Creating Your First Compact Disc Interactive Project." Press release. Laytonsville, MD: Nov. 1990.

Gleick, James. *Chaos: Making a New Science*. New York: Penguin, 1987.

Gray, Ed. "Better Business Through Creative Freedom." *Audio-Visual Communications* (June 1981).

Gregory, Mollie. *Making Films Your Business*. New York: Schocken, 1979.

*Grierson, John. *Grierson on Documentary*. Ed. and comp. Forsyth Hardy. New York: Praeger, 1975.

Harvey, Lloyd. "Thoughts on Making Short Films and Other Pleasures." *Business Screen* (Sept.–Oct. 1975).

Hayward, Stan. *Scriptwriting for Animation*. New York: Focal, 1977.

Henderson, Brian. *A Critique of Film Theory*. New York: Dutton, 1980.

Herdeg, Walter, ed. *Film and TV Graphics: An International Survey of the Art of Film Animation*. 2nd ed. New York: Hastings, 1976.

Hilliard, Robert L. *Writing for Television and Radio*. 4th ed. Belmont, CA: Wadsworth, 1984.

Hoban, Charles F., Jr. "The State of the Art of Film in Instruction: A Second Look." *Audiovisual Instruction* (Apr. 1975): 30–34.

*Hoban, Charles F., Jr., and Edward B. Van Ormer. *Instructional Film Research (Rapid Mass Learning) 1918–1950*. University Park: Pennsylvania State College, 1951.

Imke, Steven. *Interactive Video Management & Production*. New York: Educational Technology, 1991.

International Quorum of Motion Picture Producers. *Standard Motion Picture Production Contract*. Oakton, VA: IQ, 1984.

Iuppa, Nicholas V. *A Practical Guide to Interactive Video Design*. Stoneham, MA: Focal, 1984.

Jones, Everett L. "Subject A: The Class Increases." *Los Angeles Times* 8 Dec. 1984.

Key, Wilson Bryan. *Subliminal Seduction*. New York: Plume, 1973.

Killoran, J. D. *NWC Procurement Guidelines*. China Lake, CA: Naval Weapons Center, 1977.

Klapper, Joseph T. *The Effects of Mass Communication*. New York: Free, 1960.

Klein, J. Walter. *The Sponsored Film*. New York: Hastings, 1976.

Kolowski, Nathan. "Development of Effective Interactive Instruction Materials." *Instruction Delivery Systems* 1.2 (Mar.–Apr. 1987).

Kracauer, Siegfried. *Theory of Film: The Redemption of Physical Reality*. London: Oxford UP, 1978.

Lazerfield, Paul, and Robert Merton. "Mass Communication, Popular Taste, and Organized Social Action." In *The Communication of Ideas: A Series of Addresses*. Ed. Lyman Bryson. New York: Institute for Religious and Social Studies, 1948.

Lazzareschi, Clara. "AT&T Enters Race to Offer Interactive TV." *Los Angeles Times* (6 May 1993): D1–D3.

———. "TV Till You." *Los Angeles Times Magazine* (16 May 1993): 12–16.

Lee, Robert, and Robert Misiorowski. *Script Models: A Handbook for the Media Writer*. New York: Hastings, 1984.

Leyda, Jay. *Kino*. New York: Collier, 1973.

*Leyda, Jay, and Zina Joynow. *Eisenstein at Work*. New York: Pantheon, 1982.

Lipton, Russell. *Multimedia Tool Kit*. New York: Random, 1992.

Loomis, Andrew. *Creative Illustration*. New York: Viking, 1947.

*Lorentz, Pare. *FDR's Moviemaker: Memoirs and Scripts*. Reno: U of Nevada P, 1992.

*———. *Lorentz on Film: Movies 1927 to 1941*. New York: Hopkinson, 1975.

*Low, Rachel. *Documentary and Educational Films of the 1930s*. London: Allen, 1979.

Lusk, Harold F., et al. *Business Law Principles and Cases*. 3rd U.C.C. ed. Homewood, IL: Irwin, 1974.

MacCann, Richard Dyer. *The People's Films*. New York: Hastings, 1973.

MacFarlan, Greg, and Edward Pulsifer. *Navy Research and Development Contracting*. Washington, DC: Sterling Institute (DAC), 1976.

MacLeod, David. "Creativity: The Essence of Communication." *COMM-TEX International NAVA/AECT Daily* (22 Jan. 1984).

Maher, Charles. "3 Key Elements in All Contracts." *Los Angeles Times* (10 Sep. 1980).

Manvell, Roger. *The Film and the Public*. Harmondsworth, Engl.: Penguin, 1955.

———. *Films and the Second World War*. New York: Dell, 1974.

*Mascelli, Joseph V., *The Five C's of Cinematography: Motion Picture Filming Techniques*. 1965. Rpt. Los Angeles: Silman, 1998.

Matrazza, Donna. *The Corporate Scriptwriting Book*. Boston: Media Concepts, 1976.

McLuhan, Marshall. *Understanding Media: The Extensions of Man.* 2nd ed. New York: New American, 1964.

Metzner, Ralph. "Video Vanities." *Audio-Visual Communications* (Nov. 1986).

Mezey, Phiz. *Multi-Image Design and Production.* Stoneham, MA: Focal, 1988.

Montagu, Ivor. *Film World: A Guide to Cinema.* Baltimore: Penguin, 1964.

Morley, John. *Scriptwriting for High-Impact Videos.* Belmont, CA: Wadsworth, 1992.

Naisbitt, John. *Megatrends.* New York: Warner, 1984.

Negroponte, Nicholas. Speech. "The Future of TV and the Electronic Communication Media." International Television Association's Twenty-third International Conference. Boston. 30 May 1991.

Nicoll, Allardyce. "Film Reality: The Cinema and the Theatre." In *Film: An Anthology.* Edited by Daniel Talbot. Berkeley: U of California P, 1972.

Orbanz, Eva. *Journey to a Legend and Back.* Berlin: Edition Bolker Spiess, 1977.

Pahuta, Mark. "Perceptions of the In-House Film Unit by an Audiovisual Apprentice." *Proceedings, 25th International Technical Communication Conference May 10–13, 1978.* Washington, DC: Soc. for Technical Communication, 1978.

Palmer, Charles "Cap." "Open Mike." *Film World and AV News* (Feb. 1965).

———. "A Personal Philosophy about 'Business Films.'" *Exit Lines: A Personal Philosophy about Factual Films.* Ames: Iowa State University, 1982.

———. "Single Concept Comes of Age." *Educational Screen and Audiovisual Guide* (Dec. 1963).

Peter, Lawrence J. *The Peter Principle.* Toronto: Hull, 1970.

Producers' Guild Ethics Committee. "The Work Ethic." *Audio-Visual Communications* (June 1987).

Rabiger, Michael. *Directing the Documentary.* Boston: Focal, 1987.

Reid, J. Christopher, and Donald W. MacLennan, eds. *Research in Instructional Television and Film.* Catalogue No. 234-34041. Washington, DC: GPO, 1967.

Reile, Louis, SM. "Movies Major Prophet of Our Time." *Gold and Blue* (Oct. 1978): 2.

Reiser, Robert A., and Robert M. Gange. *Selecting Media for Instruction.* Englewood Cliffs, NJ: Educational Technology, 1983.

Reisz, Karel. *The Techniques of Film Editing.* New York: Visual Arts, 1953.

*Rifkin, Jeremy. *Entropy*. New York: Bantam, 1981.

Rosenberg, Victoria. *Guide to Multimedia*. New York: New Riders, 1993.

Rosenthal, Alan. *The New Documentary in Action: A Casebook in Film Making*. Berkeley: U of California P, 1971.

Rotha, Paul. *Documentary Diary*. New York: Hilland, 1972.

———. *The Film till Now*. London: Spring, 1967.

Rotha, Paul, and Richard Griffith. *Documentary Film*. 3rd ed. New York: Hastings, 1952.

Saltzman, Barbara. "Sinatra Credits German 'Stranger.'" *Los Angeles Times* (11 Sept. 1982).

Shannon, C. L., and Warren Weaver. "A Mathematical Theory of Communications." *Bell System Technical Journal* (July–Oct. 1948).

Shelton, S. Martin. "What Happens When the Lights Come On?" *Proceedings of the 27th International Technical Communication Conference, May 14–17, 1980, Minneapolis, Minnesota*. Washington, DC: Society for Technical Communication, 1980.

Sherman, Susan, and Jay Libby. "Meeting the Client's Needs." *Video Systems* (Feb. 1986).

Snyder, Robert L. *Pare Lorentz and the Documentary Film*. Norman: U of Oklahoma P, 1968.

Stalos, Sam. "Stalos: AV Shrink." *Audiovisual Directions* (Jan. 1984).

Steinberg, Charles S., *Mass Media and Communication*. 2nd ed. New York: Hastings, 1972.

Stephenson, Ralph, and J. R. Debrix. *The Cinema as Art*. Baltimore: Penguin, 1969.

Stover, Dawn. "Hypermedia." *Popular Science* 234.5 (May 1989): 122–24, 160.

*Sussex, Elizabeth. *Rise and Fall of the British Documentary*. Berkeley: U of California P, 1975.

Swain, Dwight V. *Film Scriptwriting: A Practical Manual*. Boston: Focal, 1976.

———. *Scripting for the New AV Technologies*. 2nd ed. Stoneham, MA: Focal, 1991.

Toffler, Alvin. *Future Shock*. New York: Bantam, 1972.

*Tufte, Edward R. *Envisioning Information*. Cheshire, CT: Graphic, 1990.

———. *The Visual Display of Quantitative Information*. Cheshire, CT: Graphic, 1983.

———. *Visual Explanations*. Cheshire, CT: Graphic, 1997.

Vaughn, Tav. *Multimedia: Making It Work*. New York: Osborne, 1993.

von Baeyer, Hans Christian. *Maxwell's Demon: Why Warmth Dispenses and Time Passes*. New York: Random, 1998.

Wallace, Mike. "Would CBS' Mike Wallace Switch Off His Own Show?"
    Los Angeles Times (10 Mar. 1976).
Williams, Frederick. *The Communication Revolution*. Rev. ed. New York:
    New American, 1983.
Wolf, Rilla. *The Writer and the Screen*. New York: Morrow, 1974.
Wright, Charles R. *Mass Communications*. New York: Random, 1959.
Wright, Eleanor. "How Creativity Turns Facts into Usable Information."
    Technical Communication (1985).
Zettl, Herbert. *Sight, Sound, Motion: Applied Media Aesthetics*. Belmont,
    CA: Wadsworth, 1973.

Index

Page numbers in *italics* refer to figures.

S. Martin "Marty" Shelton retired from active participation in information and documentary motion-media production. He has thirty-five years of experience in all phases of film and video planning, production, and management. He is a frequent lecturer, seminar/workshop leader, and speaker at professional organization conferences, corporate training sessions, military groups, civic clubs, and universities. He earned his M.A. in cinema at the University of Southern California.